The Middle Way

ALSO BY DEREK CHOLLET

The Long Game: How Obama Defied Washington and Redefined America's Role in the World

America Between the Wars: From 11/9 to 9/11 (coauthor with James Goldgeier)

The Road to the Dayton Accords: A Study of American Statecraft

The Unquiet American: Richard Holbrooke in the World (coeditor with Samantha Power)

Bridging the Foreign Policy Divide (coeditor with Tod Lindberg and David Shorr)

The Middle Way

How Three Presidents Shaped America's Role in the World

DEREK CHOLLET

OXFORD
UNIVERSITY PRESS

Oxford University Press is a department of the University of Oxford. It furthers
the University's objective of excellence in research, scholarship, and education
by publishing worldwide. Oxford is a registered trade mark of Oxford University
Press in the UK and certain other countries.

Published in the United States of America by Oxford University Press
198 Madison Avenue, New York, NY 10016, United States of America.

Library of Congress Cataloging-in-Publication Data
Names: Chollet, Derek H., author.
Title: The middle way : how three presidents shaped
America's role in the world / Derek Chollet.
Description: New York, NY : Oxford University Press, 2021. |
Includes bibliographical references and index.
Identifiers: LCCN 2020027027 (print) | LCCN 2020027028 (ebook) |
ISBN 9780190092887 (hardback) | ISBN 9780190092900 (epub) | ISBN 9780190092917
Subjects: LCSH: Eisenhower, Dwight D. (Dwight David), 1890–1969. |
Bush, George, 1924–2018. | Obama, Barack. | Political leadership—United States. |
Presidents—United States—Decision making. | United States—Foreign relations—1953–1961. |
United States—Foreign relations—1989–1993. | United States—Foreign relations—2009–2017.
Classification: LCC E835 .C48 2021 (print) | LCC E835 (ebook) | DDC 327.73—dc23
LC record available at https://lccn.loc.gov/2020027027
LC ebook record available at https://lccn.loc.gov/2020027028

9 8 7 6 5 4 3 2 1

Printed by LSC Communications, United States of America

For Heather

CONTENTS

"We pray for all who have authority in the world, for the leaders of our nation and for those who bear office in all the nations, that they may seek the peaceable fruits of justice; grant that they may know the limits of human wisdom in the perplexities of this day, and calling upon you in humility, and acknowledging your majesty, may learn the wisdom of restraint and the justice of charity."

—Reinhold Niebuhr

THREE PRESIDENTS

ON MARCH 27, 1990, President George H. W. Bush appeared to be fumbling the chance to show resolve.

That Tuesday, Red Army paratroopers expanded their presence in the capital of Lithuania—then one of the Soviet Union's fifteen republics—threatening to quash the nascent movement toward independence. Yet the United States barely mustered a response. "It would be presumptuous and arrogant," Bush cautioned, for the US to try to "fine-tune" how the two sides resolve their differences.

Bush's restraint angered his fellow conservatives and many Democrats. They bellowed that he was too enamored with Soviet leader Mikhail Gorbachev and therefore too willing to write off freedom in the Baltics, whose liberation was a long-standing goal of America's Cold War policy. Pundits declared this as one of the "great moral moments in modern history." And to Lithuania's president, who feared a larger crackdown looming, the verdict was clear. Bush, he said, "sold us out."[1]

As Lithuania pulsed with tension, on the other side of the world, Washington officials gathered on Capitol Hill for a happier occasion. They came together to honor the legacy of another president who, over three decades earlier, endured charges of his own weakness in the face of Soviet aggression in Europe: Dwight D. Eisenhower.

It was the centennial celebration of Ike's birthday. That morning, Congress took a break from its schedule to hold a special joint session to commemorate him. For nearly three hours, the packed House chamber gushed with testimonials of Eisenhower's leadership. The cast of characters lauding the former president ranged from Winston Churchill's grandson to professional golf champion Arnold Palmer. At a time of rising partisan tensions, Democrats and Republicans together donned the iconic red-white-and-blue "I Like Ike" buttons and recalled gauzy memories of more tranquil times.

After the Capitol Hill rituals, dignitaries and Eisenhower's friends and family made their way down Pennsylvania Avenue to the White House for a presidential luncheon. Welcoming the celebrants gathered in the State Dining Room, Bush delivered short remarks to honor the occasion and praise Eisenhower's style of leadership. He extolled Ike's character and cracked jokes about their shared affinity for fractured syntax. He described Eisenhower as a "giant of foreign affairs," a leader who entered office having already faced the most stringent tests, and who made the world a better place.

"Today I say it loudly and very proudly: I have always liked Ike." George H. W. Bush speaks at a White House luncheon commemorating Dwight Eisenhower's centennial on March 27, 1990. Sitting among the distinguished guests is Eisenhower's son, John, at bottom left. (Courtesy of George H. W. Bush Library and Museum)

As Bush considered his own response to world events, he might have thought of Eisenhower's doubters, who often pummeled him for being too soft. "You know, some critics can't figure out how Eisenhower was so successful as a President without that *vision thing*," Bush said, with a dollop of sarcasm. This knowing reference to his own perceived struggle with articulating big ideas, which had become a staple of late-night comedy jokes, left the audience chuckling.

"Well, his vision was etched on a plaque, sitting on his desk . . . 'Gently in manner, strong in deed,'" Bush emphasized. "And he used that vision not to demagogue, but deliver." The 41st president would have been delighted to hear others use those words to describe himself.[2]

TWENTY-ONE YEARS LATER, George H. W. Bush returned to the White House, this time to receive his own honor. It would be one of his last visits.

Weakened by age and walking with a cane, Bush traveled from Texas to accept the Presidential Medal of Freedom from Barack Obama. He was surprised when the 44th president called him several months earlier to offer the nation's highest civilian honor. "To say I was touched by your call today is a classic understatement," Bush responded in one of his customary handwritten notes. Although he had all but stopped traveling, he would not miss this occasion.[3]

Entering into the crowded East Room in February 2011, just down the hall from where Eisenhower was honored two decades before, a military aide assisted Bush onto the stage with other awardees. In many ways, the medal recipients represented a composite of the leadership traits and history Obama most admired and sought to emulate. The writer Maya Angelou sat alongside the midwestern billionaire value-investor Warren Buffett. Baseball great Stan Musial was there with basketball legend Bill Russell. Congressman John Lewis, the civil rights hero, also received an award, as did Obama's closest international partner, German chancellor Angela Merkel. As the last to be honored, Bush was the undisputed star of the afternoon, receiving a rousing ovation.

Speaking to an audience that included the entire Bush family, including the 43rd president, George W. Bush, Obama described the elder Bush's life as a "testament that public service is a noble calling." He praised Bush's humility, generosity, and decency, calling special attention to his skill in forging the international coalition to expel Iraq from Kuwait, and his handling of the collapse of the Soviet Union and the peaceful end of the Cold War. Harkening back to Bush's response to the revolutions that swept across Eastern Europe, Obama credited his "steady diplomatic hand that made possible an achievement once thought impossible."

"It was the steady diplomatic hand . . . that made possible an achievement once thought impossible, ending the Cold War without firing a shot." Barack Obama awards Bush the Presidential Medal of Freedom on February 15, 2011.
(Photo by Chip Somodevilla/Getty Images)

Obama obviously enjoyed this celebration of talent, and in Bush's case, his example held particular relevance. For just as the 41st President grappled with the sudden wave of political revolutions in Eastern Europe starting in 1989—often remembered as the "Prague Spring"—the 44th President had spent the previous three weeks responding to the unexpected unraveling of the existing order in the Middle East, or the so-called "Arab Spring."

The velocity of regional change was overwhelming. At the time, the possibilities seemed as hopeful as those in Eastern Europe a generation earlier. Only a few days before the February 2011 East Room ceremony, the Egyptian people forced longtime ruler Hosni Mubarak from office, and the Libyan uprising against Muammar Qadhafi was underway. Thousands of people took to the parks, squares, and streets of the Arab world. Freedom seemed on the march.

Like Eisenhower and Bush, Obama found himself on the defensive. Critics accused him of being too cautious and always a step behind events—or worse, willing to stand aside while tyrants crushed democratic aspirations.

At a White House press conference the morning of the Medal of Freedom ceremony, journalists pressed Obama about this perception of timidity. They pointedly asked whether he favored autocratic stability over freedom. In response, he defended his "calibrated" approach. He argued the United States had to be prudent in how it tried to shape events. Indeed, he said, America needed to pursue policies that looked beyond knee-jerk reactions and toward a strategy that achieved long-term success.

Obama made a case for the same kind of "steady diplomatic hand" that Bush displayed during his own tumultuous term, acting gently in manner and strong in deed. At that moment, Obama tied himself to the foreign policy legacy left by Bush—and, by extension, Eisenhower.[4]

REFLECTING ON THE STATE OF AMERICAN POLITICS and foreign policy in the early 2020s, a lot has changed since the heartfelt celebrations of Eisenhower in the nation's capital in March 1990. We seem a long way from the warmth of a White House Presidential Medal of Freedom ceremony in 2011, with Obama honoring Bush.

Many people question the future of America in the world. They wonder if the American era is over and whether the country can ever re-create the influence that fostered so many decades of success and prosperity. Such concerns are especially relevant in the wake of the cataclysm generated by the coronavirus pandemic of 2020, when many rightfully ask what kind of global power America should aim to be and what one should expect from presidential leadership, and when American democracy itself seems imperiled.

In such troubling times, the lessons of Eisenhower, Bush, and Obama can be a guide. While divided by background, generation, and political party, they exemplify an underappreciated tradition of political leadership and distinct vision for America's global role. They represent a foreign policy archetype, one too often obscured by partisan blinders, historical amnesia and, indeed, racism. Therefore, considering these presidents as a distinct cohort, tied together by perspective and disposition, is not only historically revealing, but urgent for America's future.

Governing during their own moments of geopolitical uncertainty, these three leaders demonstrated both how the United States can exercise prudent and powerful leadership in the world and stand as pillars of decency, humility, and strength. They set the bar for the kind of global role the country should aspire toward—and amid moments of deep cynicism and despair, their example can remind Americans and the world that their proud legacy exists within us.

This tradition may seem contrary to recent history. We live in an era that rewards outrage, spectacle, conflict, instant gratification, scorched-earth politics, and an abundance of anger. Yet there is another path. For America to build a sound strategy to pursue a successful foreign policy—one that is inspirational and practical, unapologetic about the exercise of power but humble about its limits, unafraid of bold strokes, but aware of their risks, and sustainable over time—requires a certain kind of presidential leadership, one that is more critical than ever. Rooted in pragmatism, optimism, humility, and common sense, this presidential lineage is a reminder of what leadership *can* be, and how the right tools and expectations can fix American foreign policy.

Introduction

The Middle Way

What connects Dwight Eisenhower, George H. W. Bush, and Barack Obama? What can we learn from the character of their leadership? How can their examples help us think about the possibilities for, and challenges to, American foreign policy today?

At first glance, these leaders—the five-star general who led the greatest generation, the presidential paterfamilias of one of America's most acclaimed political dynasties, and the first African American commander-in-chief—may appear to have little in common, and even less to offer for today's politics. Yet upon closer inspection, their similarities are revealing and their lessons newly relevant.

All three embraced bold ambitions and saw their country as exceptional, but remained focused on not overextending it. Each operated within a policy ecosystem that had little patience for nuance and often pushed for "more" of everything, frequently with little regard to managing trade-offs or maintaining strategic solvency between the nation's international commitments and its domestic resources. All three labored over wrangling cantankerous allies and calibrating controversial military interventions. They practiced a governing style that was famously, and often defiantly, no-drama. And each grappled with toxic forces at home that roiled the political debate over foreign policy, ultimately undermining their presidencies.

These presidents struggled with what one of the shrewdest observers of American statecraft, Leslie Gelb, once described as the three demons of foreign policy: ideology, domestic politics, and the arrogance of power. "These demons ensnare our leaders into thinking about what they 'must' do, rather than about what they can do," Gelb explained. "They create seeming necessities or imperatives that rob us of our choice and thus of the essence of our common sense."[1]

Seen this way, a deeper inquiry into the ties among these presidents helps illuminate three critical issues: presidential leadership, America's place in the world, and the political debates we have about both. These leaders set an example for how one should measure presidential performance and define the specific qualities it takes to be a successful foreign policy president. Yet their experiences also reveal how elusive success can be.

I.

Each President shared an outlook that Eisenhower described as the "Middle Way." Ike started talking about this idea in the late 1940s and continued to champion its principles during his two terms in office and through his final days. His first effort to articulate the concept in public came in 1949 when, as president of Columbia University, he delivered a speech before the American Bar Association in St. Louis. While his subject that day mainly concerned the US political system and the structure of the domestic economy, it reflected a disposition that shaped Eisenhower's outlook on America's global role.

In retrospect, this speech was the retired General's political debut. He argued the principles of the American system "dictate progress down the center," which is where "the contest is hottest, [and] the progress sometimes discouragingly slow." He warned against those who "run to the flanks, straggling out of the battle under the cover of slogans, false formulas and appeals to passion." Ike laid out the stakes starkly: "When the center weakens piecemeal," he said, "disintegration and annihilation are only steps away." The audience ate it up—interrupting Ike nine times with applause and three standing ovations. The speech attracted wide attention, featuring prominently on the front page of the *New York Times*. Ike later remembered the speech as one of the two or three most important of his career.[2]

When Eisenhower entered the White House in 1953, he was determined to develop the Middle Way, briefly referencing his idea at the end of his first State of the Union address before Congress. But it was never easy. His frustrations with its critics were evident throughout his letters and diaries from these years. For example, in the early 1950s, as McCarthyism poisoned Washington and consumed the country with vitriol and suspicion, Ike wrote to a close friend about the importance of finding "the path that works the way of logic between conflicting arguments advanced by extremists." He observed that while people often want problems to bend to black or white solutions, the task of a political leader is to realize that perfection is unrealistic and that the best political path is often " 'gray' or 'middle-of-the-road.' "[3]

When Eisenhower left office in 1961, he believed he set an example for what the Middle Way could be. After all, he had been elected twice and remained popular, and the country enjoyed eight years of relative peace and prosperity. But his hopes went unrealized. "In recent times," Ike wrote in 1964, "it has become fashionable to deride such words as conciliation, compromise, and coordination. By the unthinking these are seemingly used to define indecision, fence straddling, and wishy-washy action. Yet without them, constructive progress is impossible." At one point, he grew so exasperated with "unthinking" partisanship that he considered creating a new political party under a centrist banner. While Eisenhower never followed through, his political tradition inspired a new generation of acolytes who were ready to carry it forward—including a rising star in Texas.[4]

MORE THAN ANY MODERN REPUBLICAN LEADER, George H. W. Bush explicitly linked his political heritage to Eisenhower. His father, Prescott Bush, had been a US senator from Connecticut and one of Ike's closest political allies (and a favorite golfing buddy). Bush recalled his father speaking of Ike in glowing terms, and got his start in politics by raising money for Eisenhower's campaigns in West Texas. This was an uphill battle, as the GOP barely existed in Lyndon B. Johnson's Texas, and Republicans were especially scarce in its oil-rich plains. Bush nevertheless established himself as a political player, raising money and meeting Eisenhower several times at conventions and fundraisers.

Eisenhower grew to admire the budding leader. After a disappointing loss in a tough 1964 race for the US Senate, Bush ran for the House in 1966. The two exchanged encouraging letters throughout the 1960s, met at the 1964 Republican Convention, and visited at Ike's home in Gettysburg. Building on this personal rapport, Ike offered his explicit endorsement and urged his friends to donate to Bush's campaigns. Eisenhower considered Bush among the "finest young leaders to enter politics," and told him that his campaign policy platform was "one of the best I have seen."[5]

"Gently in manner, strong in deed." As Bush's political career began, he sought Eisenhower's counsel and support. Here they meet at the July 1964 Republican National Convention in San Francisco.

(Courtesy of George H. W. Bush Library and Museum)

By the end of the decade, the two were seen as generational bookends of the GOP. In January 1968, they appeared on the same nationally televised special to respond to President Johnson's State of the Union address. While Bush represented the future, vibrant and hopeful, the visibly aged Eisenhower symbolized the proud past. Ike would only live for another year, but the political torch had been passed.[6]

Bush consistently used Eisenhower's legacy as a touchstone—he was one of the first national politicians to place Eisenhower in the pantheon of Republican presidential greats like Lincoln and Teddy Roosevelt. For example, in his speech announcing his 1980 run for president, Bush cited Eisenhower's Middle Way, quoting a line from Ike's 1953 State of the Union address to summarize the kind of politics and foreign policy he aspired to achieve. "There is in world affairs," Bush said, in reference to Eisenhower's example, "a steady course to be followed between an assertion of strength that is truculent and a confession of helplessness that is cowardly."

At the 1980 Republican Convention, Eisenhower-style moderation had taken a backseat to Ronald Reagan's ideological revolution. Bush noticed how little Ike was even mentioned, let alone embraced, so when accepting the nomination to be Reagan's vice president, he went out of his way to place his candidacy within Eisenhower's tradition. Recalling Ike, Bush said he wanted to be a leader of "decency, compassion and strength," who led the country "into a new eve of peace, prosperity, and progress." Nine years later, when asked in one of his first presidential press conferences about which predecessors he admired most, Bush again singled out Eisenhower, praising his success in bringing a "certain stability" to the office.[7]

Like Ike, Bush positioned himself as highly experienced, moderate, practical, comfortable on the job, and willing to pursue consensus at the expense of partisan gain. This kind of leadership served Bush well as president and helped end the Cold War peacefully. Despite his successes, commentators often derided these qualities, criticizing Bush for lacking strong, deep-rooted convictions. The critics would ultimately prevail, and after the fierce political currents of the early 1990s had capsized Bush, he lost office after one term.[8]

Yet the circle would be unbroken. Just as Bush explicitly placed his foreign policy in the Eisenhower tradition, a young politician named Barack Obama harnessed his lineage to both Eisenhower and Bush.

FOR A PRESIDENT OFTEN VILIFIED by his enemies for being a radical leftist, it may seem implausible to suggest that Obama pursued foreign policy more in the tradition of a moderate Republican. But Obama appreciated the world as a small-c conservative, or what is sometimes described as a "dispositional conservative": ambitious in outlook while cautious in action; skeptical of sudden, sweeping change; aware of people's fallibility and the world's complexity; believing in the power of incremental progress; and continuously searching for consensus. During Obama's presidency, numerous analysts noted the similarities between his foreign policy and that of Eisenhower and Bush, especially their common instinct for strategic restraint and their intuitive "realist" approach.[9]

Obama welcomed the comparison. He often framed his most consequential foreign policy decisions by citing the examples of Eisenhower and Bush. For instance, in a 2009 speech at West Point announcing his decision to send additional troops to Afghanistan, he invoked Eisenhower's emphasis on balancing all tools of national power. Speaking again at West Point in 2014, Obama once more drew upon this tradition to remind graduating cadets that "tough talk draws headlines, but war rarely conforms to slogans." Quoting Eisenhower, he said that "war is mankind's most tragic and stupid folly; to seek or advise its deliberate provocation is a black crime against all men."[10]

Obama was even more expressive about the lessons he took from Bush, often going out of his way to praise the former president and laud his accomplishments (so much so that when some of Obama's advisers read early drafts of his 2006 book, *The Audacity of Hope*, they suggested he dial-back the effusive praise of the former Republican president). Although Obama framed his 2008 campaign as a repudiation of Bush's eldest son, he said at the time that he had "enormous sympathy" for his father's foreign policy. "I don't have a lot of complaints about their handling of Desert Storm," Obama said of the 1991 war against Iraq. "I don't have a lot of complaints with their handling of the fall of the Berlin Wall." Obama later recalled Bush as "one of our most underrated Presidents," having left an "extraordinary legacy." He said Bush's foreign policy was "as important and as deft and as effective as anyone could ask," handling the end of the Cold War "in a way that gave the world its best opportunity for stability and peace and openness."[11]

Obama described Bush's foreign policy as "important and as deft and as effective as anyone could ask." Here the two presidents confer in the Oval Office.
(Official White House Photo by Pete Souza. Courtesy of the Barack Obama Presidential Library)

While Obama was a far more rhetorically gifted speaker than Eisenhower or Bush, his approach to foreign policy shared their more understated disposition. He prized deliberative thinking, pragmatism, and, as much as anything else, patience. "We have to be careful in balancing . . . bold ideas with also recognizing that typically change happens in steps," Obama said in an observation that could have been plucked verbatim from one of Eisenhower's letters. "And if you want to skip steps, you can. Historically, what's ended up happening is sometimes if you skip too many steps you end up having bad outcomes."[12]

Although Obama never referenced the Middle Way, his outlook rested squarely within its tradition, explaining his views in terms both Eisenhower and Bush would recognize. "Some would have America retreat from our responsibility as an anchor of global security and embrace an isolation that ignores the very real threats that we face," he said in 2011. In contrast, "others would have America overextended, confronting every evil that can be found abroad. We must chart a more centered course . . . be as pragmatic as we are passionate, as strategic as we are resolute."[13]

II.

Exploring the links between Eisenhower, Bush, and Obama reveals a distinct foreign policy through line. Of course, they were not the only presidents who saw some value in centrist approaches—FDR, Harry Truman, Richard Nixon, and Bill Clinton each took pride in their pragmatism. But these three presidents still stand apart; their outlooks, leadership styles, and foreign policy strategies are strikingly similar and their connections more explicit. Moreover, considering them together illuminates the importance of presidential leadership in defining America's foreign policy during three pivotal eras: the early Cold War, the end of the Cold War, and the end of the post–Cold War era.

Eight years after the end of World War II, Eisenhower solidified America's Cold War strategy. Upon assuming office in 1953, he inherited the first draft of an international system cobbled together amid the aftermath of total war and the rising menace of communist aggression. And while the age of Eisenhower is commonly misremembered as one of boring tranquility and small pursuits, it was actually a tinderbox, with considerable tumult at home and abroad.

Throughout his presidency, Ike personified the contrasts of the era. His political image was a throwback to modest middle-class simplicity—he had "cornball tastes," in the words of his son John—yet he helped invent the modern campaign with slick TV commercials and Madison Avenue image advisers. He accelerated the development of the national security state, but then eloquently warned of its dangers. He sought to rein in the defense budget and restrain the use of military power, but diversified and deepened American engagements and expanded its global commitments—using the CIA to help overthrow governments, increasing foreign military assistance so others could do the fighting for the United

States, and doubling down on the use of invasive intelligence assets like the U-2 spy plane.[14]

Yet at the same time, a powerful myth took hold: America was losing, it lacked resolve, and it needed to be more aggressive in the world and put itself "first." Prominent media pundits like newspaper columnist Joseph Alsop peddled claims about a "missile gap" with the Soviets, and politicians like John F. Kennedy built careers upon these exaggerations. At the end of his presidency, Ike's efforts to project calm and patience were no match for the passions of the moment. He no longer exuded the air of a confident sentinel or master statesman. Instead, restraint was seen as weakness, pragmatism as lacking conviction, and humility as defeatism. Despite Eisenhower's frustrations with what he considered a "cult of professional pessimists," his legacy proved vulnerable to the argument that it required a new generation to provide intellectual and moral strength.

THREE DECADES LATER, the early 1990s represented another turning point in American history. In 1989, the Iron Curtain still divided the world and many Americans worried about the country's decline. Yet in four short years, the Berlin Wall fell, Germany reunified, the first Gulf War ended in triumph, and the Soviet Union collapsed. In the wake of these events, America faced an intense debate about its global role and whether it should do less, and if Bush's aspirations for what he called a "new world order" could ever, or should ever, be realized.

Bush possessed a fundamental optimism about America in the world, believing that with the right kind of leadership, the United States could be a force for good. Despite this, Bush was derided as out of step, accused of lacking ambition, or being a wimp. He frequently expressed frustration with what he called "the empty cannons of rhetoric" that dominated Washington punditry, remained wary of the foreign policy establishment, and resisted getting "stampeded" into doing things that might garner headlines at the risk of making things worse. At the same time, he carefully tended to alliance partners and was willing to talk to adversaries. And while Bush proved willing to use force, he remained keenly aware of its limits and careful not to overextend the military or bluff his way into an unintended conflict.

Bush appeared politically bulletproof for a moment. Basking in the afterglow of the first Gulf War, he reached the highest public approval rating of any president—a staggering 89 percent—midway through 1991. But just a year later, his polls plummeted sixty-eight points. As Bush limped into his 1992 reelection campaign, *Time* magazine summed up the mood by describing him as the "incredible shrinking president."[15]

So instead of being an exemplar for the post–Cold War world, this moment proved to be its high-water mark. By the time Bush left office in 1993, the unraveling was underway—in the Balkans, where Serbia launched a war against its neighbors; in Somalia, where US troops deployed in late 1992 to feed a starving population; in Sudan, where in early 1992 the Al Qaeda leadership issued its first fatwa against the West; or at home, where in 1992 Los Angeles erupted in riots and the presidential contest was rocked by a Republican rival who argued for "America First" and a billionaire Texas huckster named Ross Perot who campaigned against free-trade deals like NAFTA and rode the cable news wave with a promise to wash over a corrupt Washington.

IF THE EARLY 1990S SEEMED TO BE A BEGINNING, we might remember the Obama years as an end. During the 2010s, the once soaring hopes of the post–Cold War era finally crashed back down to earth. These years witnessed a historic change in geopolitics, whether with the rise of China and India, or the resurgence of Russia, the meltdown of order in the Middle East, or the emergence of global threats like climate change and pandemics. Faced with the prospect of the United States in decline—from the 2008 financial crisis to costly wars in Iraq and Afghanistan—Obama entered office determined to resuscitate American power at home and abroad.

Like Eisenhower and Bush, Obama prized prudence in foreign policy. His infamous warning not to "do stupid shit" is just a cruder version of Bush's equally mocked "wouldn't be prudent" mantra. When grappling with the historic global changes that occurred during his presidency, Obama's first instinct, like Bush's, was to do no harm. He pursued what historian Jeffrey Engel has described as "Hippocratic diplomacy."[16]

Obama's achievements were impressive: an economy rescued from the brink of depression; instituting a "rebalance" of US military, diplomatic, and economic attention to the challenges of the Asia-Pacific; and diplomatic triumphs like the Paris climate change agreement and the Iran nuclear deal. Yet the foundations of Obama's strategy proved brittle, and this era will be remembered for having set the stage for the drama that followed.

Seen this way, this is not merely a story about presidential success. It is also about failure. The journey of these presidents shows that the pursuit of Middle Way leadership is fraught with difficulties, blunders, setbacks, and formidable obstacles. Most notably, politics often stands in the way. After all, Eisenhower, Bush, and Obama were followed by successors who talked tough, promised bold strokes, and tried to set a new course for foreign policy – which usually led to something worse.

III.

Because the historical record of these presidencies is already so rich, what follows does not presume to be a chronological survey or comprehensive account of their foreign policies. Rather, it offers both a wide-angle perspective on their leadership and a close-up analysis of some of the key moments they shaped. Building on previous scholarship and new archival research, and drawing as much as possible on these presidents' own words, this book examines their statecraft thematically from five different angles.

It begins by taking a close look at their leadership styles and worldviews, asking how presidents from such different backgrounds and life experiences ended up in the White House embracing a similar Middle Way approach. By revisiting these leaders' outlook and exploring some experiences that shaped them, one can see how they understood the global challenges and opportunities they faced.

Second, we will explore what they set out to do in foreign policy— explaining the initial strategic choices they made once in office, how they formulated them, and what influenced their thinking. This includes analyzing Eisenhower's effort to build a foundation for US national security strategy in the early Cold War years and devise a sustainable concept of containment; Bush's attempts to understand the nature of change in the Soviet Union and the possibilities for superpower cooperation, especially how to define American foreign policy after the Cold War; and Obama's work to promote a foreign policy based on "smart power" and to "rebalance" US foreign policy to address twenty-first-century geopolitical shifts after inheriting a tough situation abroad and a catastrophic economic crisis at home.

Third, we will assess how these presidents reacted when their strategies and instincts were tested. How did they handle crises and unexpected events—or try, as Eisenhower once put it, "to do the normal thing when everybody else is going nuts"?[17]

The book examines six crises, taking a fresh look at familiar stories. We will revisit how Eisenhower approached aiding besieged French forces at Dien Bien Phu in Vietnam in 1954, and how he handled the stunning confluence of crises in October 1956 over Suez and the Soviet invasion of Hungary, just days before his reelection. For Bush, we will explore his leadership during the critical months of 1991—with the aftermath of the first Persian Gulf War and the collapse of the Soviet Union after the failed coup in August 1991. And for Obama, we will focus on his approach to the 2011 Arab Spring, specifically his response to the crises in Libya and Syria.

Fourth, we will zero in on the politics of foreign policy. Too often, foreign policy matters are thought to be somehow compartmentalized from politics, but in reality, the two are intrinsically related. And Eisenhower, Bush, and Obama each engaged in bitter, and ultimately crippling, political brawls over their foreign policies—and these fights reverberate today.

Eisenhower faced a two-sided struggle with "America First" nationalists, who had been ascendant in the GOP during the 1930s and 1940s, and confrontional interventionists who wanted to wage a more intense Cold War. These battles over national security featured prominent antagonists like Senators Robert A. Taft and Joseph McCarthy.

Ike tried to remake the GOP into a party of "Modern Republicanism," lifting it out of the political ditch it had been stuck in during its two decades out of power before his election. Yet he ultimately failed to build a lasting consensus. Moreover, the antibodies to Ike's brand of centrist conservatism would only become more dominant, eventually coming to define the Republican Party in the twenty-first century, pursuing a foreign policy unrecognizable to Ike's.

While Bush was a rare Republican leader unafraid to carry Eisenhower's foreign policy mantle, he faced similar opponents. Simultaneously admired and derided for being a "foreign policy president," Bush was gravely wounded inside the Republican Party by the revised "America First" surge of political operative-turned-commentator Pat Buchanan, as well as the surprise independent candidacy of Perot. Bush ultimately suffered a humiliating defeat after only one term in office.

The politics that consumed Bush in the early 1990s foreshadowed the severe political turbulence of the Obama years in the 2010s. Obama tried to define himself as a different kind of political figure—like Eisenhower, he saw himself as an outsider who could transcend traditional partisan politics, and like Ike, he remained personally popular but fell short of his larger goals. And like Eisenhower and Bush, Obama's defining struggle was against those who ridiculed his foreign policies as weak and defeatist, and worse, unleashed a devastating strain of toxicity within American politics. In many ways, Obama confronted a combustible mix of Taft, McCarthy, Buchanan, and Perot, who were the linear ancestors of the foreign policy politics of the 2010s.

Fifth and finally, we will ask what legacies these presidents left behind. How did our perceptions of them change, and why? How do their examples of presidential leadership look in history's light? What lessons do they offer for US foreign policy today?

Eisenhower departed the White House seemingly tired and enfeebled, blamed for an approach to the world that lacked ambition and felt out of step with the challenges of the era. Yet now he is widely respected for his wisdom and skill in navigating through significant geopolitical turbulence, and his decision-making process is lauded for its strategic foresight and rigor.

The interest in and admiration for Eisenhower—which stretches back decades, to the March 1990 birthday centennial celebration over which Bush presided—reveals something about modern political culture. Despite the apparent success of a politics defined by anger, paranoia, and fear—the very same forces Ike had to confront—many Americans now long for his leadership style of dignity, strong vision, careful discipline, hardheaded practicality, and fundamental decency.

Bush's narrative arc has been similar. While most presidents who lose reelection—like Jimmy Carter and Herbert Hoover—are by definition failures, such a verdict doesn't quite work for Bush. He presided over a remarkably successful era for America in the world, and today Bush's global leadership is heralded and his administration praised for setting the standard in formulating and implementing foreign policy.

Obama's legacy is still being written. In fact, overturning the 44th president's stamp on foreign policy seemed to be the single most potent rationale behind his successor's approach. How will this look in retrospect? It is important to place Obama's decisions into broader historical perspective—taking a clear-eyed view of what he tried to achieve, the strategy he pursued, how he handled crises, what mistakes he made, where he found success, and the ways he came up short.[18]

* * *

Speaking in St. Louis in 1949, when he first began to articulate the Middle Way, Eisenhower described his approach as "rooted in the hopes and allegiance of the vast majority" of the American people. He placed his aspirations in the context of the sacrifices of world war, in which millions of average Americans risked "all that they possessed in defense of ideas and ideals." These sacrifices, Ike warned, could not be forgotten. Instead, they should become a "symbol of our dedication to political, economic, and social freedom."[19]

George H. W. Bush was one of those Americans who answered the call of service to join the forces that Eisenhower led, and he always remembered the larger lessons. In notes he prepared for his 1988 speech to accept the Republican nomination for president, Bush wrote that as the "strongest, freest nation in the world," the United States had a "special obligation to lead. We must not forget our responsibility." A big part of that responsibility meant not succumbing to cynicism and pessimism, and when it came to defending America's ideas and ideals, Bush maintained relentless optimism. "I don't fear the future," he wrote.[20]

Barack Obama did not fear the future either. He remained an ardent believer in the idea of progress and maintained faith that foreign policy could reflect the best of America—thinking beyond narrow self-interest, galvanizing others, and serving as an inspiration. He saw the United States fulfilling the same kind of global role Eisenhower and Bush aspired to achieve. Toward the end of his presidency, Obama described the country as a "rare superpower in human history," explaining that because "we have strived, sometimes at great sacrifice, to align better our actions with our ideals," the United States has been a "force for good."[21]

Eisenhower, Bush, and Obama came to the presidency from very different backgrounds and faced very different circumstances. Yet they shared a similar Middle Way perspective on foreign policy and politics, as well as for the requirements of successful leadership, that is necessary today. To understand how this outlook has shaped America's role in the world, we will first explore its intellectual DNA.

Worldview

I t was August 1951, and a feverish air weighed upon the army recruits
of the 47th Infantry in Fort Dix, New Jersey. For Private Gabriel Stilian,
however, neither basic training nor the summer heat was top of mind.

Between the marches and marksmanship practice, he worried about
global dangers, especially the Soviet Union, wondering how the United
States intended to navigate an intensifying Cold War. Contemplating the
larger meaning of his training, he asked whether America's survival rested
solely on the simple notion of "kill or be killed."

Resolving to address these thoughts, he did what few junior enlisted
soldiers would do in such a situation—he wrote to the five-star general and
supreme allied commander of armed forces in Europe, then headquartered
in Paris. He mailed the letter, not expecting a response.

Dwight Eisenhower believed that the young private's questions were
important—and since he habitually used his correspondence and diaries
to sort through his ideas and fine-tune his convictions, he saw it as an opportunity. Imagine the surprise the twenty-two-year-old Stilian felt when

he opened his mail to find a lengthy, soul-searching missive from a global icon about the state of the world and America's role in it.

It is a testament to Ike's character that he offered such candid thoughts to someone he'd never met, a young man looking for answers about the future. Replying to his new pen pal at the bottom of the chain of command, Eisenhower articulated a broad definition of the national interest.

"True human objectives comprise something far richer and more constructive than mere survival of the strong," he wrote. The nuclear age cast a dark shadow, yet America's goals had to be about more than self-preservation. The country needed to remember what it was fighting for. Ike explained it must aspire to something bigger, that "the security of spiritual and cultural values, including national and individual freedom, human rights and the history of our nation and civilization, are included."

The principal purpose of American strength, Eisenhower wrote, was to preserve the peace, and, in that effort, ensure unity among free nations. Unlike the Soviets, who saw cooperation as a matter of coercion—attained through "the threat of the slave camp and the whipping post"—Ike stressed that the United States needed to work with others to achieve mutual understanding and "common determination to meet the threat sanely and reasonably." He believed world opinion was a source of power, as was America's moral posture.[1]

Just as important, Eisenhower underscored the necessities of patience and persistence. He had a fundamental optimism about the direction of history and knew progress took time. Since he believed the Soviet Union carried within itself the seeds of its own demise, the challenge was "if we can be strong enough, if we can endure enough." Victory, he wrote, would allow the United States to "devote less and less of our energies, our wealth, and our thinking to matters of self-preservation and protection."

Eisenhower concluded the letter with his typical humility and practical wisdom. The business of living, he explained, "seems to be the business of attempting to solve in decency, in fairness, and in justice the multitude of problems that constantly present themselves to us."

He hoped his words would offer a "small bit of optimism and of faith." They certainly inspired Stilian, who a year later chaired his local "Young Voters for Eisenhower" chapter. But in retrospect, this letter—and the many like it that Eisenhower wrote over the years—did much more. It crystallized the outlook that guided his foreign policy approach, one that remained remarkably consistent over time, illuminating themes he would return to again and again. It reflected, as the scholar Richard Immerman has observed, the "raison d'être for his public service and the organizing principle for his national security strategy."[2]

I. STATECRAFT'S COMPASS

What makes the worldviews of Eisenhower, Bush, and Obama distinct? And what can we learn by exploring some of the ways their outlooks were shaped?

Every president approaches foreign policy with a certain set of assumptions about the world and how the United States should (or should not) act to advance its interests. These become the prism through which they diagnose problems, decide what to do about them, how to do it, and judge whether their policies work. Put together, these assumptions function as the navigational tools of statecraft.

Each worldview is unique. Reflecting on his own journey from scholar to statesman, Henry Kissinger once observed that every leader is a "prisoner of necessity." A president enters office, he explained, "shaped by personal history he can no longer change," carrying a learned experience that influences his or her outlook. Some political scientists formally describe this unique mindset as an "operational code." This clunky phrase can be a bit misleading, as it implies that some secret recipe exists to formulate and execute a nation's foreign policy. Instead, it is better to think of this as a subtler concept, one that refers to a leader's general beliefs "about fundamental issues of history and central questions of politics."[3]

Usually formed early in one's life or career, scholars explain, these beliefs provide the "norms, standards, and guidelines that influence [their] choice of strategy and tactics . . . structuring and weighing of alternative courses in action." Implicit in this concept are ideas that encompass not only how the world works, but judgments about how it *should* work. It therefore serves as a kind of mental grammar decision-makers use to guide them—even if, like the rules of language, they may not be able to articulate its details explicitly. Another way to think of this is as a foreign policy "checklist." Like anyone facing a highly complex situation with a degree of uncertainty—such as astronauts, physicians, and soldiers—foreign policymakers can use their own mental checklists, even if only implicitly, to help them prioritize goals and adapt to change.[4]

Of course, Eisenhower, Bush and Obama's views on fundamental questions of history and politics, and subsequently, their approaches to foreign policy, are not exactly identical. Their outlooks are shaped by their unique backgrounds, experiences, training, and interpretation of the past.[5]

Yet they do possess significant similarities that warrant consideration as a distinct tradition of US foreign policy leadership. After examining some of the origins of their worldviews more closely, one discovers several revealing, and surprising, parallels.

As his letter to the young private makes clear, Eisenhower always considered America's security holistically. Being the last president born in the nineteenth century, he seemed to personify the modesties of simpler times, yet he was also thoroughly modern. Most historians rightly credit him with being the first president to have articulated a comprehensive approach to matters of war and peace in the nuclear age.

But Ike focused on more than physical security; he prioritized economic vitality as well as the strength of community, values, and basic rights at home. "I believe that world order can be established only by the practice of true cooperation among the sovereign nations," Eisenhower wrote to one of his boyhood friends in 1947, and "American leadership toward this goal depends upon her strength—her strength of will, her moral, social and economic strength and . . . military strength."[6]

This was a broad agenda, and Eisenhower boiled it down to a simple formula: "spiritual force, multiplied by economic force, multiplied by military force, is roughly equal to security." This meant not merely pre-vailing against a foe, he explained, but "defending a way of life," in which everything "must be weighed and gauged in light of their long-term, in-ternal, effect." These ideas were easier to express mathematically than to implement in reality. Therefore, he wrote in a letter to another friend in 1952, "it is exceedingly important that American leadership be wise as well as strong."[7]

Given his military experience, it is hardly surprising that Eisenhower considered cooperation with other countries as essential to effective lead-ership. Before becoming president, Ike's signature accomplishments was leading allies to liberate Europe and serving as the founding commander of NATO. He saw collective security as a core requirement of the emerging world order. The "only sound basis from which America can afford to con-sider her relationship [with] any other nation," he wrote in 1952, "is from that of enlightened self-interest," looking out for others as much as oneself.

Because of its economic and military power, the United States has an advantage in pursuing collective security. But Ike believed the country's "spiritual strength"—by which he meant its blend of "patriotism, self-confidence, intellectual capacities, integrity and forthrightness, courage and stamina"—was its super power. By appealing to the "soul and spirit of men," Ike was confident other nations would be drawn to the United States because they thought they would benefit as well.[8]

Although collective security would only work with active US leader-ship, Eisenhower recognized the United States could not do everything everywhere. He understood the temptation of isolationism, writing that he "shared emphatically the average American's understanding that this country cannot carry the world on its own shoulders." The United States had to do its part and also "assert its full influence" to ensure that other countries contributed too. "The greatest deterrent to an aggressor," Eisenhower wrote in an August 1954 letter, "is a united free world, com-posed of free nations standing on their own feet." Therefore, he believed that to put America first, the country needed capable allies, strong inter-national institutions, and generous foreign aid programs—all of which he championed to complement a strong defense.

Eisenhower saw that this "middle ground solution"—an engaged American leadership, but within limits—would not be satisfying either to the "do-gooders" or the "strict isolationists." But it offered the only realistic chance to bring about the kind of global cooperation he thought essential.[9]

Translating these core views into practice, Eisenhower once declared that his "biggest worry" was "doing the right thing," especially when problems were so complex and challenging. As a decision maker, Ike displayed both out-of-the-box thinking and extreme caution—an unusual combination that often left even his closest colleagues confused. He was "very bold, imaginative, and uninhibited in suggesting and discussing new and completely unconventional approaches to problems," observed Richard Nixon, who served eight years as Ike's vice president. Despite his considerable flaws, Nixon was an astute observer of leadership and power. "Because of [Ike's] military experience, he was always thinking in terms of alternatives, action and counteraction, attack and counterattack," Nixon wrote in his first book of memoirs. "He could be very enthusiastic about half-baked ideas in the discussion stage, but when it came to making a final decision, he was the coldest, most unemotional and analytical man in the world."[10]

ALTHOUGH GEORGE BUSH had been a heroic naval aviator during World War II, he did not begin to think seriously about America's global role until his forties, when his political career began to take off. Even then, Bush had a limited appetite for abstract concepts or theorizing. He never felt comfortable uttering "flowery phrases" written by speechwriters. Unlike Eisenhower, his letters and diaries are not filled with searching ruminations on philosophy or world affairs. Bush defined himself more by temperament than big ideas. "Labels are for cans," he once said to his wife, Barbara. As he entered politics, his policy views were better described as "tendencies."[11]

Bush's political career had a meteoric rise, and in the decade between the mid-1960s and the mid-1970s, he went from a failed Senate candidate to CIA director. Bush's worldview—forged by his experiences in World War II, serving in Congress during the Vietnam War, as US ambassador to the

UN, as envoy to China, and then as head of the intelligence community—embraced the tradition Eisenhower helped define: defending the set of global rules and institutions built and fostered by the United States after World War II, sometimes known as the "liberal international order."

Bush championed this outlook when he ran for president in 1980, which was the first time he delineated a global vision for the United States. In his maiden foreign policy speech as a candidate in June 1979, Bush described post-World War II America in terms of its generosity, magnanimity, and optimism. To him, this meant being strong at home, committed to allies, and firm with enemies. While he did not use the phrase "greatest generation," Bush promoted a heroic narrative for American foreign policy, reminding audiences that "no nation has used its power, by and large, with greater vision, restraint, responsibility and courage." But just as important as its raw power, he echoed Eisenhower: the United States, he said, "must have an inner spirit, an essence that catapults us forward."[12]

Such convictions may seem vague when applied to policy. But they had several implications. First, while Bush exuded optimism and pride about America's role, he did not take it for granted. He understood that it was not enough to be powerful and expect other countries to bend to America's will. Bush said it was a mistake to conduct policy in ways that made countries "wonder if they must conform to our every desire in order to have our friendship and support." He believed America's willingness to seek others out, listen, and gain their trust was a critical ingredient of its strength. To his mind, the conduct of foreign policy was no different than personal relations. Leadership would never work by simple assertion. It had to be earned.[13]

Second, Bush thought the nation's influence depended on its ability to avoid bad decisions and overreach. The United States could not do it all, and to believe otherwise would be a grave error. The country had to understand its limits. Bush's views were shaped by his experiences coming of age in government during the Vietnam War and amid the tumult of the 1970s. While hardly a dove on Vietnam, Bush saw the conflict as a mistake, even if the United States had entered it with good intentions. From this perspective, Bush drew a simple lesson: the United States must not become "committed in wars we shouldn't be involved in, where we'd have no support from the American people."[14]

Third, Bush promoted the concept of collective security. He saw this as essential to sustaining American power and enabling the United States to achieve its aims while recognizing its limits. He considered the country always stronger when it worked with others and within global institutions.

Nevertheless, at the beginning of his political career in the early 1960s, Bush dabbled with some of the more paranoid rhetoric about the United Nations to attract support from the far-right John Birch Society wing of the Republican Party, which was then a formidable force in conservative politics, especially in places like Texas. This failed utterly. Bush conceded this mistake of political expedience, set out to remove the Birchers from party leadership posts, and publicly expressed regret for not confronting the "irresponsibility" of these "nuts." He then went on to champion the UN, and as the US ambassador in New York in the early 1970s, he spoke of the organization as "one of the greatest instruments of peace" and as a unique asset of America's strength. Yet he understood that organizations like the UN could not function independently as some kind of "automatic peace machine." Instead, to operate effectively, international institutions required a committed, active United States.[15]

And finally, for Bush, the *ways* the United States stayed engaged—how it exercised its leadership—were the crucial components of a successful foreign policy. He recalled that his time in New York at the UN "taught him a lot about treating nations, large and small, with respect," which he believed was a far stronger foundation for success than "bullying." Bush thought the best policy comes from "your willingness to 'go to others,' to ask advice, to be grateful, to get here earlier and leave later than the rest of the people." The single most distinct component of Bush's approach to foreign policy was his abiding faith in the power of personal diplomacy.[16]

WHEN COMPARED WITH EISENHOWER AND BUSH, Barack Obama's worldview started from a very different place. In terms of pre-presidential foreign policy experience, Eisenhower and Bush entered the White House

with as much as any person in US history. Obama was among those with
the least. He had not commanded mass armies in battle or risen from a
long career in politics and Washington's bureaucratic trenches.

Yet Obama's diverse background—growing up outside the continental
United States, with a mother dedicated to international development and
a Kenyan father he barely knew, and, of course, as an African American—
gave him a perspective that reflects nearly every aspect of modern
American power, whether for good or ill.[17]

Despite the assertions of many conservatives that Obama was ide-
ologically un-American, or the hopes of some liberals who believed he
wanted to refashion America's global role completely, Obama's basic foreign policy views were comfortably nested in the post–World War II tradition. Obama believed that the United States was the "indispensable
nation," or the "underwriter" of the international order. He thought it
must assert leadership to solve problems, address threats, and bring countries together in common cause. "Even our adversaries expect us to solve
problems and keep things going," Obama once said. "Nobody looks to
Moscow or Beijing." He believed in strong institutions like NATO and the
UN, a commitment to allies, and the central role of US military might
alongside reinvigorated diplomacy and development.[18]

Obama often stressed the importance of using American power wisely
and appreciating its limits—which meant seeing the world, in his words,
"as it is." This did not mean he believed the United States could withdraw —isolationism, he argued, was "untenable." Obama saw himself as
an internationalist and an idealist. He believed it essential for the United
States to promote democracy and human rights, both because it was good
for the country, and it inherently made the world better.

At the same time, he thought of himself as a realist, because he believed
"we can't, at any given moment, relieve all the world's misery . . . we have
to choose where we can make a real impact." However, acknowledging the
world "as it is" did not mean forsaking how things should be. For Obama,
seeing the world "as it is" was a core part of his theory of ambitious yet incremental change, the kind that required an understanding of power and
an appeal to self-interest. Perhaps this outlook stemmed from his early

career as a community organizer in Chicago, where he worked to advance social justice and end hardship at the grass roots. Obama's experience in those South Side Chicago neighborhoods tempered his idealism with reality, and is where he learned the first rule of change was to "start from where the world is, as it is, not as [one] would like it to be . . . That means working in the system."[19]

But Obama always aspired to make that system better—more effective, fair, and just. Like Eisenhower and Bush, Obama maintained a fundamental optimism about America abroad. Before becoming president, he argued the United States needed a foreign policy "that matches the boldness and scope" of America's post–World War II approach. He believed in the power of America as a force for good despite its "warts." He had great confidence in the strength and wisdom of the American people. He thought, as he often said, that over time history bent toward progress, confirmed by the fact that, as an African American, he was elected president. One of his favorite quotes—Dr. Martin Luther King, Jr.'s "the arc of the moral universe is long, but it bends toward justice"—was woven into the customized carpet in the Oval Office. Equally profound was his conviction that the United States needed to confront its flaws directly. Doing so, Obama believed, was not an admission of weakness; it was the key to renewal.[20]

Looking out at the global landscape of the early twenty-first century, Obama saw a lot of change for the better—millions of people lifted out of poverty, diseases eradicated, greater economic opportunity, and social mobility. But he also acknowledged globalization's dark underbelly and the unfinished business of social justice at home. Progress could be very jolting, especially for those most dislocated by change; rapid modernization and cultural flattening tempted many to revert to tribe. Obama's life experience had taught him about the power of fear and tribalism's resilience—having discovered how it had destroyed his father's life in Kenya, he said understanding tribalism's centripetal force was part of his genetic makeup.

"I've been navigating tribal divisions my whole life," Obama observed. He felt this experience enabled him to understand better what was going on around the world—as well as at home. When people are under stress and social order weakens, he explained, "the default position is tribe—us/them, a hostility toward the unfamiliar or unknown." Obama believed that one of the central challenges of global politics—and increasingly, American politics—was to resist the tribal impulse to "push back and strike out against those who are different." While Obama remained attuned to tribalism's enduring power—which helps explain his caution in using American military might to solve tribal conflicts—he also projected optimism that with the right approaches, such attitudes could be overcome.[21]

This mix of traits—the idealism and realism; the optimism about America as a force for good, coupled with a keen awareness of its capacity for mistakes; the confidence in the exercise of power, while acknowledging its limits; and the patience that comes from understanding that progress is not linear—comprised the core of Obama's worldview.

Obama was confident. He had plenty of ambition. But at the same time, he had an acute modesty about his ability to bring change. Perhaps because he was a careful student of history, or because he grew up looking at the continental United States from afar, or had experienced the challenges of bringing change to struggling communities in Chicago, he was comfortable with the world's complexities and keenly aware of both the possibilities and the perils of America's use of power abroad.

II. ORIGINS

Considering the worldviews of Eisenhower, Bush, and Obama side-by-side, one sees several unifying threads: the broad perspective of America's interests; the connective tissue between foreign policy and domestic priorities; the sense of proportion and clear-eyed practicality; the belief in America as exceptional; a faith in collective security; and an awareness of the temptation for overreach. Although one cannot presume there is a single path that leads to such an outlook, we can discern a few common origins.

At crucial moments in their lives, they went abroad. When thinking about how their worldviews took shape—and how they would approach foreign policy—it is instructive to look back at these first experiences living in other countries, far from the comforts of home: as a mid-career military officer stationed in Panama; as an envoy in China having been stung by political scandal at home; and as a young boy in Indonesia.

Their experiences did not affect them the same way. Nor were they necessarily the most critical moments in their intellectual development. There's no question Eisenhower's time working alongside Douglas MacArthur and commanding forces on D-Day, Bush's service as the navy's youngest fighter pilot in World War II and eight years as Reagan's vice president, and Obama's work in Chicago as a community organizer and time spent in the Illinois state legislature each shaped their outlooks profoundly.

Yet what's striking is that, years later, each of them would underscore these early foreign experiences as being pivotal. By understanding what happened during these formative phases in their lives, we can see how they incorporated these lessons into their leadership style.

To HIS REGRET, EISENHOWER missed action in World War I. In the early 1920s, he found himself as a major in the peacetime army with a career stuck in neutral. His professional fortunes changed in 1922 when he received his first assignment abroad. Shipped off to Panama, he was to serve as the executive officer to the commander of the 20th Infantry Brigade and one of the brightest intellects in the army, Brigadier General Fox Conner.

Although the living conditions were hard—the flimsy, makeshift houses leaked and were filled with vermin and bats—Eisenhower looked back on this experience as "one of the most interesting and constructive of my life." It changed the way he thought about leadership, history, strategy, and his own potential. In his letters and diaries, Eisenhower frequently referred back to what he learned in his early thirties from Conner, describing him as "the ablest man I ever knew."[22]

Conner had requested Eisenhower's deployment to Panama's Camp Gaillard, and after facing resistance from the army brass, pulled strings to get him there. Yet what makes Eisenhower's time in Panama so important is not so much what he learned from a foreign land—he apparently didn't interact with many locals or see much outside the confines of his narrow military duties. What mattered most was that for the first time, Ike had a mentor who inspired him to think deeply.

Beyond his formal staff duties, Conner treated Eisenhower to a twenty-month tutorial in history, philosophy, and leadership. Over long evenings sitting in Conner's overstuffed library, or together on eight-hour horseback reconnaissance rides, the two would talk about the Civil War, Napoleon, Plato, and Nietzsche, with the learned general peppering the young major like a Socratic professor. Such conversations, Eisenhower recalled, often started as "bull sessions," but they soon evolved into exhaustive colloquies "about the long history of man, his ideas, and works."[23]

Ike was once an indifferent student, turned off by the rote learning he was subjected to as a cadet at West Point. Under Conner's tutelage in the Panama Canal Zone, he became impassioned. He devoured historical novels and studied battlefield histories. He recited Shakespeare. He read Carl von Clausewitz's strategic opus *On War* three times. Quizzed by Conner on its maxims, he would subsequently recite them throughout his military career and as president. From Clausewitz he learned to balance means and ends, as well as to grasp the fundamentally political nature of military force.

Conner's training boosted Eisenhower's sagging military career. This was Ike's first real professional success. From Panama, he would go on to thrive at military staff college and then garner a series of prominent assignments. Conner acted as Ike's guardian, outfoxing army bureaucrats who wanted to place him in lesser roles, and Eisenhower repeatedly turned to Conner for advice. Fox Conner taught Ike how to think about the world and, more importantly, himself.

For example, Eisenhower later explained how Conner's instruction on the "art of persuasion" influenced his leadership during World War II, especially about how "you get allies of different nations to march and think as a nation." Several of Conner's truisms about how to be a leader— most notably, "always take your job seriously, never yourself"—became Eisenhower's standards by which he judged his own behavior and that of others. He also internalized Conner's broader lessons for war and peace, like "never fight unless you have to," "never fight alone," and "never fight long." Eisenhower emulated Conner's attributes—stern discipline, intense self-study, attention to detail, appreciation for historical context, and the ruthless cunning to maneuver around bureaucratic obstacles and manipulate personalities—for the rest of his career.

Beyond what he acquired in knowledge and experience, Eisenhower left Panama with something more intangible yet essential: confidence. Through this unorthodox apprenticeship with Conner, Ike developed the tools to think critically. He gained the encouragement to look beyond the rigid confines of the peacetime army. He subsequently credited this intensive experience as the cornerstone for his successes, saying that aside from his parents, no one influenced him more than Conner. As Eisenhower later reflected, "it took me years before I fully realized the value of what he had led me through."[24]

GEORGE BUSH COULD HAVE GONE to the United Kingdom or France, but he wanted to go to China. After enjoying his first taste of diplomacy as US ambassador to the UN in the early 1970s, he had endured an unhappy tenure as chair of a Republican Party roiled by the Watergate scandal. As a reward for his suffering, in 1974 President Gerald Ford offered him an ambassadorship to London or Paris. Instead, the fifty-year-old Bush asked to go to Beijing—a place he saw as the future. It didn't hurt that China was about as far away from the post-Nixon carnage as one could go.

His friends thought he was crazy, warning that he would be bored stiff. The US Liaison Office in Beijing—there would not be an Embassy there until 1979—was a small outfit on the remote diplomatic frontier. In the mid-1970s, China was a hardship post. Bush described it as a "land of contrasts," characterized by striking natural beauty but plenty of dirt and drabness.

Bush's time in Beijing coincided with significant tumult for the US position in Asia. Saigon fell in April 1975, and the United States appeared in full retreat. Just six months after he arrived in China, Bush saw up close the ramifications of South Vietnam's collapse and how it diminished the image of American power. He reflected on the domino theory, worrying that other countries would distance themselves from Washington and side with the Soviets or Chinese. Watching the chaos in Saigon from the viewpoint of the small diplomatic community in Beijing, Bush pondered America's global role. "We must not lose sight of our own perspective and our own raison d'etre as a nation," Bush recorded in his diary in February 1975. "So much of the world depends on the United States. So much depends on our own self-confidence and in our ability to cope. If we project this confusion and failure and discouragement, it will show up all around the world."[25]

As for the conduct of diplomacy, Bush's tenure in Beijing was relatively uneventful. China was just coming out of its shell, and its officials remained aloof and reluctant to meet. When he wasn't entertaining a steady stream of friends and dignitaries from Washington or Texas, Bush spent his time hobnobbing with other diplomats and biking with his wife Barbara through Beijing's crowded streets. From this vantage, he gleaned another perspective on how the United States looked from the outside. "The American people do not have any concept of how others around the world view America," he noted in his diary in May 1975. "We think we are good, honorable, decent, freedom-loving. Others are firmly convinced . . . that we are embarking on policies anathema to them."[26]

Bush saw the boundaries of American influence and understood the flawed presumption that the United States could exert total control over events in faraway places. "We have got to be realistic," he reflected; "we have to have our eyes wide open." He recalled with fury the debate about the United States "losing" China, which had cast such a pall over the Eisenhower years and animated American strategy in Asia for decades. "China was not ours to lose and that has been part of the problem," he recorded in his diary.[27]

Looking back on this first diplomatic posting, Bush described himself as a practical man who held a dim view for what he considered the "airy and abstract." Never possessing formal diplomatic training, he said his approach to international affairs did not "have anything to do with diplomacy; it has to do with life." When asked years later where this perspective came from, Bush recalled it came from his mother's advice: "Be kind. Don't be a big shot. Listen, don't talk. Reach out to people . . . This isn't some great diplomatic study from the Fletcher school or something."[28]

According to Jeffrey Engel, the outlook Bush took to the presidency fifteen years later was, in many ways, "made in China." What stands out is Bush's "overriding belief in stability over radical change; a willingness to engage the perspectives of other nations; and a desire to promote an American model through example rather than force."[29] One can see all the attributes of Bush's approach to the world at work during his fourteen months in Beijing: a leader committed to values yet coming to grips with the limits of power, always keeping an eye on how the United States appears to others, remaining firm with the conviction that personal relationships are vital to diplomacy.

BARACK OBAMA'S FIRST EXPERIENCE LIVING ABROAD was far different from the genteel diplomatic community of China in the 1970s or the dingy military barracks of Panama in the 1920s. Landing from Hawaii in Jakarta in 1967 at age six, Obama recalls clutching his mother's hand on a "tarmac rippling with heat," mesmerized by the chaotic congestion of motorbikes on the streets. He lived in a home with a mango tree in the front yard, played in fields with water buffaloes, and tasted the delicacies of dog meat, snake, and roasted grasshopper.[30]

While he was too young to appreciate it, Obama's four years in Indonesia—a complex tapestry of regions and ethnicities, with thousands of islands and hundreds of languages—indelibly shaped his worldview. "When you spend time in Jakarta growing up as I did, and see the masses of humanity in a place like that," Obama mused to a few aides in a quiet moment as president, "it makes it harder for you to think purely of yourself."[31]

It's revealing that in Obama's first two books, he uses his time in Jakarta as a portal to describe the evolution of his own identity as well as his outlook on global politics. His recollections of life in Indonesia's bustling capital, which he remembered as a "magical place," are filled with images of whimsy and wonder alongside punishing hardship. It is there that he started to wrestle with race and economic injustice. It is where he learned to defend himself. It is where he came to appreciate the common humanity of all people. And it is where he also discovered what it meant to be an American, with all the privileges and opportunities that afforded.

At the same time, the young Obama encountered life's roughest edges, from witnessing crushing poverty and the dysfunction of a developing country, to understanding the unspoken fears of a people still recovering from the legacy of recent violent political upheaval. This was the first time Obama contemplated raw power, which in Indonesia he recalled as "undisguised, indiscriminate, naked, always fresh in memory." He saw it directly in the struggles of his stepfather, who was conscripted into the Indonesian army, but who then enjoyed the fruits of prosperity with a job working for an American oil company. He saw it on the streets, in what he later described as an education "in the potential oppressiveness of power and the inequality of wealth."[32]

Although Obama's memories of Indonesia consisted mainly of childhood impressions, he came to see US relations with the country as encapsulating many of the hopes, successes, failures, and contradictions of American foreign policy.

"Our record is mixed," Obama later observed. America's approach to the world was often farsighted, "simultaneously serving our interests, our ideals, and the interests of other nations." However, at other moments its actions "had been misguided, based on false assumptions that ignore the legitimate aspirations of other peoples, undermine our own credibility, and make for a more dangerous world." In Indonesia he came to appreciate the blessings of opportunity that came from being an American, and grew to disdain the "blend of ignorance and arrogance that too often characterizes Americans abroad." Such awareness of the good things the US could do and admiration for how others see it—but also understanding its blind spots, excesses, and how it can look very different on the receiving end—became the core of Obama's outlook.[33]

Some observers would later attribute Obama's cool restraint and Spock-like reluctance to display emotions to his experience with Indonesian culture, especially from his relationship with his stepfather. Perhaps. Obama tended to opine more on the external lessons, especially the grinding everyday struggles he witnessed. By focusing on what Indonesia and the United States shared, he also found optimism, reminding him of the strength that comes from diversity and the importance of tolerance. Indonesia demonstrated that "nations show that hundreds of millions who hold different beliefs can be united in freedom under one flag."[34]

THESE EXPERIENCES ABROAD MEANT something different to each of them: for Eisenhower, it was an opportunity to practice rigorous thinking under a demanding mentor; for Bush, it was the appreciation for how others see America, especially when it is faltering; for Obama, it was living with the complexity and contradictions of US power. Being away from the United States, if only for a few years, gave them a different sense of place—providing a perspective on what their country was and what it could be.

A sense of place influenced their worldviews in another way—a perspective not from outside America, but from within. All three of them, to varying degrees, express some of the lessons drawn from their exposure to the mindset of America's heartland—or what the writer Robert D. Kaplan calls the "frontier ethos."

In terms of American foreign policy, the heartland is usually considered a breeding ground for a very different outlook than the one promoted by Eisenhower, Bush, and Obama. Shielded and geographically insulated from the world, for decades Midwest politicians have been depicted as the true "center of the American spirit," suspicious of foreign entanglements and the ambitions of internationalism. By this rendering, the Midwest has been a center of dissent and resistance to the idea of America's Cold War leadership and post–Cold War indispensability.[35]

Yet the idea of the Midwest as static and inward-looking has always been more myth than reality. Instead, the Midwest reflects a duality that is at the core of America's approach to global affairs: the sense of distance and isolation yet a reliance on others; a place where cruelty and danger rest alongside kindness and opportunity; and a connection to the world and advantageous strategic position that enhances US leadership. Shaped by its history, it is a place of tradition, practicality, experimentation, community, resilience and renewal. One can see how the lessons of the frontier, however indirect, influenced each president's approach to foreign policy.[36]

"The frontier," Kaplan observes, "was about being frugal with our assets. It was about pushing out over the boundary line, but only while tending to our own. It was about maintaining supply lines, however much that slowed us up. It was about reaching but not overreaching, even as it was about not being timid. Above all, it was about pragmatism."[37]

This ethos is most obvious and deeply felt by Eisenhower, who grew up in the hardscrabble Kansas prairie town of Abilene. Ike never lost connection to Abilene and idealized his boyhood there, remembering those years as a "golden time." He remained extraordinarily close to his family and childhood friends, exchanging long letters with them throughout his life, and often referred to the life lessons Abilene taught him. "Concern for others was natural in our small community," he reflected. So was "ambition without arrogance." Moreover, Ike's understanding of the frontier's lessons shaped his ideas on the proper role of government and his thinking behind the Middle Way. "My personal commitment to [this philosophy] stems back from my earlier years on the Kansas prairie," he recalled. The Midwest ethos prized self-sufficiency, responsibility, and personal initiative, Eisenhower's brother Milton once observed, and "radicalism was unheard of." As Ike's longtime aide Andrew Goodpaster, another midwesterner, later remembered, "we thought coming from the Midwest [meant] . . . that we were pretty close to understanding the thinking of the American people."[38]

We see something similar with Bush. He was raised in the cradle of East Coast privilege, yet started his career and family in West Texas, near the hundredth meridian of longitude, considered the defining midpoint of American geography and gateway to the West. He lived there for over a decade in the 1950s, finding riches by wildcatting in the oil business and getting an early taste of politics. Life there was hardly idyllic—with its sandstorms and dirt roads, things were not too far removed from frontier living during the days of the wagon train. Yet the relative isolation and harsh environment fostered a sense of community. Bush soaked it all in, thriving while many others retreated, inhaling the food and lore and lingo, drawing lessons from his successes and the friends he made there. He formed his Texas identity, one that he faithfully maintained, even if it was always a bit of an awkward fit in his patrician shell.[39]

It may seem incongruous to find that Obama, the first American president who grew up outside the continental United States, has such a keen sense of the frontier sensibility. Yet he was deeply influenced by his mother's Kansan parents, who helped raise him; he embraced his adopted home of Chicago with the same fervor that Bush embraced Texas; and his first elected office was in the Illinois legislature, downstate in Springfield. Obama often referred to how his grandparents' homespun virtues of humility, honesty, hard work, and optimism shaped him. From them, he saw the possibility of self-renewal as well as its limits. While Obama cherished these lessons, he never romanticized their origins. He understood that his grandparents came from a place "where decency and endurance and the pioneer spirit were joined at the hip with conformity and suspicion and the potential for unblinking cruelty." One can apply this observation to his outlook on the potential and peril of America in the world.[40]

Along with Eisenhower and Bush, Obama grew to understand that when we forget the lessons of this sensibility, we get ourselves in trouble. All three saw that while the United States should act abroad with ambition and confidence, it also needed to exercise the kind of restraint necessary for survival on the frontier.

Considered this way, this ethos is not about embracing the mythologies of rugged individualism or manifest destiny, nor is it a denial of the racism and violence intrinsic to America's history of westward expansion. Instead, it reflects a simple perspective, one that, as Kaplan explains, was "about doing rather than imagining and living according to an applied wisdom of common sense."[41]

III. PRAGMATISM, EMPATHY, AND TRAGEDY

Examining the worldviews of Eisenhower, Bush, and Obama reveals several generalizable attributes: their patience, humility, and optimism; their firm commitment to the importance of working with others; their conception of power as multifaceted; their ambitions for their country and the world; and their recognition that even the powerful must have limits.

All of these attributes shaped the course and conduct of their foreign policy. Nevertheless, when thinking about what makes them distinct, three characteristics should be highlighted.

The first is their spirit of pragmatism. This is meant not only in the colloquial sense—in that they are merely practical—but because they embraced pragmatism actively as an outlook on the world and as a philosophy for solving problems. This is not unprincipled opportunism focused on the short-term. Instead, it is an approach with a distinct intellectual tradition in America's democracy—and one that scholars have considered a vital component of the American foreign policy "style."[42]

Pragmatism accepts uncertainty, acknowledging that even the most well-intentioned leaders are fallible. It therefore demands the continuous testing of assumptions. While pragmatic thinkers maintain faith in the possibility of progress, they rely on experience, understand the importance of process, and acknowledge the inevitability of contingency and chance. To be pragmatic is to be suspicious of certainties and absolutist dogmas. All ideas must show their utility and have a chance of achieving the intended effect. In other words, they should work.

Pragmatism is as much a method as it is an outlook. The ways one approaches problems and makes decisions are as important as the outcome. Pragmatists are comfortable enough in their own skin to seek a diverse range of views and can admit when they are wrong. As intellectual historian James Kloppenberg observes, pragmatists "build support slowly, gradually, through compromise and painstaking consensus building." This can be easily caricatured as excessive caution or indecision—a charge from critics that each of these presidents had to endure. Therefore, to be a pragmatist, Kloppenberg explains, "requires a more enduring toughness than our impatient culture of the present, ever in search of quick fixes, is likely either to recognize or respect."[43]

To be sure, these three presidents were not equally steeped in pragmatism's intellectual origins or adherents of philosophers like John

Dewey or William James. Eisenhower was familiar with Dewey yet had mixed views of his educational methods (having been exposed to them while serving as president of Columbia); Bush apparently gave them (or for that matter, any other philosophers) little thought; while Obama engaged these ideas in college and law school and showed a more profound understanding of them. Yet whether or not they considered themselves as part of pragmatism's philosophical lineage, they prided themselves on being seen as adhering to its lessons.[44]

Eisenhower often expressed the importance of "making progress through compromise." Bush pushed back against the notion that he didn't possess a vision and defended the importance of getting results, however incremental: "what's wrong with trying to help people, what's wrong with trying to bring peace, what's wrong with trying to make the world a little better?" he asked. And Obama probed policy options in a way described as "consequentialist," always asking if they would have the intended effect, and often skeptical of those promising quick and easy answers. "Every morning and every night I'm taking measure of my actions against the options and possibilities available to me," Obama once said, in an observation summed up by one of his favorite mottos: "better is good." He explained that "better may not be as good as the best, but better is surprisingly hard to obtain. And better is actually harder than worse."[45]

Pragmatism is evolutionary, not revolutionary; it is rooted in humility, compromise, and results. It is therefore anathema to those on the political extremes. So it is not surprising Eisenhower, Bush, and Obama shared deep frustrations and waged endless struggles with polarized politics. "I have no patience whatsoever with the extremes in political thinking," Eisenhower wrote in 1960, expressing a sentiment they all shared. Their challenge would be figuring out how to get traction for a policy of pragmatism within the context of absolutes, which sometimes proved too powerful to overcome.[46]

THIS BRINGS US TO THE SECOND ELEMENT of their outlook worth underscoring: empathy. By dint of background and experience, they all understood the importance of seeing things from another vantage. Their ability to empathize with others was key to their political success, and it was also a core attribute of their foreign policies. They considered empathy as important for understanding nations as it is to engaging with people. They believed empathy was key to preventing misperceptions, to finding common ground, and to getting things done. It made them aware; it taught them patience; it gave them perspective. These presidents saw, as the theologian Reinhold Niebuhr once observed, that all great nations are "caught in a web of history in which many desires, hopes, wills and ambitions, other than their own, are operative."[47]

Empathy should *not* be misconstrued with sympathy, thereby rationalizing or justifying others' actions, or even taking their side. Too often, empathy is seen as a weakness in foreign policy debates. Yet these presidents saw the advantage of trying to get inside other people's minds to discern their motivations, priorities, needs, and fears. "It all starts with being able to relate," Obama said. "Don't confuse being soft with seeing the other guy's point of view," Bush once advised his sons.[48]

Each of these presidents valued his ability to understand another perspective, considering their foreign policy moves by anticipating how others would react, and at times allowing others to enjoy the spotlight. This was an essential component of their alliance management. They were comfortable exercising leadership in sometimes humble, subtle, less visible ways: Eisenhower famously wielded power with a "hidden-hand"; Bush often extolled the virtue of "giving the other guy credit"; and Obama understood the importance of occasionally "leading from behind" the scenes.[49]

THIRD, ALL THREE PRESIDENTS shared a tragic sensibility—they recognized the world could be messy and mean and harsh. They understood that despite the best intentions, things go wrong. This is not to say they were pessimistic. They did not believe every initiative was destined to fail and, therefore, not worth trying. In fact they were each preternaturally optimistic, constantly looking on the bright side and trying to buoy the spirits of those around them. Yet they grasped they must take nothing for granted; in international affairs, as in life, hardship and danger lurked and success was not assured.[50]

They learned these lessons from history. But at a deeper, more emotional level, they suffered tragedy personally—and therefore knew its lessons intimately. They were not strangers to grief and recovery. They experienced what loss felt like, and knew what it meant to submit to uncontrollable events, adapt, recover, move forward, and work to make things better. Their experience with adversity imbued them with a submerged strength.

Eisenhower and Bush both endured hardship up close during World War II. Ike made decisions that sent thousands to their deaths, and Bush lost two of his crewmates, and nearly his own life, when his fighter plane was shot down over the Pacific in 1944. They also shared the trauma of losing young children to disease: Eisenhower's first son, Icky, died at age three from scarlet fever; Bush's first daughter, Robin, died after suffering from leukemia, also at age three.

They carried the weight of their loss for the rest of their lives. Eisenhower recalled his son's death "the greatest disappointment and disaster in my life . . . a tragedy from which we never recovered." For Bush, the meaning of his daughter's death "taught me that life is unpredictable and fragile," and the pain always rested just beneath the surface. Until their last days, these two men were overwhelmed with emotion by these memories. When a reporter once questioned Bush if he had ever faced personal adversity, he coldly stared back and asked, "Have you ever sat and watched your child die? I did, for six months." Visiting their gravesites today, one finds that along with their loving spouse, each rests next to their lost child.[51]

Obama's experience with tragedy was different, but no less profound. He grew up with a void caused by a father who left when he was young. While seeking to discover his own identity, Obama lived in Indonesia and worked on Chicago's South Side, where he saw the desperation and disorder of the powerless, and observed the narrow path "between humiliation and untrammeled fury." As an African American coming of age in the 1970s and 80s, he was very familiar with what he called "the bitter pill of swallowed back anger," and the brutality, injustice, and oppression engendered by systemic racism. Because of this, Obama understood how hard it was "to acknowledge the sins of the past and the challenges of the present without becoming trapped in cynicism and despair."[52]

Suffering hardship like the death of a child or enduring the sting of racism might trigger doubt or dampen hope. Obama sometimes wondered, when faced with such cruelty and injustice, "whether we progress from one stage to the next in an upward course or whether we just ride the cycles of boom and bust, war and peace, ascent and decline." Concluding that these were thoughts of an "old man," he knew his only choice was to move forward; to be resilient, "keep going, charging ahead," as Bush would say. In a 1956 letter to his older brother who had lost his own son, Eisenhower reflected on his own suffering and noted that while some terrible things could never be explained, the pain "must be accepted and absorbed into the philosophy that a man develops as he goes along." Understanding tragedy did not cause them to cower in pessimism; on the contrary, it made them forward-thinking, determined, creative, and, perhaps paradoxically, hopeful.[53]

This impacted their foreign policy fundamentally. Having a tragic sensibility inspired prudence, a recognition that few problems could be solved quickly, and some not at all. They knew most answers were imperfect. They understood many choices they faced were not between good and bad, but bad and worse. Difficult trade-offs between priorities were inevitable. Yet they believed the United States still had the power to make a difference if it endured sacrifice and worked with others. Mitigating tragedy requires relentless energy, unceasing effort, and resilience. A foreign policy leader must never forget that while things might get better, danger—and failure—is never far away.

Toward the end of his presidency, Obama summarized this in a way to which Eisenhower and Bush could surely relate. "The world is a tough, complicated, messy, mean place, and full of hardship and tragedy," he said. "And in order to advance both our security interests and those ideals and values that we care about, we've got to be hardheaded at the same time we're bighearted, and pick and choose our spots, and recognize that there are going to be times where the best that we can do is to shine a spotlight on something that's terrible, but not believe that we can automatically solve it. There are going to be times where our security interests conflict with our concerns about human rights. There are going to be times when we can do something about innocent people being killed, but there are going to be times when we can't."[54]

In other words, a central challenge, especially for a country as powerful as the United States, is to maintain a sense of proportion. Excessive ambition can be as dangerous as insufficient courage. Wisdom means knowing when and how to act, balancing between doing too much or too little, and navigating between hubris and fear. Thinking tragically requires getting the balance right—connecting the dots from means to ends, understanding how actions in a particular circumstance fits within a broader context of a nation's goals. All this constitutes the foundation of strategy.

Strategy

On a blustery morning in downtown Chicago, the week before Christmas 2008, Barack Obama sat down with his new national security team to sketch out a strategy to revitalize American power and redefine its global role. Following a presidential race fueled by hope and possibility, the Obama team faced a reality much like the weather outside—cold and grim.

Four years earlier, Obama had been one of the fifty-nine members of the Illinois state senate. Now the forty-seven-year-old president-elect gathered with his newly selected top aides, most of whom were long-standing pillars of official Washington, such as the incoming secretary of state, Hillary Clinton; and Robert Gates, the first secretary of defense ever asked by a new commander-in-chief to stay in the job. Obama hardly knew many of them.

Meeting in a high-rise office building that served as the small Chicago outpost for Obama's Washington-based transition team, they spent the day sifting through a perilous global inbox: wars in Iraq and Afghanistan, tensions roiling the Middle East, global threats like a warming climate, and a rapidly changing geopolitical chessboard defined by rising powers like China and India.

The discussion was sober and business-like. Given the task, there wasn't much of Obama's campaign "yes-we-can" enthusiasm. The president-elect asked probing questions, challenged assumptions, and encouraged vigorous debate. Everyone sitting in that stale conference room understood the future of American power hung in the balance.

Yet worldwide tumult was not the most urgent of Obama's worries, or even the most important. The next morning, he convened another set of advisers to discuss a topic not formally about foreign policy, but that had everything to do with the future of America's international role: the Great Recession of 2008. The president-elect's incoming economic team laid out the stakes in blunt terms: they told him it was his "holy shit moment." If he did not act decisively, they warned, the financial system would crater and he would not be able to do anything else. Obama's foreign policy strategy had to start with saving the economy.[1]

IN ANOTHER DECEMBER FIFTY-SIX YEARS EARLIER, president-elect Dwight Eisenhower enjoyed more convivial surroundings when he first gathered with his newly appointed national security team. Far removed from any nondescript downtown conference room, they convened in the elegant admiral's quarters aboard the USS *Helena*, at sea on the Pacific Ocean.

The circumstances they inherited, however, were similarly daunting. Eisenhower faced a hot war abroad and economic fragility at home. Returning from visiting the American commanders and troops in Korea, a visit he famously pledged to make during the 1952 campaign to end that war, Ike's principal policy advisers joined him for the journey, including John Foster Dulles, his nominee for secretary of state. As they sailed across the Pacific in the navy cruiser, the administration-in-waiting spent hours sitting around a green felt-covered table, getting comfortable with one another, playing some bridge, and discussing the key issues facing the nation—and the strategies needed to address them.

The media breathlessly reported on this "epic mid-Pacific conference" as one of high drama, a depiction no doubt encouraged by Ike's press team eager to show the president-elect taking charge. However, other than some ambassadorial appointments and budget disputes, the group made few policy decisions. Like Obama's transition session in 2008, this was Ike's chance to size up his new advisers and hear their views. Nevertheless, the discussion proved important when considering the broad contours of Eisenhower's future strategy.

This floating seminar tackled the moment's essential issue: the nature of the Soviet threat and an appropriate response. Dulles did most of the talking. He argued the Soviets intended to "exhaust our resources and our patience and divide us internally," chiefly by forcing the United States on the defensive by "mounting a series of local actions around the world at times and places of their choosing." Eisenhower shared this perception of the threat, but worried about the larger trade-offs. He stressed the need to balance the resources required for US military strength with those needed to fuel a vibrant economy. This balancing act—referred to as the "great equation"—became the cornerstone of his strategic approach. "To amass military power without regard to our economic capacity would be to defend ourselves against one kind of disaster by inviting another," Eisenhower said a few months later in his first State of the Union address, the drafting of which began aboard the *Helena*.[2]

FOR GEORGE H. W. BUSH, the weeks after his 1988 election were characterized by simmering anxieties rather than urgent concerns. After eight years as vice president, Bush did not represent a clean break from the past, nor did he inherit an unpopular war or a massive economic crisis. He knew his incoming team because it included some of his oldest friends and colleagues. But the president-elect still had to put his stamp on foreign policy, especially as it concerned the principal strategic question of the time—how to respond to the rapid transformation of the Soviet Union, led by Mikhail Gorbachev.

On the Sunday before Thanksgiving, Bush invited James A. Baker III and Brent Scowcroft to meet with him at the vice president's residence at the Naval Observatory in Northwest Washington, DC. Bush already named his old friend Baker as secretary of state, and that November morning, he asked Scowcroft to join the White House as his national security adviser. When the three men took their seats by the fire in Bush's small study, they began to wrestle with a world on the cusp of fundamental change. Baker would later reflect that it was a moment when "long-held beliefs about grand strategy were being turned upside down."

They faced the same fundamental questions that Eisenhower's team discussed on the *Helena*: what was Moscow up to and what should the United States do about it? Bush's two advisers presented different answers. Baker was bullish about Soviet intentions, while Scowcroft was skeptical, worried that Gorbachev was a "clever bear" who, by making the Soviet Union seem less threatening, could undermine alliances and deflate the rationale for robust American leadership.

Bush remained unsure. Frustrated by the Soviets, who were setting the pace of events and forcing the United States into merely reacting, the president-elect sought to regain the initiative without, as he explained, "do[ing] anything foolish" in the process. And before he engaged Gorbachev, he wanted to shore up American alliances. As Bush prepared to enter the White House, he conceded he had "a vision of the world" that he wanted to see, but "no fixed 'ten-point plan'" to get there.[3]

EISENHOWER, BUSH, AND OBAMA each became president at an inflection point for the United States in the world—inheriting situations in which the country seemed to be falling behind. Eisenhower and Obama found a nation deeply wounded by unpopular ongoing wars. Eisenhower took office at the dawn of the nuclear age and decolonization, and he wondered about the economic sustainability of long-term confrontation with the Soviet Union. Obama dealt with the possibility of a second Great Depression and a changing global chessboard. Bush inherited a country on the cusp of winning the Cold War but worried about losing the peace.

All of them wanted to reposition the United States so it could better project influence across a shifting geopolitical landscape. They worried about American decline, the seductive pull of isolationism, and the corrosive effect of partisan politics on sound strategic thinking. And they each wanted to put their own stamp on strategy. For Eisenhower and Obama, it was about charting a new course following unpopular presidents who were considered failures; for Bush, it was about finally emerging from his predecessors' long shadow.

Of the three, Eisenhower spent the most time formally studying strategy as a discipline. He preferred a simple definition, considering it as "the art and science of applying resources to accomplish national objectives." True enough. But as Ike well understood, the requirements of national security are more complex and demanding.[4]

Presidents require a "grand strategy," which is a big phrase for a simple concept. A grand strategy is a coherent set of ideas about what one wants to achieve in foreign policy and how to do it. It is the way a president translates a worldview into concrete policies by setting objectives, prioritizing them, and adjudicating among those that come into conflict. What makes a strategy "grand" is in how it accounts for the totality of the nation's interests at home and abroad, and in the way it designs an integrated approach to pursue them. While a country's foreign policy goals could potentially be unlimited, the means for achieving them are necessarily limited—so a successful grand strategy aligns the two. "Whatever balance you strike," the historian John Lewis Gaddis observes, "there'll be a link between what's real and what's imagined: between your current location and your intended destination." A president must connect the dots.[5]

Forging a grand strategy isn't easy. Implementing one is even harder. From the moment of their election, Eisenhower, Bush, and Obama thought deeply about their approaches to national security. Eisenhower and Obama did so systematically, interrogating ideas exhaustively by relying on a carefully managed process, while Bush was more informal and instinctual. They all consulted widely, challenged conventional wisdom, and tried to think big. They subsequently strove to articulate their strategies in speeches and public statements. They did their best to stick with their decisions, yet also took advantage of opportunities that emerged to adjust course. Nevertheless, all three were criticized for being too cautious, indecisive, and unimaginative—or, occasionally, for not having a strategy at all.

I. EISENHOWER: STRATEGIC SOLVENCY

During Dwight Eisenhower's eight years in the White House, the National Security Council (NSC) met 366 times, gathering in the Cabinet Room at the same time almost every Thursday morning. Eisenhower presided over 329 of these sessions. The voluminous record of minutes from these meetings shows an actively engaged commander-in-chief, who steered the conversation by asking incisive questions, testing ideas, and sometimes contradicting himself. The rigor and discipline with which Eisenhower and his team approached strategic questions (and documented their discussions in ample records) is a standard no administration has yet matched.[6]

Throughout these discussions, which usually lasted as long as two hours, Eisenhower emphasized one theme above all: strategic solvency. He repeatedly stressed the nation's commitments must balance with its capabilities and resources. As he clarified on the *Helena*, Eisenhower thought his most important task was to design an approach the United States could afford to sustain over time without bankrupting the nation. In one of his first NSC meetings in early 1953, Eisenhower explained that his basic purpose was to "reverse a growing complacency in the country that the U.S. could go on spending as it pleased, without regard for its income."[7]

Although Eisenhower campaigned in 1952 by excoriating Harry Truman's policies, he shared his predecessor's basic outlook. A Truman strategy paper, known as NSC-68, articulated their common view, stating the nation's survival rested on active global leadership to counter the Soviet Union. Yet Eisenhower thought Truman's strategy ceded agency to the pull of different emergencies and an imprecise definition of the threat, allowing policy to lurch along unsustainably at the cost of long-term prosperity. Since NSC-68 did not distinguish between core and peripheral interests, the implication was the United States would respond to everything everywhere. The costs were clear: in less than three years, defense spending tripled, and the size of US forces doubled, prompting the new president to ask just how much military power was sufficient to secure the country.

Eisenhower ran for office promising to restore a sense of predictability and balance to foreign affairs; "Eisenhower, Man of Peace" was his 1952 campaign slogan. He worried the United States suffered from what he described as an "enough-ness" problem—he accepted the premise of containment, but wanted to take a "new look" at its conduct. He did not doubt the magnitude of global danger. However, he questioned how much sacrifice Americans could tolerate. If the price of internationalism proved too costly—as he believed the Korean War exemplified—the public might find solace in isolationism. Ike also thought about the trade-offs between military spending and economic health.[8]

This was about more than budget arithmetic. As Eisenhower saw it, how one answered such questions would shape the fundamental nature of American society. "The essential dilemma," he explained, was that by "defending this way of life we would find ourselves resorting to methods that endangered this way of life." Therefore, Ike argued, the United States needed to confront the Soviet threat with a strategy "that would not result in our transformation into a garrison state," becoming a nation "mighty in arms that is lacking in liberty and bankrupt in resources."[9]

FOR MOST OF HIS FIRST YEAR as president, Eisenhower and his aides methodically hashed out a blueprint for dealing with the Soviets through a process now regarded as a master class in strategic planning. They spent hours in meetings and produced mountains of documents.

The most revealing public statement of Eisenhower's strategic approach, however, came just a few months after he took office, in response to the unexpected death of Soviet leader Joseph Stalin in March 1953. Despite the interruption to their review, Eisenhower welcomed the opportunity to reframe the Cold War, or perhaps end it altogether. He sought to use his first major foreign policy speech to declare this "chance for peace."

Eisenhower spent weeks deliberating with his team about what to say. They argued about the speech's timing, substance, how it might be used to jump-start negotiations with the Soviets, and whether it was even a good idea at all. Ike focused less on the specifics than the larger purpose: to transcend the entrenched military, political and economic rivalry between the world's two most powerful countries. He also grew frustrated with his aides' second-guessing and lack of bold thinking. "I'm responsible for this country's goddamn foreign policy," he lashed out in one conversation. "Now we either cut out all this fooling around and make a serious bid for peace—or we forget the whole thing."

This process reflected Eisenhower's deep anxieties about the costs of the Cold War. "What world can afford this sort of thing for long?" he said with exasperation to his speechwriter as they talked in the Oval Office one late afternoon. Pacing impatiently around the room, Ike dictated themes he already rehearsed in his mind. Rehashing another indictment of the Soviet regime would be "asinine," he said. "What matters is this—what have we got to offer the world? What are we trying to achieve?"

Ike wanted to frame the choice between two divergent paths. The current course could lead to nuclear war or, at best, a militarized state, in which "every nation on earth is being deprived of the fruits of its own toil." Alternatively, there was a path of "disarmament," which he hoped would rekindle the kind of optimism last felt eight years prior, at the end of World War II. Although Ike realized complete disarmament was unrealistic, he wanted to offer the Soviets a bold deal: if they could reach an agreement on reducing hostilities and thereby lowering defense spending, the United States would be prepared to devote most of the savings to aid and reconstruction.[10]

Delivered on April 16, 1953, at the annual meeting of the American Society of Newspaper Editors at the Statler Hotel in Washington, DC, the "chance for peace" speech received worldwide acclaim, admired for its eloquence and moral clarity. The administration widely publicized the address, rebroadcasting it in forty-five languages and circulating the text in 3 million sleek brochures. One of the most influential observers of the Washington scene, and an avowed Eisenhower skeptic, Richard Rovere, raved about the "immense triumph" of the new president. He asserted the president's address "firmly established his leadership in America and reestablished American leadership in the world."[11]

In hindsight, one can see in this speech the themes that animated Eisenhower's foreign policy for the next eight years: a determination to be tough with an adversary, while also being willing to reach out and talk concretely about reducing military tensions; a desire to arrest the escalating rise of defense spending; and a deep concern about what he would later call the military-industrial complex and its threat to the American way of life. "All lie like seeds in this address," one of Ike's aides, William Ewald, later observed.[12]

The speech's most lasting contribution was Eisenhower's framing of national security's fundamental choice: the high price of war and how those resources could be better used. Using language he instructed his speechwriter to include, Ike passionately described the social costs of military spending in a way no commander-in-chief had before, and few have since. He talked about how the cost of one bomber could build thirty schools or pave fifty miles of highway, or how the price of a single fighter jet could pay for a half-million bushels of wheat, or how a naval destroyer cost the same as homes for thousands of people.

"Every gun that is made, every warship launched, every rocket fired signifies, in the final sense, a theft from those who hunger and are not fed, those who are cold and are not clothed," Eisenhower said in one of the most quoted sections of the speech. "This is not a way of life at all . . . Under the cloud of threatening war, it is humanity hanging from a cross of iron." Seeking to solve the "essential dilemma," or "great equation," between security, economic health, and liberal democracy, this speech represented the conceptual heart of Eisenhower's aspirations for US foreign policy. These words are also how he wanted to be remembered. Decades later, Eisenhower had them chiseled into the marble of his burial site just steps from his boyhood home in Abilene, Kansas.[13]

"This is not a way of life at all . . . Under the cloud of threatening war, it is humanity hanging from a cross of iron." Dwight Eisenhower outlines the "chance for peace" on April 16, 1953.
(Photo by Hank Walker/The LIFE Picture Collection via Getty Image)

Despite its powerful words, the speech did not have its intended effect. While there might have been a chance for peace, few wanted to seize it. The climate of fear and mutual suspicion proved too great. Moscow failed to reciprocate, and Eisenhower's administration remained deeply divided about how to follow up practically on its rhetoric. Just two days after the address, Secretary of State Dulles gave a far more belligerent speech promising that the United States would not be a "supplicant." The structural, political, and ideological divide between the United States and the Soviets proved too much to overcome, and Ike's appeal to reshape the Cold War sputtered.

Nonetheless, Eisenhower's response to Stalin's death became the template for the rest of his presidency, one which adhered to the same strategic principles he learned from Fox Conner and honed as a successful general: setting lofty goals, carefully planning, building resources, maintaining the ability to maneuver, and always acting from a position of strength. While Eisenhower dreamed about the possibilities for peace— and ceaselessly worried about the sacrifices required in its absence, and how those may jeopardize the American way of life—he never stopped preparing to wage a long war.[14]

EISENHOWER'S STRATEGY OUTLINED several ambitious goals to meet the perceived Soviet threat to US security. He aimed to build the strength and cohesion of European allies, especially by restoring confidence in the US role in NATO and assisting the continent in consolidating the post-World War II peace. He needed to craft an approach to deal with an untested and unpredictable new leadership in Moscow, which was keen to project Soviet influence in Europe and Asia. He had to come up with an approach to address weak states and the emergence of newly established nations in the wake of decolonization (which were then described as the "uncommitted areas of the world"). He had to handle the exponential development of nuclear weapons and rapid modernization of missiles. And perhaps most important, he aspired to achieve all this in a sustainable way—to seek, as he liked to quote George Washington, "a respectable posture of defense" for the long haul. Ike's explicit goal was to cut the price of Truman's conventional and strategic buildup—costs that he believed threatened US solvency—while also waging the Cold War more aggressively.[15]

Eisenhower probed these issues thoroughly, establishing task forces to assess competing approaches through a process known as "Project Solarium," which is unquestionably the most heralded strategic review in US history. When completed in October 1953, the strategy it produced— known bureaucratically as NSC Document 162/2, but more commonly as the "New Look"—provided the basic framework for Eisenhower's foreign policy for the next seven years.

The strategy embraced the core lessons of the Great Depression and World War II: that long-term US prosperity required leadership to nurture an open, lawful, and stable political economy and a global balance of power in favor of freedom. Accordingly, no adversary should be allowed to dominate key regions—meaning Europe, the Middle East, and Asia—and the United States should work to create strong allies who shared its perspective and foster a broader collective security. In essence, this strategy aimed to preserve and expand the American way of life while thwarting the appeal of command economies, socialism, and communism. By doing so, it established the primary means to wage the Cold War followed by subsequent presidents—and in many respects, still influences foreign policy in the twenty-first century.[16]

THIS STRATEGY CONTAINED SEVERAL COMPONENTS worth highlighting, starting with the best-known aspect of the New Look—nuclear weapons.

Eisenhower's views on nuclear weapons continue to arouse a considerable amount of controversy and confusion. His strategy envisioned nuclear arms to be "as available for use as other munitions," yet he harbored no illusions about their dangers and firmly believed they would "destroy civilization" if used in an all-out war. Although Ike held on to the dream of disarmament, he resigned himself to the logic that the best way to prevent the use of such weapons was to threaten nuclear war—thus establishing deterrence as the bedrock for American strategy.

He argued the United States needed to show a "manifest determination . . . to use its atomic capability and massive retaliatory striking power." As much as Eisenhower abhorred nuclear weapons, he understood their utility as a tool of statecraft, hoping that the terrible prospect of absolute war, one in which no one could win, would help prevent conflict generally. Eisenhower translated this into practice by pouring substantial resources into modernizing America's nuclear arsenal (establishing the nuclear "triad" of weapons delivered by missiles, from aircraft, or at sea), hardening homeland defenses to ensure the United States could survive a Soviet attack and launch a "second strike," and integrating nuclear weapons as a core component of US defense planning.[17]

However, as the "chance for peace" speech illustrated, Eisenhower relied on more than bluster -- he sought opportunities to engage the

Soviet leadership to reduce tensions, constrain the arms race, and resolve differences over time on America's terms. This steadfast commitment to "waging peace," as Ike called it, was a second component of the New Look.

This derived from his pragmatism. "You don't promote the cause of peace by talking only to people with whom you agree," Eisenhower said. "You've got to meet face-to-face the people with whom you disagree at times, to determine whether or not there is a way of working out the differences and reaching a better understanding." Although Ike pushed several initiatives to spark talks—such as meeting with the Soviet leadership at three summits, and proposing ideas like "open skies" (a proposal to allow the United States and Soviets to fly reconnaissance missions over each other's territory) to build confidence and trust—his efforts to wage peace garnered little success.[18]

Third, the New Look stressed the importance of strong relations with allies, helping them develop greater capacity to defend themselves and fight alongside the United States. Despite his initial hope the US military presence in Europe could be temporary, Eisenhower strived to maintain a substantial force deployed there. He prioritized integrating West Germany into NATO, actively supported the continent's evolution into a European Community (the forerunner of today's EU), and sought ways for European allies to contribute to the nuclear deterrent. Ike also prioritized US assistance to developing countries, both to make them less vulnerable to Soviet influence and better "able and willing to participate in the defense of the free world." Such spending remained a tough sell politically at home. Nevertheless, Eisenhower argued, "when we are investing in other countries . . . it is not charity—it is a security expenditure."[19]

Fourth, Eisenhower's strategy essentially invented the modern US intelligence community and fully integrated covert operations into the execution of American foreign policy. Eisenhower poured resources into the CIA and unleashed it to wage a hidden war against communism. At the same time, he invested heavily in new technologies to better understand Soviet capabilities and intentions. Most controversially, he authorized US involvement in coup plots in Iran in 1953 and Guatemala in 1954, and personally approved risky U2 reconnaissance flights over the Soviet Union.

Eisenhower instituted a clandestine toolkit of considerable breadth. As historian William Hitchcock explains, "from coups to economic warfare, and sabotage, propaganda, and underground resistance, U.S. plans took aim at every aspect of communist power across the globe." Ike's enthusiasm for the dark arts stemmed from several factors: they were a relatively cheap way to project influence; they were supposed to remain secret, and therefore preserved deniability; and they were deemed to be less risky, since, even if discovered, the Soviets were less likely to retaliate through escalation.[20]

Ike's reliance on covert actions as an alternative tool of American power was crucial for a fifth element of his strategy: ensuring that the United States could assert its influence and prevent Soviet gains in Europe, the Middle East, and Asia at a reasonable price and without getting bogged down in a costly, open-ended conflict. He assumed office with 300,000 US troops deployed to Korea to fight a war in which 45,000 Americans were killed or missing. That was not something he intended to repeat. "No more Koreas" became one of his administration's maxims. Moreover, this fear of another regional war is further reason Eisenhower's strategy emphasized nuclear weapons. If covert action broadened options, the reliance on nuclear weapons limited them—the United States would have to think twice before getting itself involved in a conflict that could escalate into Armageddon.[21]

Sixth, Eisenhower understood that the New Look could not be accepted by acclamation or promulgated without explanation—it required, as he wrote in a 1953 memo to Dulles, "the enlightened support of Americans and the informed understanding of our friends." Ike acknowledged that since common citizens "felt helpless to do anything about the foreign threat," he had to conduct a "vigorous campaign" to educate the public. He did so with major policy speeches, nationally televised addresses, and weekly press conferences. He believed such an effort was "indispensable if we are to do anything but drift aimlessly, probably to our own eventual destruction."

Eisenhower set out to explain the basic contours of his strategy in simple, often folksy terms, casting himself as a soldier of peace. Americans needed a clear picture of the global landscape in order to support the rationale for the sacrifices being asked of them and know why the government would act in some circumstances and not in others. Moreover, Eisenhower thought, the rest of the world also needed to understand US goals better, since "abroad we and our intentions are suspect because we are known to be big and wealthy, and believed to be impulsive and truculent."[22]

Eisenhower considered maintaining public support to be about much more than boosting his personal popularity or political fortunes; it was a manifestation of his concerns about how much sacrifice the American people could tolerate. "Leadership has the chore of informing people and attempting to inspire them to real sacrifice," he wrote in a 1953 letter, emphasizing the need to push back against those who appealed to "man's natural fear of the future." The requirements of national security could be endless, yet the country's democratic system could only withstand so much. The means had to match the ends—and both had to be sustainable.[23]

In a meeting with his NSC at Camp David in 1955, Eisenhower told his colleagues it was their duty to "clearly realize that he is engaged in defending a way of life over a prolonged period," and to be "constantly aware of the weight of the financial burden that our citizens are able to bear." Absent public support, Eisenhower observed, they could "force upon our citizens defense and other spending at much higher levels," but over the long term, this "would require an authoritarian system of government, and destroy the health of our free society." In other words, strategic solvency remained paramount for American democracy to endure.[24]

However wise, this approach exposed Eisenhower to the charge that his strategic choices did not add up; that he lacked the will to fulfill his ambition. Sometimes the messaging—with slogans like "massive retaliation" and talk of "liberation" and "winning" the Cold War—obscured his more calibrated policy substance. Observers were quick to note the gap between the Eisenhower administration's words and deeds. "It had promised to do more than its predecessors with less money," James Reston wrote in 1955. "It implied that it was going to 'roll back' the Communist tide while at the same time it was cutting the military budget." Such overstatement was a key flaw of Eisenhower's otherwise coherent strategy—and it is a challenge both Bush and Obama wrestled with as well.[25]

II. BUSH: ENLIGHTENED PRIMACY

George H. W. Bush understood the importance of strategy. But compared to Eisenhower, he preferred a far looser, inductive approach to developing one. To Bush, foreign policy was less about big ideas and more about people, personalities, and places. He loved the high drama and intrigue far more than abstract debates that felt too academic and often left him tongue-tied.

Broadly speaking, Bush's strategy rested on three pillars: first, to support the Soviet Union's peaceful transformation and the liberation of Eastern Europe in a way that prevented backlash or instability; second, to sustain America's unique strength and preeminent geopolitical position, especially by maintaining its active leadership in Europe; and third, to use American influence to promote the kind of global cooperation envisioned after World War II, but undermined by the Cold War stalemate.

Bush's first challenge in 1989 was adapting America's posture toward a rapidly transforming Soviet Union. He prized personal relationships— "where would we be without friends?" he often said—and the most important one of his presidency proved to be with an unlikely partner: the General Secretary of the Communist Party of the Soviet Union.

Bush was initially skeptical of Gorbachev. Ronald Reagan left the White House convinced the Soviet leader's reform efforts were the real deal, saying that all his talk about the Soviet Union as an evil empire was from "another time and another era." However, Bush only met Gorbachev a few times before taking office and found him to be a bit of a showboat, and top White House advisers thought Gorbachev was relaxing tensions not to make peace, but to buy time to revitalize Soviet strength and drive a wedge between the United States and Europe.[26]

So the new administration tried to slow things down. Bush wanted to engage Gorbachev on his own terms and with allies' active support. He used his early conversations with fellow world leaders to stress the need to proceed with caution and reclaim the initiative. "We must take the offensive," Bush told his good friend, Canadian Prime Minister Brian Mulroney, soon after entering the White House, adding that "[we can] not just be seen as reacting to yet another [Gorbachev] move."[27]

Like Eisenhower, Bush ordered his administration to initiate a comprehensive internal review of its policy toward the Soviet Union. Not satisfied with simply sticking with the status quo, they asked what kind of relationship they wanted to see in the year 2000 and devised a set of initiatives (such as arms control measures and proposed troop withdrawals from Europe) to test Moscow's intentions. Given the stakes of the ongoing review, pursuing a temporary "pause" in the relationship seemed to make sense. Yet this fed the perception that Bush was timid, ambivalent, and, perhaps, wished for Gorbachev to fail. The president chafed at such impatience, privately complaining he was "trying to do things in a thoughtful way, not through the editorial page of the *New York Times*."[28]

Bush eventually warmed to the Soviet leader, sympathizing with his plight and admiring his courage. By the end of 1989, Bush reached a clear strategic conclusion: he wanted Gorbachev to succeed. He once described his counterpart as a surfer riding waves of global support; in the late 1980s, the enthusiasm for "Gorbymania" seemed to be everywhere. Yet when the tides quickly changed and the Soviet empire started to falter, Bush worried any triumphalism would backfire. He needed Gorbachev as a partner, not a defeated, aggrieved, and embittered foe. Bush wanted to promote peaceful change within the Soviet Union and encourage its cooperation abroad—to move, as he put it, "beyond containment."[29]

"I want the American people to say the Soviet Union is not the enemy," he told the Soviet leader. Publicly and privately, Bush said he wanted to handle things "properly" and exercise restraint. Stability mattered above all else. "It is true I am a cautious man," he admitted to Gorbachev during their shipboard summit off the Maltese coast in December 1989. "But I am not a coward. We are in favor of reserved behavior." Bush wanted to nudge Gorbachev along, but not too hard. As long as Bush saw events moving his way, he did not want to overreach and screw things up.[30]

THIS PENCHANT FOR AVOIDING RISK TO DO NO HARM—or his "Hippocratic diplomacy"—did not always apply, especially when grappling with two of the most consequential strategic decisions of his presidency: what to do about a divided Germany and whether to confront Saddam Hussein's Iraq. In both instances, the president departed from his usual course and took a big gamble. This risk tolerance highlights the final two components of Bush's strategy, which were reminiscent of Eisenhower's: a commitment to sustaining American leadership to promote greater freedom and prosperity, and an aspiration to forge a new system of international cooperation to solve common problems.[31]

Bush viewed the end of the Cold War as validation of decades of America's containment policy. Moreover, he believed it created an imperative for even more US leadership. Seeing vigilance and strength as essential to secure lasting peace, Bush did not subscribe to minimalist interpretations of American power. As he wrote at the time, his "vision" for world leadership sought "to guarantee" that people live free from fear and "know the blessings of democracy of freedom." This required the United States to stand up for its values, maintain a strong military, promote free markets, be an "active leader," and understand that "[American] security comes first but the security of other friends around the world is vital too." Bush sought to renew the "spirit of America," which appealed to "the better nature of man, a concept of neighbor helping neighbor."[32]

"It is true I am a cautious man. But I am not a coward." Bush confers with National Security Adviser Brent Scowcroft (at left) and Secretary of State James A. Baker III (at right). (Photo by David Valdez/White House/The LIFE Picture Collection via Getty Images)

Bush considered Europe's fate central to American interests. Communism's rapid collapse reignited decades-old debates over the proper US role on the continent: if the Soviet Union was no longer an overriding threat, were the continued costs and sacrifices of US leadership in Europe worth it? Shouldn't the Europeans do more on their own? Although Bush supported some modest scaling back of the US military presence, he viewed maintaining a strong transatlantic alliance as one of the essential lessons of the twentieth century. He thought the United States "bears a disproportionate responsibility for peace in Europe," and that it learned the "hard way that it was a mistake to withdraw into isolation after World War I."[33]

After the fall of the Berlin Wall in November 1989, Bush considered East and West Germany's post–Cold War future through this lens. Instead of following a cautious approach—which would entail stepping back and allowing Germany to remain either divided or neutral—Bush championed its reunification inside NATO. At the same time, he pushed nervous partners, such as the United Kingdom, France, and the Soviet Union, to do the same, despite historial anxieties about renewed German power. Bush's assiduous support for German unity stemmed from his belief that the country's fate would determine Europe's future, and that its citizens should determine their own destiny. For Bush, a united Germany had to be embedded within the Western Alliance—which was an extension of Eisenhower's thinking about the key importance of West Germany in the 1950s.

It wasn't all for the benefit of others, however. German reunification was also good for the United States. Bush worried the end of the Cold War would erode the case for supporting institutions like NATO and sustaining an active US role in Europe. He lamented the "euphoria" surrounding expectations of a peace dividend and dismissed the "weirdos" who "don't want our troops in Europe at all." To him, these individuals "sounded like the isolationists of old."[34]

Therefore, a reunified Germany inside NATO would be vital to maintaining US leadership in Europe and outmaneuvering domestic critics of US global engagement. "I've got to look after the U.S. interest in all this," Bush dictated to his diary at the time, "without reverting to a kind of isolationist or stupid peace-nik view of where we stand in the world." The decision to keep a reunified Germany in NATO—which planted seeds for the alliance's enlargement over the next three decades to thirty members—proved controversial and remains a source of Russian grievance against the West. However, Bush saw this achievement as a key component of his strategy. Solving the Germany puzzle ensured the survival of NATO, which allowed the United States to maintain its leadership in Europe and sustain—and transform—its political and economic influence.[35]

AMERICAN LEADERSHIP WOULD NOT ENDURE through dominance alone. It needed other nations to go along, seeing it to be in their interests too. This was the logic behind the third component of Bush's strategy: the somewhat misunderstood, and much maligned, "new world order."

The idea's straightforward premise—that the more countries solved problems together, the better it was for the United States and the world—was instinctual to Bush, reinforced by his experiences as an envoy abroad and at the UN. "It is my theory that the more [other countries] are included in the take-off, the more we get their opinion, the more we reach out no matter what is involved, in terms of time involved, the better it is," Bush told his diary. "Everyone has his place in the sun—large country or small, they should be consulted, the opinions considered."[36]

As a matter of strategy, allied buy-in was necessary for two interrelated reasons: first, because the United States needed other countries to share the burden; and second, because greater cooperation was required to sustain the American people's support for an assertive foreign policy. In contrast to influence by coercion, which was more the Soviet model, leadership by consent is what made the United States unique. Bush saw the Cold War's end as an opening to allow for the type of international cooperation many hoped to see after 1945. Seen this way, Bush thought he had an opportunity to do something his predecessors never could achieve: consolidate the victory of World War II into a workable and lasting peace.

Bush and his team kicked around several ideas for how this revived geopolitical construct might work—"creative responsibility sharing" was one early and inelegant variant—but it did not come into focus until the fall of 1990, in response to Iraq's invasion of Kuwait. Bush could have dismissed this crisis as a Gulf family squabble, or embraced more modest goals like deterring Iraq from moving against Saudi Arabia. Yet in this instance, Bush set aside his predilection for caution and set the bold objective of forcing Iraq out of Kuwait, even if it meant war.

The prospect of conflict bitterly divided the country, with most Democrats warning of another Vietnam. Less than two decades removed from that Southeast Asian quagmire that had caused so much turmoil—leading many to question not only the wisdom of intervention, but whether the US military could ever win such wars—Bush knew that failure in Iraq would have catastrophic consequences. He even wondered if it would lead to his impeachment. But Bush believed US interests justified the risks.

Even more, he hoped that by working with the Soviet Union and other powers through the United Nations, his response to Iraq's actions would serve as an example for how the post–Cold War world could function, with collectively enforced shared rules.

This was what Bush meant by a new world order. He first discussed the concept with Brent Scowcroft while fishing off the coast of Maine in August 1990, as they pondered the possible implications of the Gulf crisis. The idea itself wasn't particularly new. It reflected the same potential for global cooperation that Bush first hoped for while serving as the US ambassador to the UN, only to be tied up in knots by the superpower struggle. Now, with Gorbachev in the Kremlin, he thought it could finally work.

"I want to go to the American people . . . to close the book on the Cold War and offer them the vision of this new world order in which we will cooperate," he told the Soviet leader in September 1990. Speaking to a joint session of Congress, Bush explained this aspiration as one "quite different from the world we've known," a place where the "rule of law supplants the rule of the jungle . . . Nations recognize the shared responsibility of freedom and justice . . . [and] the strong respect the rights of the weak."[37]

This was heady stuff, especially for a president who usually steered clear of grandiose rhetoric. But it was entirely consistent with his self-image of alliance leader. And for a moment, the Gulf War's stunning success in early 1991 seemed to justify such lofty goals. At last, Bush believed, the country had "kicked the Vietnam Syndrome" and realized the post-1945 dream of nations coming together in practical ways to solve common problems. To capitalize on this momentum, Bush and his team tried to make their concept of a new world order stick—in less than a year, they used the phrase over three hundred times.

Yet the idea proved too confusing. Some thought Bush was suggesting the world had reached a state of perpetual peace. Others saw his message as an ominous desire to concede US sovereignty to the UN or some globalist cabal (tapping into the paranoid right-wing conspiracies that dogged Bush throughout his political career). In the end, pushing the new world order concept became more trouble than it was worth—as Scowcroft later

said, it was "described, defended, dissected, debunked and dissolved"—
and eventually, the president stopped talking about it altogether.[38]

While Bush abandoned the branding exercise, he never diverted from
the underlying logic of his strategy. He remained committed to leadership defined by persuasion rather than coercion—and the idea that the
American-led international order, built on cooperation and a sense of
common interests, depended on legitimacy. For Bush, such "enlightened
primacy" could leverage unique American capabilities alongside strong
partners to solve shared problems.[39]

III. OBAMA: RESTORING BALANCE

Barack Obama's approach to grand strategy blended that of Eisenhower
and Bush. Like Eisenhower, he thought deeply and conceptually about the
world, tested his assumptions and arguments, felt comfortable tackling big
questions, and relied on speeches to explain his thinking and articulate his
strategy. He understood that framing his decisions in a broader narrative
about America's history, interests, values, and global role—or, as he once
put it, "to tell a really good story about who we are"—was essential.

While Obama cherished "regular order" and adhered to a disciplined,
no-drama decision-making process, his overall strategy was neither the
product of rigorous, formal NSC deliberations nor litigated through the
drafting of lengthy official documents. Like Bush, Obama could be dismissive of the very notion of a grand strategy. "I don't really even need
George Kennan right now," he once said, referring to the diplomat-
strategist known as the father of containment. He preferred to refine his
views more informally, either alone, thinking aloud with a small group of
his closest advisers, or through the writing of speeches.[40]

He had plenty to ponder. Every new president inherits a daunting
inbox, and certainly Eisenhower and Bush felt the weight of responsibility
at the Cold War's beginning and at its end. Obama's inheritance, however,
seemed especially unforgiving, especially for a leader with little global experience and, therefore, a lot to prove.

In January 2009, the country was in the midst of what was then the worst economic meltdown since the 1930s. Millions of Americans were out of work. The unemployment rate soared to 10 percent and nearly eight hundred thousand Americans lost their jobs each month. Major financial institutions collapsed, and the auto industry teetered on the brink. Meanwhile, 150,000 US troops were fighting wars in Iraq and Afghanistan that were not going well and had been paid for using an overdrawn credit card; Iran and North Korea were on an aggressive track to nuclear proliferation; the threat of violent Islamic extremism was metastasizing; and transnational challenges like climate change and possible pandemics got too little attention despite the clear risks.

Strategically, Obama faced a dual challenge: much like its over-leveraged economy, America's strategic standing faced a solvency crisis. Spending so much blood and treasure in Iraq and Afghanistan depleted its ability to project power and maintain credibility. At the same time, issues requiring the country's global leadership piled up. Reflecting on their first year in office, Secretary of State Hillary Clinton conceded that the administration underestimated the implications of the transforming global geopolitical picture. "The world has changed, and our capacity to shape it has eroded," she wrote in an informal, hand-delivered assessment to the president in early 2010. "The constraints on our ability to drive our preferred outcome are greater . . . and our leverage is less. Some of these are attributable to the mistakes of the past Administration, and therefore recoverable, but some are attributable to systemic changes, especially the diffusion of power across states and non-state actors . . . and our policy approaches need to be conceived and implemented against this emerging backdrop."[41]

Within this new geopolitical context, Obama followed the same strategic lodestar as Eisenhower and Bush: to maintain American "primacy" in the international system. Although Obama avoided the term—he likely understood the baggage it carried—he embraced its fundamental precepts. He often said his "number-one" goal was that the "U.S. remains the most powerful, wealthiest nation on Earth." He saw America's interests and values, at home and abroad, as interrelated.

This did not stem from presumptive arrogance or an inclination for dominance. Instead, Obama saw it as a manifestation of America's unique power and therefore a necessity for upholding the global order to promote greater freedom and prosperity. He considered it essential the US champion "a set of rules and norms that everyone can follow and that everyone can benefit from." It is for this reason, he explained, that he aimed to promote a "clear belief among other nations that the United States continues to be the one indispensable nation when tackling major international problems."[42]

This was not a significant departure from the past, but a return to the tradition of presidents like Eisenhower and Bush. During his campaign for president in 2008, Obama praised the elder Bush's team for their "clear-eyed view of how the world works," explaining that observing them in action shaped his views. Obama said he admired how the 41st president recognized "that it is always in our interests to engage, to listen, [and] to build alliances." This did not mean subsuming national interests to others—the United States needed, he said, to "be fierce" in protecting them. But at the same time, Obama understood Bush's lesson to be "that we understand it's very difficult for us to, as powerful as we are, to deal with all these issues by ourselves."[43]

So, what did this mean in practice? Presidents find it hard to resist the temptation to come up with the pithy word or phrase to describe their foreign policy. Eisenhower had the "New Look" and Bush tried the "new world order." Obama and his team never landed on the right slogan. Instead, they sought to design a strategy that reflected the complexity of challenges they inherited, which is part of the reason why their approach could be hard to explain and easily ridiculed.

"If you were to boil it down to a bumper sticker," one of Obama's closest advisers, Ben Rhodes, once explained, "it's 'Wind down these two wars, reestablish American standing and leadership in the world, and focus on a broader set of priorities, from Asia to the global economy to a nuclear non-proliferation regime.'" Or, thinking about it more broadly—and in the spirit of finding something that might actually fit on a fender—one can understand Obama's strategy along the lines of four broad themes: rebalance, reset, rethink, and recalibrate.[44]

"Rebalance" was the heart of Obama's foreign policy. It reflected the view that Obama inherited a set of policies that were fundamentally *imbalanced* when it concerned America's long-term interests. Although this "rebalance" is most often associated with the shift of diplomatic, economic, and military emphasis to the rising challenges of Asia away from a decade of preoccupation with Middle East wars, its meaning is far broader. Obama wanted to bring about greater balance between the tools of American power, elevating diplomacy and development to work alongside defense as the "3Ds" of American power. Greater balance meant doing more to address global problems like climate change, the threat of pandemics, and the spread of weapons of mass destruction. More fundamentally, Obama set out to achieve greater balance between US goals abroad and its attention to problems at home.

The link between saving the American economy and forging a sustainable foreign policy should be self-evident, but it is striking how often those assessing Obama's strategy overlook it. "Our whole foreign policy has to be anchored in economic strength here at home," he once explained. "If we don't maintain the upward mobility and equality of opportunity that underwrites our political stability and makes us a beacon for the world, then our foreign policy leadership will diminish as well." Much more so than 1953 or 1989, by almost every measure, the United States was a declining power in 2009—which is why Obama's success in addressing the economic crisis is arguably his most consequential strategic achievement.[45]

While Obama never warmed to the explicit concept of grand strategy, he intuitively adhered to its essential elements: prioritizing goals, making choices, allocating limited resources, and carefully balancing means and ends. Inherent to the idea of balance is that, as powerful as the United States may be, its resources are finite. Therefore, while stressing balance reflects an understanding of the limits of power, it is also a manifestation of America's unique global role. This is because so much is expected of the United States—it must grapple with more demands, diverse goals, and interests than any other country. As Obama experienced, the cumulative effect of these demands makes maintaining balance quite hard.[46]

THE IDEA OF A "RESET" WAS A SECOND COMPONENT of Obama's strategy. The United States needed to turn the page from the bitterly divisive, and ultimately misguided, post-9/11 years. In many ways, the election of an African American who campaigned on hope and optimism itself symbolized a reset to the world. (One testament to these high expectations was that several hundred thousand happy Germans who crammed into Berlin's Tiergarten in July 2008 to cheer Obama, four months *before* he was elected.) After nearly a decade of American foreign policy wrapped around the axle of Iraq and the war on terrorism, Obama set out to pursue a broad policy agenda. He used a series of speeches around the world in 2009 to outline his ideas and create a new narrative for American leadership.

The result was as ambitious a collection of foreign policy rhetoric as any president has delivered in a single year: in Prague, Obama outlined his aspirations for a nuclear weapons–free world; in Ankara, he pledged that the United States was not at war with Islam; in Cairo, he outlined a "new beginning" with the Muslim world, taking a risk by admitting US culpability in past misdeeds; in Accra, he explained his hopes for democracy and development, especially in Africa; and in Moscow, Obama spoke of his hopes for greater global cooperation and moving beyond "zero-sum" politics. Through these efforts, Obama aimed to capture the imaginations of ordinary people, hoping that his background, his identity, and his message could project a new way forward for America in the world.[47]

Some of the policy specifics of these speeches—such as the "new beginning" with the Muslim world and the infamous "reset" with Russia— generated lasting controversy. Obama approached both issues from a starting point of pragmatism. In the Middle East, Obama didn't set out to dictate change, which he viewed as a folly of his predecessor's democracy agenda. Instead, he hoped to inspire Muslims to address the roots of their own problems. As Obama later explained, he wanted to "advance the goals of a practical, successful Arab agenda that provided a better life for ordinary people." The core logic of the Russia "reset" was, as Hillary Clinton later put it, "straight up transactional diplomacy." Washington aimed to work with Moscow where interests converged (like reducing nuclear weapons stockpiles), stand firm where they did not, and engage directly with the Russian people as they pressed for political freedom and economic reforms. The problem, however, was that despite some modest accomplishments, neither of these resets realized the full potential Obama once hoped for.[48]

THIS RELATES TO THE THIRD ELEMENT of Obama's strategy: an enthusiasm to rethink some time-honored, if politically expedient, approaches to American statecraft. This is most evident in Obama's willingness to speak openly about failures of American foreign policy—from recent ones like Iraq, to older ones like the bombing of Laos in the 1970s, or US culpability in coups in the Middle East like Eisenhower's involvement in Iran in 1953. Although this exposed Obama to shallow critiques that he somehow didn't love America and went on "apology tours," Obama believed that rethinking the past, and admitting mistakes, was an essential part of restoring credibility and rejuvenating US leadership.

For the best examples of how this translated into policy, consider Obama's diplomatic approach to two long-standing enemies, Cuba and Iran.

Obama didn't have any illusions about the malign intentions of either regime, and he possessed a clear perspective of the national interest. Nevertheless, he concluded the past approach of isolation and non-engagement failed to achieve results. "The notion that somehow not talking to countries is punishment to them . . . is ridiculous," he said, pointing out that leaders like Eisenhower and Bush met with their Soviet counterparts while the Cold War raged. "We don't want to be imprisoned by the past," he once argued regarding his approach to Cuba. "When something doesn't work for fifty years, you don't just keep on doing it, you try something new." Among his aides, Obama often summed up his view with nine words, punctuated for emphasis: "It. Is. Not. A. Reward. To. Talk. To. Folks."[49]

In his first inaugural address, Obama offered to "extend a hand" to foes (a phrase that echoed a line from Bush's 1989 inaugural, where he said "goodwill begets goodwill. Good faith can be a spiral that endlessly moves on"). The logic was clear: such engagement would either elicit a positive response, and the two sides could negotiate, or it would not, and the other sides' intransigence would betray their true intentions. In this way, engagement was a practical means to generate leverage—a form of pressure to reposition the United States and give it the upper hand.[50]

FINALLY, OBAMA'S STRATEGY SOUGHT TO RECALIBRATE the use of military force as an instrument of American power. This did not mean he was (as Bush might have said) a peacenik. Two of Obama's most important, and contested, strategic decisions concerned the wars he inherited: winding down the US presence in Iraq, leading to the complete military withdrawal by the end of 2011; and the 2009 decision to surge seventy thousand additional troops into Afghanistan. Despite widespread criticism, Obama also proved ready to take big risks with the use of force—consider the 2011 air campaign over Libya, the raid to kill Osama bin Laden, the hundreds of counterterrorism operations with drones or special operations forces, or the thousands of airstrikes against ISIL targets in Syria and Iraq after 2014. Nevertheless, he often said he did not want to be "a president who is comfortable and at ease with killing people." While Obama remained a president at war, he was determined not to become a "war president." He did not want armed conflict to subsume all other aspects of his foreign policy.[51]

This caution with using force frustrated those who felt the United States needed to gamble more. Yet Obama wanted to heed the lessons of the past. After over a decade of war since the 9/11 attacks, he argued the country had to think very carefully about where and how to be militarily engaged, especially in the Middle East. Leaders cannot make decisions in a vacuum, Obama explained, and "any thoughtful president would hesitate about making a renewed commitment in the exact same region of the world with some of the exact same dynamics and the same probability of an unsatisfactory outcome."[52]

TO BETTER UNDERSTAND OBAMA'S VIEWS on the use of force, it is useful to return to two of his speeches from December 2009. Delivered more than a week apart, Obama's remarks at West Point (where he announced his decision to surge troops to Afghanistan) and in Oslo (where, by his own admission, he prematurely received the Nobel Peace Prize), illuminate how he saw his role as commander-in-chief. Both addresses encapsulate the themes that undergirded his grand strategy and the role of military power in foreign policy. Years later, his closest aides often referred to them as the best windows into his thinking.

Obama used these speeches to outline his vision of American power and speak plainly about the inherent dilemmas in exercising it. "The American people are idealists," he said to his speechwriters during one drafting session. "But their leaders have to be realistic and hard-headed." Therefore, Obama felt it imperative to explain that making tough choices was the essence of strategy. Referencing Eisenhower, he said that when approaching foreign policy decisions, a president always needed to consider the totality of American interests.[53]

"I refuse to set goals that go beyond our responsibility, our means, or our interests," Obama explained at West Point, in a speech he later described as a "gut punch" because he stood before many cadets he was about to send off to battle. "I must weigh all of the challenges that our nation faces. I don't have the luxury of committing to just one." He lamented the steep price of losing balance in foreign policy, clarifying that the United States could no longer afford to ignore the costs of war.[54]

Yet sometimes the price must be paid. Obama's Nobel address was an unsentimental statement on the necessity of force. He pulled an all-nighter, writing the speech by hand (one of the only times his speechwriters recalled him doing so, and something Obama swore he would never do again). Having decided to deploy tens of thousands of young Americans to war in Afghanistan, Obama wanted to confront big questions and discuss hard truths, reflecting philosophically on the dilemmas of realism versus idealism, the nature of human imperfection, and the limits of reason. "I know why war is not popular," he wrote, "but I also know [the] belief that peace is rarely enough to achieve it. Peace requires responsibility."

When considered together, these speeches, like Obama's grand strategy itself, were bold, optimistic statements about the imperative of American leadership. He outlined an activist agenda for the United States—more engagement, in more places, on more issues, in more ways. But America would execute this with a more diverse array of tools and tactics, and with the full awareness that while few problems can be solved alone, some cannot be solved at all. Believing the United States needed to restore balance between its means and ends, and subordinate tactics to strategy, Obama shared Eisenhower's basic emphasis on solvency. This reflects his determination to transform an extraordinarily challenging inheritance into a sustainable foreign policy more relevant to twenty-first-century challenges.

Critics saw the opposite. They derided Obama for apologizing for America, shirking leadership, lacking confidence, and withdrawing from the world. Perhaps this was a response to his willingness to acknowledge imperfections. Or maybe it was a reaction to his desire to address uncomfortable truths about the limits of American power. Or it could have been because of Obama's determination to be, in his words, "sober and adult" and not beat his chest unapologetically.

Whatever the reason, many analysts took umbrage with Obama's suggestion that the United States made mistakes, overextended itself, and therefore needed to adjust accordingly. Some commentators call this "retrenchment." In plain meaning, the word refers to reducing costs in response to resource constraints. In foreign policy terms, however, it is not usually a compliment; instead, it is just another way of saying an even more loaded term, retreat.

Yet retrenchment, like "restraint"—another concept experts appropriated to advocate the US do less abroad—oversimplifies most of the choices policymakers actually face. Such terms suggest every decision can be boiled down to a binary all-or-nothing answer, when the reality is somewhere in between. They also reflect a bias toward assessing American influence solely through a military lens—as measured by interventions, deployments, capabilities, and basing—while discounting the economic, political, diplomatic, and developmental aspects of American power—the kinds of tools that Obama, like Eisenhower and Bush, sought to elevate and make stronger. This kind of nuanced leadership—better described as "recalibration," rather than retrenchment or restraint—is often harder to measure or characterize, which is why it is so frequently misunderstood.[55]

* * *

EISENHOWER, BUSH, AND OBAMA faced dramatically different strategic contexts. In 1953, Eisenhower inherited a bipolar world, with the US-Soviet rivalry intensifying. In the early 1990s, Bush's world was moving from bipolarity to a unipolar one, and the possibilities seemed endless. In 2008, Obama found something wholly different—with geopolitics moving from unipolarity to something far more uncertain, in which the United States faced the rise of other powers, a greater diversity of threats, a battered and restive public, and far messier choices. Nevertheless, their approaches had important parallels in both means and ends. Comparing their strategies, five broad themes stand out.[56]

First, each president shared the conviction that because of its power, interests, and ideals, the United States must pursue a unique leadership role in shaping the world order. They embraced the fundamental view that US interests—financial, geopolitical, and ideological—demanded a stable, balanced, open political economy. And they believed America's power gave it special responsibilities to address global problems. Therefore, the United States needed to maintain an active forward presence abroad, whether through energetic diplomacy, military posture, more foreign assistance, or leadership in multilateral institutions.

In this way, they all championed the same principles of American-led internationalism—in which capable partners, strong alliances, and a common set of rules were a prerequisite. As Eisenhower wrote in a 1952 letter to Dulles, because it was America's "enlightened self-interest" to uphold the global order, "we must be successful in developing collective security measures that will encourage . . . countries to develop [their] own political and spiritual strength."[57]

This was a forerunner of Bush's new world order. Although Bush largely dispensed with the slogan, he and his team defended the idea during his 1992 reelection campaign, describing the concept as a "quest for a world in which nations settle disputes through cooperation, not confrontation; where the strong protect the weak; [and] where people are governed by the rule of law and not the tyranny of despots." Some Bush officials described this "collective engagement" as a way to marry the imperative of American leadership with the new possibilities for coalition diplomacy.[58]

Obama's strategy built on these themes. He described his "main goal" was to work with partners "to promote a system of rules so that conflicts can be resolved peacefully . . . so that whether you're a big country or a small country, you know that there are certain principles that are observed—that might just doesn't make right, but that there's justice both inside countries and between countries."[59]

These presidents' common perspective on American leadership—establishing shared rules of the road, promoting collective security and engagement, supporting strong partners, and building enduring alliances—was less a matter of ideology than their sense of how to get things get done. The more countries worked together, the better. They saw such leadership as not only necessary to solve foreign policy problems, but as critical to establishing conditions for the US to thrive economically, to sustain the necessary resources, and, crucially, to maintain the American people's support for their strategy.[60]

SECOND, EISENHOWER, BUSH, AND OBAMA all emphasized the importance of strategic balance—to varying degrees, they each inherited a situation in which US global efforts had become lopsided to dangerous and unsustainable levels. They each felt the need to remedy the denial of hard choices. Therefore, their strategies tried to address these imbalances: between America's interests and values; among its goals at home and abroad; concerning its competing objectives in different regions; and between US responsibilities and burden-sharing with others. This meant pursuing policies oriented toward investing in partners, strengthening global institutions, and maintaining solvency.[61]

All three faced a formidable strategic task: to balance a bold vision for American leadership with more limited resources. Acknowledging limits and making trade-offs among competing goals is one of the hardest aspects of statecraft. Every leader faces significant psychological incentives to avoid tough choices and to think they can have their cake and eat it too. This is especially true when the consequences of decisions are hard to predict or only clear in the future. In foreign policy, this is also distinctly American: because of the country's relative economic success, geographic advantages, and optimistic, can-do cultural ethos, US leaders tend to be slow to perceive trade-offs and less vocal about the necessity of sacrificing some things in order to achieve others. Too often, leaders want to have it all.[62]

These presidents led during moments of national security budget austerity. Eisenhower and Obama both labored to get spending under control, and were forthright about the costs. Obama once described how he approached these strategic dilemmas by quoting one of Eisenhower's admonitions, reminding that "each proposal must be weighed in light of a broader consideration: the need to maintain balance in and among national programs."[63]

So they each took significant steps to steady the ship: Eisenhower cut defense spending by 27% but doubled funding for research and development (although defense expenditures remained over 10% of GDP for most of Ike's tenure). Obama followed a similar course, scaling back defense spending by 23% while investing in modernization, all at a lower level of total GDP (around 3%). For Bush, the trade-offs were easier to manage, as he sought to give American taxpayers a "hunk of the glory" for winning the Cold War, trading deep defense cuts for more domestic spending (he slashed the Pentagon budget by about 15%, taking it to under 5% of GDP, and reduced active duty troops by 400,000).[64]

Yet however hard they each tried to align strategic means and ends, success proved elusive. Critics lambasted Eisenhower and Obama for starving their strategies (despite the fact they increased US defense capabilities), while Bush lost reelection in large part because he did not dedicate enough resources to domestic priorities.[65]

THIRD, A SIMILAR MIX OF PRAGMATISM AND IDEALISM characterized their strategies. This is especially evident in the ways each president grappled with the role of nuclear weapons and the goal of disarmament—which in the case of Eisenhower and Obama, proved most disappointing.

While Eisenhower placed nuclear weapons at the center of his national security strategy, believing they were critically important to defend American interests in Europe and Asia, he remained anguished about the implications. Ike sometimes wondered aloud about the use of nuclear weapons in specific crises, such as Korea and Vietnam; nevertheless he thought keeping a nuclear war limited was inconceivable and winning a total nuclear war impossible. In a nuclear conflict, he said in 1954, "there is no victory except through our imaginations."

Ike's goal was deterrence—and since he faced claims the United States was falling behind in the arms race, he oversaw a buildup of nuclear weapons he ultimately thought neither necessary nor wise, conceding to his aides that their elaborate planning for nuclear war "no longer makes any sense." Even that was still not enough to satisfy his hawkish critics. Ike maintained faith in the goal of disarmament, yet left office deeply frustrated by his failure to make meaningful progress (in his farewell address, Ike conceded his "definite sense of disappointment") and worried about the monumental challenge he bequeathed to his young successor, who had far less experience handling the military.[66]

Bush enjoyed a very different strategic reality—and therefore had an opportunity to reduce nuclear danger in ways Eisenhower could only wish. Bush often expressed his hope to build a future "free from the fear of nuclear war," and with the Soviet Union in sharp decline, lowering nuclear weapons stockpiles became the most significant means to ease Cold War tensions. Bush revived Ike's "Open Skies" proposal (which was signed in 1992) and aimed to reduce nuclear weapons in a way, he said, that "promotes stability at the lowest feasible level."

Bush negotiated several landmark arms control agreements with the Soviets, eliminating thousands of nuclear warheads. In 1991, Bush announced the most comprehensive change in US nuclear weapons strategy since the Eisenhower era, unilaterally de-alerting strategic bombers, cancelling missile programs, and removing tactical nuclear weapons at sea. While Bush did not necessarily create the conditions for such dramatic reductions—Gorbachev's own unilateral cuts opened the door—his vigorous pursuit of nuclear disarmament was one of his most lasting, if underappreciated, achievements.[67]

Obama's strategy sought to fulfill Ike's idealistic dreams. Captivated by the idea of nuclear arms control since his college days, when he wrote student newspaper articles criticizing the "billion dollar erector sets" of the nuclear weapons complex, Obama outlined his ambitious vision for a world without nuclear weapons during his first year in office. In his final year, Obama became the first sitting president to visit Hiroshima, where he called for a "moral revolution" to eliminate nuclear arms. Obama organized security summits to galvanize world leaders to lock down nuclear materials, launched new initiatives to bolster nonproliferation, and negotiated a new arms control agreement with the Russians.

Yet Obama's hopes foundered on tough geopolitical and bureaucratic obstacles. Obama shared Eisenhower's frustration with the unreality of nuclear war planning—he once began a meeting to discuss nuclear war guidance by stipulating, "this is all insane"—nevertheless he too maintained a robust nuclear deterrent and resisted unilateral US cuts. This disappointed many early champions of Obama's nuclear policies. He knew he came up short, conceding that not only did disarmament remain a distant goal, but that he had only achieved "some modest progress" in reducing nuclear stockpiles. In the end, like the early 1950s, nuclear deterrence remained a core component of US national security strategy.[68]

FOURTH, THESE PRESIDENTS BELIEVED a successful strategy required patience. It was a point perhaps best explained by Eisenhower, who spoke in his farewell address about the "element of time" and the "long lane of history" and warned against quick solutions. Ike often stressed these themes. "We face, not a temporary emergency, such as a war, but a long-term responsibility," he wrote in a 1957 letter. Therefore, he explained, America's strategy needed to be "designed for indefinite use and endurance," with elements "we must be prepared to sustain . . . for years, even decades." Bush, too, often underscored the importance of patience, often saying that sound strategy meant not getting "stampeded" into acting. And Obama reminded Americans that history showed that seemingly insoluble problems could be solved "as long as there were those who stayed steady and clear-eyed and persistent."[69]

At the same time, even though they were elected to change courses, each of these presidents' strategies embraced certain important continuities with their predecessors. Eisenhower validated Truman's Containment.

Bush built on Reagan's approach toward Gorbachev. And Obama followed many of the key aspects of George W. Bush's war on terrorism. They sought to revise these policies not to repudiate them, but to make them more effective, legitimate, and sustainable. In this sense, their pragmatism enabled them to escape the trap of campaign promises—which sometimes suggested a sharper break with the past—and recognize enduring interests and reality. They set out to construct policies that, with patience, could succeed.

FINALLY, THEIR STRATEGIES EMBRACED THE NECESSITY of building and sustaining public support. Each president labored to explain what they were doing and put things in a larger context. During their first months in office, they all sought to reframe the strategic debate and reclaim the initiative. But it proved exceedingly difficult to project a broad ambition for American interests while stressing the necessity of balance, patience, and limits. No matter how hard they tried, all of them struggled to maintain popular support for their strategies. "One of the frustrating facts of my daily existence," Ike lamented in 1956, in an observation Bush and Obama could relate to, "is the seeming inability of our people to understand our position and role in the world and what our best interests demand of us."[70]

As the scholar Stephen Sestanovich observes, these presidents' shared challenge was to figure out how to persuade "the American people that their foreign policies [were] more successful, less rudderless and reactive, than it seemed." As a consequence, whatever success they achieved in setting a distinct strategic course, and no matter how well they established a balance between goals and tactics, the results turned out to be less attractive for subsequent presidents to sustain. In the eyes of many, they were perceived to be three presidents resigned to managing weakness rather than projecting strength.[71]

This perception is partly a manifestation of the politics of foreign policy—whether it is the propensity to measure strength by the use of military power alone, or the pressure to respond to relentless calls to do "more" of everything, regardless of the costs or probability of success. As we will explore later, political struggles over each president's decisions, or perceived inactions, ultimately consumed them. Rather than being considered the better part of wisdom, their caution and desire to recalibrate were made to seem weak.

Eisenhower, Bush, and Obama tried to pursue a Middle Way strategy they believed would serve American interests while sustaining American power. They shared what Walter Lippmann called the "constant preoccupation of the true statesman," which is to achieve and maintain an equilibrium among "the nation's commitments with the nation's power." Yet they all were tested by crises which conspired to throw them off course—demanding that they reassess their desire to stay patient, maintain balance, and respect limits. How they handled these unexpected moments—and tried to adhere to a policy, in Lippmann's words, based not on accident and force but on reflection and choice—is where we must turn next.[72]

3

Crisis

I t was just after nine o'clock on a Thursday morning in April 1954, and nearly 150 journalists gathered in the Executive Office Building across West Executive Avenue from the White House. As Dwight Eisenhower opened the thirty-fifth press conference of his presidency, the dire situation facing the embattled French Army in Dien Bien Phu dominated the headlines.

The French were desperate. Nine years into their insurgency, communist forces were about to overrun fifteen thousand troops hunkered amidst the heavily fortified garrison in Vietnam (then known as Indochina). Worried about the prospect of the country becoming another Asian "domino" to fall to communism, public calls for unilateral US intervention reached a fever pitch. Resisting this pressure, the president scrambled to respond.

One reporter asked about the likelihood of using force in Vietnam. Trying to keep his options open, Eisenhower stressed the United States would continue to provide the French with technical and financial support but would not pursue military action without allied and congressional backing.

For weeks, Eisenhower had been warning of the dangers of communist victory. But he did not want to own this fight. Instead, he explained, he sought to steer "a course between two extremes . . . [the] unattainable, and the other unacceptable." The United States could not let Indochina fall to the communists. At the same time, he said, a "general Asian peace" would not be possible, so the best one could expect would be to "work out [a] practical way of getting along."

The next morning, journalist James Reston declared on the front page of the *New York Times* that the president had "charted a cautious middle course." Against the pressure of the moment, the "tenor of his remarks suggested moderation, compromise, and even reconciliation," Reston wrote, "rather than any dramatic course of intervention."

Eisenhower knew such a policy would prove unsatisfying to the jury of public opinion. But it was, he said, "the most you could ask." Within a few months, Ike's course led to the division of Vietnam, with communists in control of the North.[1]

THIRTY-SEVEN YEARS LATER, in April 1991, George H. W. Bush found himself in a similar situation. It had taken the US military and its coalition allies less than one hundred hours to expel Iraq from Kuwait. As stunning as this achievement was—after all, many had warned beforehand that Bush was leading the country into another bloody morass like Vietnam—the accomplishment seemed tarnished. Saddam Hussein remained in power. "It hasn't been a clean end," Bush admitted to his diary the day the Gulf War concluded. "There is no battleship *Missouri* surrender," he lamented, thinking back to the total defeat of Japan in World War II.

Making things worse, the Iraqi military moved to quash the uprisings of Iraqi Shia and Kurds. Long-suffering under Saddam's brutal rule, the rebels saw his Gulf War defeat as an opportunity for freedom. Bush, who never hid his disdain for the Iraqi leader, lent the insurgents his rhetorical support. Despite such encouragement, American forces were rapidly withdrawing from Iraq, and Saddam—who was defeated but not vanquished— had a free pass to act.

Critics blamed Bush for allowing Saddam to stay in power, encouraging the rebellion, raising expectations for what the US might do to help, and for not speaking the truth about what was going on inside Iraq. Democrats like Tennessee Senator Al Gore, then widely seen as a contender to challenge Bush in the 1992 election, said the president "was mortgaging U.S. policy in the Gulf to the success of tyranny in Iraq."

Bush struggled to explain his goals. He clarified that American forces only had the narrow mission of kicking Iraq out of Kuwait, nothing more. The United States "did not go there to settle all the internal affairs of Iraq," he told reporters. "Of course I feel a frustration and a sense of grief for the innocents that are being killed brutally. But we are not there to intervene. That is not our purpose; it never was our purpose. I can understand the frustration of some who think it should have been our purpose, some who never supported this in the first place on military action."

Such exchanges got testier as the situation worsened. The uprisings sparked a massive refugee crisis. The insurgents were getting slaughtered. While Bush said he still wanted Saddam gone, he remained determined to stay off the slippery slope of intervention and regime change.

"I am not going to involve any American troops in a civil war in Iraq," Bush said in frustration one April afternoon, as he stood among reporters huddled on the White House's South Portico. "They are not going to be going in there to do what some of my severest critics early on now seem to want me to do. I want these kids to come home. And that's what's going to happen. And we are going to do what is right by these refugees, and I think the American people expect that, and they want that. But I don't think they want to see us bogged down in a civil war by sending in the 82nd Airborne or the 101st or the 7th Cavalry."

Although Bush sought to use his Gulf War victory to define the new world order as a "responsibility imposed by our successes," he believed responsibility had its limits. So it would be up to the Iraqi people alone to decide their future. Bush grudgingly accepted Saddam's survival, much like Eisenhower accepted Vietnam's partition.[2]

It was the last question of the last press conference of a week-long trip to Asia, and for Obama, it became an occasion to uncork some frustration.

While Obama spent those final days of April 2014 on *Air Force One* crisscrossing the Pacific to implement his strategy to rebalance to Asia, the traveling press corps hounded him to answer criticisms that his response to numerous crises—from the war raging in Syria to Russia's invasion of Ukraine—was lackluster and weak. Obama stewed over what he saw as the disconnect between the big strategic picture and critics' insatiable appetite for US action no matter what. He wondered, had they forgotten the lessons of Iraq? So when a Fox News journalist asked how he would answer those who said that his foreign policy doctrine is one of "weakness," Obama unloaded.

"My job as Commander in Chief is to deploy military force as a last resort and to deploy it wisely," Obama said with frustration while standing next to his Filipino counterpart inside Manila's sprawling Malacañang Palace. "And frankly," he continued, "most of the foreign policy commentators that have questioned our policies would go headlong into a bunch of military adventures that the American people have no interest in participating in and would not advance our core security interests."

Obama took aim at those critics "sitting behind a desk in Washington or New York" who called for the United States to act "strong" in places like Syria and Ukraine, asserting they offered glib solutions while eliding the potential consequences. Obama said he was ready to use the full toolbox of American power if he thought it could make a difference. Yet not every tool was suitable for every problem at every moment. To advance America's interests over the long term, a president's job was to figure out which one to use, and when.

This was about more than what to do in Syria or Ukraine. It was about how to define foreign policy success. Obama pointed to what he had been doing for the previous week in Asia—practicing the kind of steady, patient, and sometimes unglamorous diplomacy in pursuit of a larger strategy. The approach "may not always be sexy," he acknowledged. "That may not always attract a lot of attention, and it doesn't make for good argument on Sunday morning shows." A wise foreign policy, Obama said, was often like good baseball: "it avoids errors. You hit singles, you hit doubles; every once in a while, we may be able to hit a home run."

The White House journalists in the audience had heard this riff from Obama before, but it had been off-the-record and slightly more colorful. One afternoon a few days before the press conference, while flying high over the South China Sea, he made a surprise visit to *Air Force One*'s press cabin to talk about the crises in Syria and Ukraine. He pushed back on recent stories suggesting that his prudence and pragmatism were nothing but weakness and fecklessness. Barely masking his anger, Obama recited the litany of errors he believed stemmed from Washington wisdom, and set out to explain how he defined foreign policy success. Obama told the assembled journalists that he could sum up his foreign policy philosophy in one phrase: "don't do stupid shit." To ensure they got the point, he asked them to repeat those words, like wayward students, in unison.[3]

IN APRIL 1954, EISENHOWER TRIED TO STEER between the unattainable and the unacceptable. In April 1991, Bush pledged not to get bogged down in another country's civil war. And in April 2014, Obama explained how he navigated crises with baseball metaphors and salty admonitions.

Although spanning sixty years, their sentiments are interchangeable. Each president remained determined to keep a firm hand at the helm of American power, maintaining a strategic direction while also responding to the unexpected in ways they thought recognized the reality of limits and did not jeopardize more important long-term interests. Each struggled to craft a policy to meet unrealistic expectations, sometimes of their own creation. And each grew deeply frustrated by the implication that their pragmatism and caution were seen as weakness.

A successful foreign policy requires a well-considered strategy—but presidencies are defined by the ways a leader responds to a crisis. How, in the face of uncertainty and heightened passion, does a president manage a slate of bad options, calibrate when to do more or less, or admit it is time to change course? This reality is vividly captured in a pearl of wisdom once offered by the famed boxer Mike Tyson: "Everyone has a plan until they get punched in the mouth."[4]

The essential challenge also brings to mind a more quotidian observation made by George Kennan, who said planning in foreign policy is a lot like managing a farm (Kennan knew this firsthand, since he maintained 235 acres in rural Pennsylvania). On any particular day, he explained, you may have an overall objective—planting the crops, for example. At the same time you must constantly juggle other priorities and surprises—a fence collapses, the hogs end up on the loose, a fox raids the henhouse. Eventually, you end up standing there, wondering where to start, asking whether you have your priorities right, weighing whether you even have the capabilities to fix things, and debating what can be done in a way that still allows you to achieve your larger objective. Of course, an added complication is that in foreign policy, one would be doing all this as the townspeople crowded around, judging and second-guessing your every move.[5]

These presidents weren't farmhands—while Ike presided over one in Gettysburg, Bush preferred speedboats and Obama favored basketball. Nevertheless, each had plenty of days when they felt buffeted by events and overwhelmed by the inescapable triage of choice.

Putting this in the language of foreign policy, one of Kennan's distinguished diplomatic successors, William Burns, writes that while successful statesmen need a sense of strategy and the discipline to stick with it, they also have to be "endlessly adaptable—quick to adjust to the unexpected, massage the anxieties of allies and partners, maneuver past adversaries, and manage change rather than be paralyzed by it."[6]

What follows is an examination of six crises each of these presidents faced—Eisenhower in Vietnam in 1954 and the twin crises in Suez and Hungary in 1956; Bush in 1991 in postwar Iraq and the Soviet Union's collapse; and Obama starting in 2011 in Libya and Syria. To be sure, these were not the only foreign crises they confronted. But they are illustrative. How they handled these crisis moments opens a window into their leadership style and provides a stark reminder about how hard—and oftentimes thankless—it can be to steer a stable, moderate Middle Way course.

I. EISENHOWER: BETWEEN THE UNATTAINABLE AND
THE UNACCEPTABLE

"Crises, there will continue to be," Eisenhower said succinctly in his 1961 farewell address. Yet in meeting them, he continued, "there is a recurring temptation to feel that some spectacular and costly action could become the miraculous solution to all our current difficulties." Eisenhower's national security strategy was predicated on resisting such temptations. Rooted in the imperative of patience and the careful balance of resources in order to achieve larger aims, it said the United States needed to respond to threats by calling its own shots—not by getting forced by others onto a certain course.[7]

Vietnam presented a critical test. By the early-1950s, France had been struggling for the better part of a decade to maintain control over the small southeast Asian country, which was one of its imperial jewels. In their first White House meeting during the 1952 post-election transition, the outgoing Truman team warned Eisenhower that Vietnam's fate was an "urgent matter upon which the new administration must be prepared to act," and Eisenhower and his advisers discussed the issue while aboard the *Helena* in December 1952, when they agreed Vietnam could not fall to communists. But then Eisenhower soon found himself in a bind. Worried the French could not hold their position in this exhausting colonial war, he began to weigh US military action, considering options from limited air strikes to a larger intervention. Ike began building a public case for greater US involvement while increasing military support for the French, deploying bombers and technicians to help. At the same time, he worried about the risks of intervention and the lack of domestic and international support.[8]

The situation steadily deteriorated until it reached a tipping point in April 1954. The French decided to make a desperate last stand at Dien Bien Phu, a cluster of valley villages one observer described as "hell in a very small place." Eisenhower's response reflected his contradictory impulses. He spoke in dramatic terms about the danger of losing Vietnam, while also stressing great caution about the risks of American action. For example, in an NSC meeting on April 6, Ike said the United States could not replace the French and there was "no possibility whatsoever" for unilateral military intervention. "We had best to face that fact," he said. At the same time, he fretted that Vietnam could be the first in a row of dominoes to fall to the communists—a metaphor he repeated in a press conference the next day, in what became one of the most famous utterances of the Cold War—suggesting the stakes were so high the United States needed to be ready to fight.[9]

Eisenhower had two preconditions for intervention: a coalition of allies and greater support from Congress. Neither proved forthcoming. Allies resisted bailing out the French—most notably, Winston Churchill dismissed Ike's personal appeal to remember the lessons of appeasement. The administration also ran into a buzz-saw of resistance in Congress, which never authorized the war in Korea and didn't want to be held responsible for another American conflict in Asia. This left Eisenhower in a lose/lose position. If the United States failed to act and Vietnam fell, his political opponents would throw his own alarmist rhetoric back in his face and blame him for "losing" another Asian country to communism. Yet if the United States moved without domestic or international support, Ike would be blamed for repeating the mistakes of Korea.[10]

Given this circumstance, the debate over what to do raged inside the administration for weeks. A key moment came on the morning of April 29, 1954, during an NSC meeting that immediately followed the press conference where Ike stated the need to navigate between the unattainable and unacceptable. Now, he had to figure out what exactly that course would be.

For three hours, Eisenhower and his team debated their next steps, with some advisers forcefully advocating the United States act alone. Eisenhower vehemently disagreed, arguing that to intervene unilaterally "amounted to an attempt to police the entire world." Ike explained that "to him the concept of leadership implied associates." Without them, he said, "the leader is just an adventurer like Genghis Khan." Eisenhower also wondered whether, once in, American forces could prevent deeper intervention. He warned about getting on a slippery slope, saying the "U.S. would never survive if it frittered away our resources in local engagements." With this, the NSC decided to postpone discussion of any intervention to see how diplomacy played out.[11]

Late that afternoon, Eisenhower joined a few aides on the White House lawn to chip some golf balls and unwind. He was pleased with that morning's press conference and said that while the NSC meeting had been "controversial," they had made the right decision to wait. "A proper political foundation for any military action was essential," Eisenhower later wrote to a friend. "Since we could not bring it about . . . I gave not even tentative approval to any plan for massive intervention."[12]

EISENHOWER'S DILEMMA CAN BE SUMMED UP this way: having made the calculation that Vietnam could not be lost to the communists, and having built a convincing public case for action, he knew his credibility was on the line. At the same time, he was well aware of the military and political risks and wary of the costs of getting sucked into another land war in Asia. US forces were already stretched thin and unprepared to take on what promised to be a massive fight against Vietnamese insurgents. Furthermore, public support would be difficult to sustain with memories of the unpopular war in Korea still fresh.

So Ike hedged his bet. He stood ready to intervene in principle, but only if the conditions were right, and he did not authorize detailed military planning for US action. Yet his combination of exercising restraint while also warning of catastrophe left many people confused. His policy rested on the uncomfortable middle ground between dire warnings of falling dominoes while pledging "no more Koreas," with the practical result being the United States providing logistical and financial support to keep the French afloat, while avoiding direct military action.

This was not enough to save Dien Bien Phu. After a valiant fight, the French forces surrendered on May 7. By the end of the summer of 1954, the French acceded to a peace deal to split the country in two, with the United States stepping in as the chief patron of a new government in the South, based in Saigon. Ike hoped this compromise would achieve the larger goal of safeguarding Southeast Asia from communism—a decision that would prove fateful by the mid-1960s.

Although public support for American intervention always remained tepid, critics predictably heaped scorn on Eisenhower after Dien Bien Phu fell. It was seen as a devastating defeat—abandoning an old ally in need, ceding critical ground to enemies, and projecting overall weakness. Influential conservatives were livid, with the Republican Senate leader decrying the outcome as "the greatest victory the communists have won in twenty years" (a ridiculous statement considering the Chinese revolution just five years prior). Democrats, still nursing wounds from Eisenhower and his Republican allies' accusations of being soft on communism, sat back and enjoyed the show. Texas Senator Lyndon Johnson ripped Eisenhower's policy as "a dismal series of reversals and confusions" that left the United States isolated in the world. "The damn Republicans blamed us for losing China and now we can blame them for losing Southeast Asia," another Democratic congressman said.[13]

This leaves something of a tragic contradiction: Ike's policy stymied communism's march; Dien Bien Phu didn't cause any dominoes to fall. Indeed, in the moment, Eisenhower and his aides celebrated their success in keeping the United States out of a war no one wanted. For the next generation of policymakers, however, such restraint taught a different lesson. By failing to stop communist aggression, this argument went, Eisenhower presided over an "Asian Munich," and therefore the United States needed to risk more to support its allies and fight communism.

Instead of using his tremendous prestige to disengage from Vietnam by arguing that its future was not a core US interest, the net effect of Eisenhower's decisions deepened America's commitment to the future of Southeast Asia. Because subsequent administrations did not want to expose themselves to perceptions of being similarly weak, the political imperative for more forceful action only grew. "We could not see the affairs of Vietnam as they really were, mired as we were in prejudices generated by our own domestic politics," the great chronicler of America's tragedy in Vietnam, David Halberstam, once observed. "We thought the war in Indochina was over; the other side knew it had just begun." It would be for future presidents—Kennedy, and especially LBJ and Nixon—to pay the

political price, and for future young Americans and Vietnamese to bear
the ultimate burden.[14]

II. EISENHOWER: THE MOST CROWDED AND
DEMANDING WEEKS

On the first day of November 1956, Washington seemed ready to ex-
plode. With Election Day less than a week away, conflict loomed on two
continents, and US leadership seemed on the verge of collapse. As the
American people prepared to go to the polls, Soviet tanks were poised to
crush a rebellion in Hungary. Meanwhile, the British, French, and Israelis
launched a surprise attack against Egypt in response to its seizure of the
Suez Canal.

When Eisenhower mounted the rostrum before eighteen thousand
ebullient supporters in Philadelphia's Convention Hall on that Thursday
evening, he aimed to rise above the partisan din and make sense of this
extraordinary confluence of crises. After a few days off the campaign trail
to oversee round-the-clock meetings in Washington, this was his opportunity to deliver his closing argument of the 1956 campaign.

He spoke to a packed house, with several thousand supporters standing
outside in a steady rain and millions more tuning into the live broadcast on
television and radio. True to form, Eisenhower's words were not those for
a rousing political rally. Instead, for thirty minutes he offered his thoughts
on geopolitics and delivered a detailed defense of his foreign policy.

Speaking in the city of the nation's founding, he applied the enduring
ideals of the early republic to the global firestorm he faced. Ike stressed the
importance of the principles undergirding his strategy: upholding collective security, resolving conflicts peacefully, ensuring both friends and foes
adhere to the rule of law, and pursuing vigorous US leadership tempered
by military restraint.

Yet events, Ike conceded, put his strategic precepts to the test. "The
damn trouble with these principles," Eisenhower said to his speechwriter
a few days earlier, "is that when you try to apply them to any situation, you

find some may conflict or you gotta give up one or two." The trade-offs were formidable.

The Soviets dared the United States to do more to help support freedom in the heart of Europe, while friends in London, Paris, and Tel Aviv brazenly defied Washington's pleas to solve their differences with Cairo peacefully. Such dilemmas would be challenging for any president, but especially one who stood on the cusp of an election—in one case having to choose between allegiance to long-standing partners and respect for the rule of law, while in another having to weigh the defense of freedom against fears of war.

"This is a classic example of how complicated these things can get," Eisenhower lamented. "We can only hope our peaceful efforts can have some effect when nations like these fall out among themselves, which we can't stop them from doing. And that's about all you can say."

As Eisenhower tried to calibrate America's response, his political opponents and leading pundits pilloried him for being out of touch and indecisive. The accusations stung, particularly since they came at such a charged political moment. Ike pushed back hard against those he called the "strident few" who sought to "turn world events into political profit." He warned the response suggested by his Democratic rival, Adlai Stevenson— who asserted that Ike's policy was as abysmal and catastrophic a failure as any in American diplomatic history -- would be a "design for disaster."

It's notable that at a time of possible war—when one might expect a president, especially one in the final throes of an election campaign, to resort to chest-thumping rhetoric—Eisenhower chose to emphasize moderation. Instead of whipping up martial emotion and rallying around the flag, Ike sought to lower the temperature and "continue to practice the peace that we preach." The larger point, he stressed to his audience in Philadelphia, was that "the power of modern weapons makes war not only perilous—but preposterous." He continued, "the only way to win World War III is to prevent it."

Eisenhower's words of calm and resolve masked the stress of the previous weeks—after a blur of continuous crisis meetings and calls, he returned home exhausted, knocking back several cocktails on the late-night train back to Washington. Five days later, the American people rewarded Ike with a landslide victory and a second term in the White House.[15]

In his typically understated way, Eisenhower recalled these weeks as "the most crowded and demanding" of his entire presidency. His chief of staff more pointedly remembered them as the "worst." Looking back, Eisenhower's response to the concurrent crises in Hungary and Suez was a defining point for his presidency, with implications that shaped foreign policy for decades.[16]

In Hungary, the United States accepted constraints over its defense of freedom against Soviet aggression, leaving questions of whether it had gone too far in raising expectations about supporting independence in the first place. In the Middle East, the Suez crisis exposed a gap between US and allied interests, and its outcome ushered in a period of growing American dominance in the region. Taken together, these crises are emblematic of the combination of bold action and deliberative caution that were the trademark of Eisenhower's leadership—but they also provided critics ample fodder to tarnish him as weak.

Like Dien Bien Phu two years earlier, the crisis in Hungary exposed the gap between Eisenhower's maximalist rhetoric and his perceived limits of what he could do about it.

Spurred on by hawkish advisers like John Foster Dulles, Eisenhower allowed rolling back Soviet influence over the "captive nations" of Central and Eastern Europe to be one of the core planks of his first campaign for president in 1952. It therefore became a focus of his administration's early efforts, from information campaigns (which they called "psychological warfare") to combat communist propaganda, to economic incentives for countries susceptible to Soviet influence, and diplomacy to strengthen alliances. Yet despite the expectations suggested by Ike's heated campaign rhetoric, these steps did not add up to a coherent policy of liberation. There was plenty of tough talk, but Ike's New Look drew the line at using American military force to free Europe from the Soviet grip.

When the Hungarian uprisings first began in late October 1956, the moment seemed tailor-made for vigorous US support. Not wanting to give the Soviets a pretext for violence, Eisenhower played things carefully, even reassuring Moscow that the United States would not seek to incorporate an independent Hungary into NATO. Ike and his team were thus optimistic after the Soviets initially appeared willing to allow the Hungarians a degree of autonomy.

By Election Day, however, all their hopes came crashing down: sixty thousand Red Army troops and thousands of tanks swept into Hungary's capital, killing as many as two thousand civilians. Moscow's brutality stunned Eisenhower. "This whole business is shocking to the point of being unbelievable," he said to his aides gathered for a meeting of the National Security Council. Nevertheless, he felt short on meaningful options to stop the bloodletting. "We can say we are at the end of our patience," he continued, "but what can we do that is really constructive?" Any moves threatened a wider conflict. In the end, the Soviets checkmated the United States by demonstrating their willingness to risk and sacrifice more for Eastern Europe, which they viewed as vital. As Ike later reflected, "we could do nothing."[17]

The Hungarian crackdown shattered any illusions Eisenhower harbored about benign Soviet intentions. It also raised questions about the consequences of his hawkish rhetoric and, as some influential commentators claimed, his hypocrisy. "There can be few in this country who have not felt how sharp is the contrast between what we have been saying about Hungary and what we are doing," the columnist Walter Lippmann wrote. Eisenhower vigorously defended his policy in public—making clear he never advocated for violent rebellion, but rather wanted to promote long-term peaceful change. He nevertheless understood how this nuance was often lost on domestic audiences, as well as the Hungarians, who believed the United States would come to their rescue.[18]

In a private moment of candor, Eisenhower conceded the United States "had excited [the] Hungarians after all these years, and now [we're] turning our backs on them." The United States could only provide humanitarian assistance and, he hoped, turn world opinion against the Soviets by publicizing their brutality. In the years to follow, the debate over what the

Eisenhower administration did or did not do to support the Hungarians—including whether it irresponsibly promoted liberation without understanding the situation on the ground—became a crucial episode in the narrative about supporting rebellions elsewhere. Its lessons would extend from Bush's handling of communism's collapse in the 1990s to Obama's dealings with Libya and Syria in the 2010s.[19]

At the time, Eisenhower's tepid response to the crackdown in Hungary had as much to do with the potential for war with the Soviets as it did with another preoccupation of the moment: trouble in the Suez.

* * *

For most of 1956, Eisenhower and his advisers worked behind the scenes to ease tensions in the Middle East. After Egyptian leader Gamal Abdel Nasser nationalized the Suez Canal, the United States focused on restraining the United Kingdom and France from forcibly retaking it from Egypt. Seeing this as the last gasp of European dominance in the region, Eisenhower worried the Brits were just looking for a way to prove their toughness. "You don't go to war to preserve your influence," he warned. For a time, Ike thought his quiet diplomacy was making progress to keep a lid on things. He failed, however, and the British and the French colluded behind his back with the Israelis to invade, retake the canal, and, they hoped, deal a decisive blow against an upstart regime in Cairo.[20]

Eisenhower felt personally betrayed by his World War II partners—especially his closest allies, the British, who were the chief instigators of the crisis. He was flabbergasted by their deception and by how badly they botched things (Ike also pointed out the incongruous circumstance in which the US was simultaneously at bitter odds with the British and French over Suez while working closely with them against Soviet aggression in Hungary). Writing to friends at the time, Ike called the British actions "stupid" and a "terrible mistake," serving only to "isolate themselves from the good opinion of the world" in a way that "will take them many years" to recover, if ever. His speechwriter Emmet Hughes recalled that the "whole Middle Eastern scene [left] him dismayed, baffled, and fearful of the great stupidity about to assert itself."[21]

"You don't go to war to preserve your influence." Eisenhower and Secretary of State John Foster Dulles in the Oval Office delivering a televised report to the nation on the Suez crisis in 1956.
(Courtesy of Dwight D. Eisenhower Library)

To force a ceasefire, Eisenhower took the unprecedented step of working against the British and the French at the UN, rallying a vote ordering them to halt their actions. To squeeze them further, he suspended US arms sales and threatened to cut off their access to oil. Eisenhower took these extraordinary actions to defend basic principles—such as the sanctity of territorial sovereignty and the peaceful resolution of disputes—even if it meant punishing friends. He understood this entailed political risk, telling his aides "he did not care in the slightest" if he was reelected or not, and if the American people "threw me out . . . so be it."[22]

Ike's motives were also consistent with his New Look strategy: he wanted to prevent the Soviets from taking advantage of the crisis to claim the upper hand in the Middle East. During a long NSC meeting on the morning of November 1—just hours before he boarded the train to Philadelphia to deliver his last campaign speech—Eisenhower warned that Moscow would pounce if the United States did not act to quell the crisis. "The Soviets must be prevented from seizing a mantle of world leadership," he later summarized in a memo for the record. Sure enough, on Election Day, word came the Soviets were preparing steps to intervene on behalf of the Egyptians. Ike told his aides that if this happened, he stood ready for a "major war."[23]

Although Eisenhower ordered careful military steps to deter Soviet action—such as putting units on alert and preparing ships and aircraft for deployment—they soon became unnecessary. The British buckled under the pressure, backed down in humiliation, and eventually withdrew their forces. But the crisis was the death blow for Europe's predominant influence in the Middle East. With them gone—and to keep the Soviets out and the oil flowing—Eisenhower felt the need to fill the void.

Determined to deny Moscow any advantage, Ike focused on the "constructive" things the United States could do to project its influence in the Middle East. As he explained at the time, he hoped to bring "more patience, more understanding and somewhat more wisdom than has yet been brought to bear in that troubled region." This set in motion a series of diplomatic, economic, and military decisions now known as the "Eisenhower Doctrine." In diary notes from November 1956, Ike summed up his goal this way: the United States needed to offer the region "information and proposals that will establish real peace in the area and, above all to exclude Communist influence from making any headway."[24]

In other words, the United States had to commit itself to the Middle East for the long haul. Therefore Eisenhower enlisted congressional support, codifying his policies into a far-reaching legislative resolution that called for a bold US assistance program as well as authorize US military power to, as Eisenhower explained, "put the entire world on notice that we are ready to move instantly if necessary." Congress's backing would make the US commitment more credible. It was also consistent with Eisenhower's views that a president's authority to use force, while substantial, should be purposely bound. In retrospect, this represented a high-water mark in modern presidential deference to Congress on war powers—although its implications over time proved, ironically, very different.

When Congress passed the Eisenhower Doctrine legislation in March 1957, just four months after the Suez crisis, it not only ushered in an era of American dominance in the Middle East, it also empowered the president with a remarkably open-ended approval to use force—authority that, while never directly invoked, still remained on the books over six decades later.[25]

EISENHOWER FELT THE WIND at his back as his second term in office began. He had won a resounding electoral victory. He had endured a profound moment of global crisis. He earned congressional backing to implement a bold vision for the US role in a critical region (importantly, he also seemed to have bounced back from several serious health scares that left him sidelined for weeks). He rose to the challenges as promised on that rainy November 1 evening in Philadelphia—"proud of our principles, persistent in peace"—doing so in ways many historians would come to herald as an example of great restraint, courage, and foresight.

At the time, however, many critics weren't convinced. They saw Eisenhower not as triumphant, but as weak. Rather than being considered as a masterclass of statesmanship, these events exposed Eisenhower's foreign policy flaws—in Hungary, by not doing enough to stand up to the Soviets after allegedly encouraging a revolt; and in Suez, by undermining the vital alliance with the United Kingdom and France. Moreover, his persistence in warning about the costs of war—and his determination to avoid taking actions that might escalate into one—was seen perversely to invite, if not encourage, further Soviet adventurism in Europe and the Middle East.[26]

III. BUSH: SQUANDERING VICTORY

George H. W. Bush was nobody's idea of a revolutionary. When crises flared, his first impulse was to deescalate. If events were breaking in one's favor, then don't screw up; if things were going against one's interests, contain the damage. When presented with a crisis, Bush once explained in a letter to a friend, "my mode, having been through history's greatest frenzy [World War II]—albeit as a spear carrier—Be calm . . . do your best and don't worry about things you can't do anything about . . . maybe your colon will have a kink or two in it from concern, but life'll go on."[27]

Bush would often say to his aides that he aimed "to do the most good I can, and the least harm," adding that he felt an "obligation to temper optimism . . . with prudence." Before entering the White House, these instincts served him well. Whether leading the Republican National Committee during the turmoil of Watergate, or serving as CIA Director in the mid-1970s when the intelligence community faced intense scrutiny after a wave of scandals, Bush had a knack for projecting confidence and providing calm in a storm.[28]

Steady stewardship was a vital ingredient of his leadership—after all, other countries looked to the United States to solve problems, not create new ones. The framework for his foreign policy, Bush later wrote, "was very deliberate: encouraging, guiding and managing change without provoking backlash and crackdown." This meant projecting the kind of "certain stability" he admired in Eisenhower. "The longer I am in this job," he dictated to his diary in November 1989, just as the Berlin Wall was coming down, "the more I think prudence is a value and experience matters."[29]

Such innate caution was easily portrayed as weakness. Bush proved willing to act forcefully, but bristled at critics who always wanted him to show emotion or just *do more*. There is no better illustration of these competing impulses at work than the 1991 conflict with Iraq.

He took the biggest gamble of his presidency in fighting the war. By ejecting Iraq from Kuwait, the United States upheld the idea that countries cannot take territory by force, safeguarded energy supplies so vital to a thriving and open global economy, and enhanced American influence in a critical part of the world. But the war's ugly aftermath—with Saddam Hussein still in power, slaughtering his opponents and threatening the region—presented one of the greatest tests to the president's concept of

Hippocratic leadership. It would also be one of the most controversial aspects of his legacy, offering lessons that would have fateful consequences when applied by his eldest son's administration a decade later.

THIS WAS NOT HOW BUSH IMAGINED VICTORY. It was March 1991 and the US-led coalition of thirty-five countries had just driven Iraq's military from Kuwait in a decisive air campaign and lightning ground invasion. Bush's public approval rating soared to 89 percent. Yet rather than fade away, Saddam Hussein's forces began to turn their sights onto their own people—the Kurds in the north and the Shia in the south.

Stunned by the rapidity of their military success, Bush and his team were caught flat-footed. Or, as they later put it, they were "psychologically unprepared" for what came next. When the US military routed Iraqi forces—with retreating Iraqi troops, vehicles, and artillery blasted away in a "turkey shoot" on a "highway of death"—Bush thought it was just a matter of time before Saddam would flee or be overthrown. It was a reasonable, though incorrect, assumption.

While the humanitarian catastrophe intensified, Bush came under mounting pressure to act. Politicians who voted against the war in the first place now pushed Bush to intervene further. Pundits thundered and world leaders weighed in. German Chancellor Helmut Kohl, one of Bush's most trusted partners, urged him to step up and show "a new kind of leadership."[30]

This was one instance when Bush's rhetoric got away from him. He privately considered the Iraqi leader a "cancer" and publicly encouraged Iraqis to "put him [Saddam] aside." For months Bush had been making the case for war by describing Saddam Hussein as a modern-day Hitler, as a tyrant who could never be appeased. But to avoid getting bogged down in conflict as well as to secure the largest possible international coalition of countries, which had UN backing and included many of Iraq's Arab neighbors, he tightly scoped the military mission to avoid regime change. "We need a surrender, we need Saddam out," he said to his diary. "And yet our objectives are to stop short of all that." When deciding the criteria for ending the war, Bush focused on the threat to Kuwait. He emphasized withdrawing US forces and letting others carry the principal security burden. As for what happened inside postwar Iraq, Bush and his top aides fully expected the Iraqi people to rise up and oust a weakened and humiliated Saddam.[31]

This outcome seemed likely when the Kurdish and Shia rebellion began. Yet while the Iraqi military proved no match for the Americans, it retained enough firepower to slaughter civilians and demolish the ragtag insurgents. The rebels misjudged Saddam's strength as well as the US commitment to their cause. Bush stood still as Saddam struck back. He was unwilling to change the mission to the far more dangerous goal of regime change, fearing this would fracture his international coalition and jeopardize the domestic support he had mobilized.

Bush defended this stance, describing his initial rhetoric of regime change not as a policy goal, but as a gesture toward the rebels. He said it wasn't meant as a "promise to aid an uprising." At the same time, Bush felt no euphoria with Saddam still in power. "Hitler is still in office, and that's the problem," he lamented to his diary.[32]

At home and abroad, critics blamed the administration for bungling the war's end. The *New York Times* columnist William Safire described Bush's "betrayal" of the Kurds as an "ignominious military defeat" that "threw away our newfound pride." The comparison of Bush's reluctance to act with Eisenhower's handling of Hungary in 1956 was obvious. For Democratic politicians who opposed the war (and most had voted against it), the president's stumble provided an opportunity to sully the victory and reestablish some political momentum. And from abroad, pressure to act increased. In Paris, thousands marched to demand action to stop the slaughter, and world leaders called the White House imploring Bush to do something—anything—to protect civilians and ease the suffering.[33]

Bush finally acknowledged he was not doing enough. He dispatched his secretary of state, James Baker, to the border between Kurdish-populated Iraq and Turkey. After spending a few harrowing moments on a rugged mountainside teeming with desperate refugees, Baker immediately called the president in Washington. "You have no idea of the human nightmare here . . . people are dying every day," he stressed, telling Bush "to do something and do it now . . . if we don't, literally thousands of people are going to die." The urgent humanitarian concern compelled Bush to move.[34]

While he still worried about the risks of deeper military intervention and getting the United States stuck in an Iraqi quagmire, Bush ordered US forces to airdrop food, blankets, and clothing to the refugees. He also worked through the UN Security Council to pass a groundbreaking resolution condemning Saddam and labeling the flow of refugees across borders as a threat to international peace and security. Most significantly, Bush used the UN resolution as legal justification for the United States to lead a twelve-nation military coalition to create safe havens and no-fly zones in northern and southern Iraq. He sent twenty thousand troops to northern Iraq to implement this mission, "Operation Provide Comfort," which was the first humanitarian military effort of the post–Cold War era.

By working with allies and using military power to alleviate suffering, the US delivered much needed aid and, at least in the short term, dissuaded Saddam from continuing his assault. Yet Bush did not disarm the dictator—for example, he refused to ground Iraq's helicopter gunships—leaving his military intact. Nor did Bush accept the recommendation from some of his advisers to continue the air campaign until Saddam personally accepted the terms of the surrender, thereby humiliating the Iraqi leader and likely leading to his downfall. Nevertheless, this playbook—using multilateral authorization for the limited use of military power to address a threat to civilians—cleared a path for future international responses to humanitarian crises, whether the following year in Somalia, later that decade in the Balkans, or in Libya in 2011.[35]

JUST TWO MONTHS AFTER American forces entered northern Iraq on a humanitarian mission, hundreds of thousands of spectators flooded Washington's National Mall to watch over eight thousand troops and a packed trail of tanks, jeeps, helicopters, fighter jets, and missiles (as well as a capability few had seen before, an unmanned drone) on display to celebrate the US military's overwhelming victory against Saddam Hussein's Iraq. On that day in June 1991, Washington witnessed its largest military spectacle since Eisenhower marched victorious American GIs down Pennsylvania Avenue to celebrate the end of World War II. The happy crowds honored the troops, and they also cheered their triumphant commander-in-chief. Sixteen years after Bush, as envoy to China, watched the US retreat in humiliation from Saigon, it seemed the United States finally exorcised the ghosts of Vietnam.[36]

Yet amid the celebration, Bush privately sensed trouble ahead. Politically, Bush knew he was vulnerable. His advisers warned of the "Churchill parallel," when another leader brought victory in war only to get tossed out of office, and Bush quietly pondered whether he even wanted to stand for reelection in 1992. While few questioned Bush's skill in handling the Gulf War, especially his effort to forge a broad international coalition and secure UN Security Council authorization, the tarnished conclusion proved deeply unsatisfying to critics and supporters alike.

The handling of postwar Iraq left the stain of unfinished business— giving Bush's political opponents a rare opportunity to chip away at one of his perceived strengths. In Bill Clinton's first major foreign policy address as a presidential candidate in April 1991, he sharply criticized Bush for encouraging and then abandoning the rebellions, while his eventual vice presidential running mate, Al Gore, asked if Bush was such a "whiz" at foreign policy, then why was Saddam thumbing his nose at the world?

The president pushed back by instructing his campaign team to stress that if he had done what critics suggested by pushing to Baghdad, American troops would still be occupying Iraq, propping up a new government and "incurring incalculable human and political costs." Dick Cheney, Bush's defense secretary who at the time supported the decision not to go to Baghdad, but a decade later emerged as the most important Iraq hawk, conceded that "we hadn't done a lot of planning for what happens after the war."[37]

Yet the damage was done. The widespread view that Bush botched the war's end—particularly by not removing Saddam Hussein when he had the chance—was seen as a kind of original sin, one that not only caused hundreds of thousands of innocents to suffer, but something that future presidents would have to atone. Moreover, the no-fly-zones over Iraq enforced by US and coalition aircraft meant the American military would remain actively engaged in the Middle East throughout the 1990s and well into the 2000s—which was, in effect, a costly turn in the Eisenhower Doctrine's evolution.

For more than a decade, Bush's postwar restraint was considered unwise and cowardly. Critics thought the president bequeathed to his successors a problem he did not have the guts to solve. The sense of guilt over the betrayal of the Iraqi Kurds and Shia lingered. The belief that American inaction was such a huge mistake—a view especially held by some Bush veterans who advocated for doing more and returned to power eight years later to serve in his son's administration—was a crucial backdrop to the decision to invade Iraq in 2003.

Of course, future events eventually vindicated Bush's caution regarding the dangers of regime change in Iraq. But that was quite hard to see in the summer of 1991. After all, another era-defining crisis was about to boil over.

IV. BUSH: "I THINK WE HANDLED IT ABOUT RIGHT."

As a hurricane barreled toward the Bush family compound on Maine's coast in August 1991, the president rushed to call his friend Brian Mulroney, the prime minister of Canada.

Bush's biggest concern wasn't the stormy weather. He was thinking about the shocking events of several hours earlier, when Soviet hardliners staged a coup against Mikhail Gorbachev. Suddenly, the future of a nuclear-armed superpower appeared perilously up for grabs. Bush knew his next move could potentially doom six years of reform efforts in the Soviet Union—leading to a return to the darker days of the Cold War, or perhaps worse, the country's chaotic collapse.

Only a year earlier, Iraq's invasion of Kuwait upended Bush's summer vacation; now he had to grapple with an even more consequential geopolitical crisis. "Every time I come to Maine," Bush sighed to Mulroney, "all hell breaks loose."[38]

FOR DECADES, AMERICAN PRESIDENTS COULD ONLY DREAM of the day the Soviet Union would finally succumb to its own internal contradictions. But when this prospect seemed imminent, Bush was apprehensive. Together, he and Gorbachev had done big things. In just two years, the Soviet leader became Bush's wingman in the emerging new world order: accepting Germany's reunification, signing historic arms control agreements, supporting the US-led effort to oust Iraq from Kuwait, and allowing Soviet domination over Eastern Europe to end peacefully.

"I felt I could trust him," Bush later reflected. "And I think he felt he could trust the West at this time of deepest, and ultimately final, crisis for the Soviet Union." Faith in Gorbachev became a central pillar of Bush's foreign policy strategy; he saw the leader as the key actor in bringing peaceful change to the USSR and working with the United States to construct a new era of geopolitics.[39]

Yet by mid-1991, just as the Gulf War crisis ebbed, a new one flowed from inside the Soviet Union itself. With the Soviet Republics agitating for greater independence from Moscow, Bush found himself walking a diplomatic high wire, trying to encourage steady reforms while avoiding anything to spark the country's implosion. Freedom and democracy were important, he believed, but not at the expense of stability. "Whatever the course and whatever its outcome," Bush remembered, "I wanted to see stable, and above all peaceful, change."[40]

Bush's careful approach was instinctive; his memories of World War II, he recalled, did "condition me as commander in chief and makes me cautious." But it also reflected the more recent lessons he took from dealing with the June 1989 massacre in Tiananmen Square, in which the Chinese military killed thousands of pro-democracy protestors. Bush thought he knew the Chinese leaders well (having gotten to know many of them during his time there in the 1970s) and was utterly shocked by their vicious crackdown. Perhaps, he worried, such brutality was a preview of things to come elsewhere. This only reinforced the president's cautious intuition—and that is a key reason why he did not "dance on the wall" in November 1989, recognize Lithuanian or Ukrainian independence in

1990–91, or rush to declare the Soviet Union dead after the August 1991 coup.[41]

WHEN BUSH AWOKE TO THE NEWS of tanks and armored personnel carriers rumbling through Moscow's streets, his response was textbook do-no-harm diplomacy. Unsure whether Gorbachev was still alive, Bush worked the phones, trying to get in touch with the Soviet president and imploring fellow world leaders not to let things spin out of control.

Bush refused to get "stampeded into some flamboyant statement" or "overexcite" people. He resisted efforts to hold an emergency NATO meeting to discuss the coup, worrying that it would "send scary military signals" and raise expectations for the Alliance's possible intervention, creating "commitments that would be a repeat of Hungary in 1956." As Bush summarized in his diary, "The best thing we can do at a time like this is calmness, firmness, adherence to principle."[42]

The coup reinforced Bush's conviction that his initial strategy of betting on the Soviet leader to promote gradual change was right: it "*totally* vindicat[ed] our policy of trying to stay with Gorbachev," he reflected. "If we had pulled the rug out from under [him] . . . you'd have seen a military crackdown far in excess of the ugliness that's taking place now." Bush appreciated the moment's gravity, but always kept perspective and tried to stay matter-of-fact, reflecting the long view. "The hurricane's gone by," he told his diary. "The Soviet Union is in turmoil. Eastern Europe is worried. But life goes on. August nineteenth. A historic day."[43]

While the coup quickly dissolved into farce—with the plotters proving incompetent, drunk, or both—it ignited three challenges: first, how to handle the political dissolution of the Soviet Union itself; second, how to manage the future of the massive Soviet nuclear arsenal and arms control efforts; and third, and perhaps most important, how to support democracy and economic reform in the newly independent former Soviet states.

Unlike the previous summer, when Iraq's invasion of Kuwait clearly violated international law and warranted a robust response, the United States didn't have a lot of policy options. "Here, I'm not sure what has to happen,"

Bush admitted to himself. "What I'd like to see is a return of Gorbachev and a continuous movement for democracy. I'm not quite sure how to get there." His top aides were divided between those (like Dick Cheney) who advocated for a quick breakup of the Soviet Union, wanting to see it in "smaller pieces," and others (like James Baker) who sought a more gradual process, perhaps with the central authority of Moscow maintaining some degree of control. While Bush quickly recognized the sovereignty of the Baltic states, which were always considered a special case, he chafed at calls to immediately support the independence of Soviet Republics like Ukraine. He didn't want to prejudge the USSR's ultimate fate.[44]

Bush thought he was staving off chaos. Yet his critics argued he was missing a historic opportunity. They weren't convinced this was a moment for more prudence. Even Bush's political allies argued the United States needed to jettison Gorbachev and throw its support behind the president of Russia, Boris Yeltsin.

"We can't put all our eggs in Gorbachev's basket," said Robert Dole, the Republican leader in the US Senate (and later, the 1996 GOP presidential nominee). Bush didn't want to lose such a valued diplomatic partner, and it did not help that Yeltsin's blustery style left him uneasy. Ultimately, Bush tried as long as he could to follow a hands-off approach, telling his foreign counterparts "we support the center or at least we support Gorbachev." In his mind, the alternative was "anarchy."[45]

Bush's desire to stick with Gorbachev and slow the disintegration process was about more than his personal feelings or predilection for order. Never before had a multinational empire imploded absent a major war. Bush was rightfully anxious about what a mismanaged, rapid dissolution would mean for a country with twenty-seven thousand nuclear warheads spread across four Republics. So he decided to take a bold step that could both enhance stability and, perhaps, throw a lifeline to Gorbachev. In September 1991, Bush announced that the United States would unilaterally eliminate its tactical nuclear weapons, de-alert all nuclear bombers, and abolish its multiple warhead missiles. Gorbachev quickly reciprocated with his own arms reductions. The result helped reduce a significant threat and stands as one of Bush's most significant long-term accomplishments in managing the Soviet Union's collapse. Yet it would not be enough to save his man in Moscow.[46]

THE END WAS SWIFT. Shortly after the Ukrainians voted in favor of independence in December 1991, the leaders of Belarus and Russia followed. Thankfully, the Soviet Union went out with a whimper, not a bang. On Christmas Day, the Soviet hammer-and-sickle flag was lowered over the Kremlin for the last time. That evening, Bush returned from Camp David to speak to the nation from the Oval Office. Reflecting on the extraordinary global tumult of the previous twelve months—from confronting Saddam Hussein's aggression to managing the collapse of the Soviet Union—he summarized the year's dramatic change: "You and I," he said, "have witnessed one of the greatest dramas of the 20th century."[47]

Despite this triumph, many Americans had a lingering sense that, once again, Bush did not seize the moment. Soviet communism may have failed, but the United States had not yet won. With Russia and the former Soviet states heading toward economic collapse, there were fears of widespread unrest and starvation; some worried that like Germany in the 1930s, a "Weimar Russia" would lead to extremism and nationalism. To prevent this, some influential voices called for the administration to step up with a massive financial assistance package on the scale of the Marshall Plan. Without this kind of "grand bargain," they warned, any hopes for a democratic Russia would be lost.

The views of one critic crystallized the argument that Bush was failing. Former President Richard Nixon, finally emerging from his long political exile back into the good graces of statesmanship, issued a damning assessment in a March 1992 memo entitled "How to Lose the Cold War." Although supposedly confidential, the critique leaked to anyone interested, sparking one of those Washington skirmishes that dominates the headlines and recasts the debate. Nixon happily basked in the attention with a series of major television appearances and interviews with influential journalists.

Describing the fate of Russia's political and economic reforms as the most important issue facing American foreign policy since the end of

World War II, the former president belittled the Bush administration's efforts to support Yeltsin as "tokenism" and "pathetically inadequate," sarcastically describing the response as only generous "if the target of our aid were a small country like Upper Volta." He warned against the dangers of a "new despotism" in Russia, arguing that while the stakes were high, Bush was "playing as if it was a penny ante game." Nixon harkened back to an earlier trope that was instrumental to his own political rise during the beginning of the Cold War and as Ike's vice president: while "the hot-button issue in the 1950s was 'who lost China?'" he wrote, "if Yeltsin goes down, the question of 'who lost Russia?' will be an infinitely more devastating issue in the 1990s."[48]

Nixon concluded his five-page broadside with an off-hand, merciful description of Bush as "uniquely qualified to meet this challenge," citing his leadership in forging the Gulf War coalition. However, the implications of his argument were clear: Bush needed to display more creativity and courage. This thrust the president on the defensive at exactly the wrong moment—just as the 1992 campaign heated up. Bush found himself parrying a strong primary challenge from Pat Buchanan, who asserted that the United States needed to spend less on its foreign policy, while at the same time, Democrats used Nixon's arguments as ammunition to attack him, declaring he was not doing enough to support Russia.

Bush maintained a brave face, implausibly saying he did not see his Republican predecessor's critique as "scathing." Privately, Bush told Nixon he agreed with his memo's core message, conceding "that we have an enormous stake with democratic Russia." Yet Bush and his team thought Nixon's memo, and the publicity he stoked around it, a cheap stunt. Because the Soviets "could not get their act together" on economic reform, they thought large-scale US assistance in the immediate aftermath of the coup to be an unwise idea. Doing so would have been simply throwing more good money after bad. Moreover, while no one wanted to "lose" Russia, the American people worried about the weakening United States economy and clamored for a peace dividend, not a victory tax. "There isn't a lot of money around," Bush conceded. "We are spending too much as it already is. So to do the things I would really like to do—I don't have a blank check for that."[49]

Bush eventually pledged billions of dollars in US assistance and worked to rally the world to do more to help Russia. Despite this, his handling of this crisis perpetuated a perception of leadership that became a liability at the time, and shaped his legacy ever since.

This impression is aptly summarized by the verdict rendered by Michael Beschloss and Strobe Talbott in their contemporaneous account of the end of the Cold War: "Bush was so intent on shoring up Gorbachev that he was slow to perceive that by the summer of 1991, the Soviet leader was largely a spent force," they wrote. "Bush created the impression that he cared more about his friend in the Kremlin than about the principles of freedom and independence. His ties to Gorbachev—and his reluctance to support Yeltsin—ultimately became a political liability in Bush's campaign for reelection." Decades later, scholars still ask whether the United States "lost" Russia, and speculate if bolder leadership in late 1991 and early 1992, especially greater economic assistance, could have led to a better outcome.[50]

Bush, of course, saw things differently. To him, none of this was inevitable. If he had handled the Soviet collapse less carefully, it could have metastasized into a much worse crisis, like Hungary in 1956 or Tiananmen Square in 1989, only this time with nuclear security at stake. "I know there's some current kind of conventional wisdom that we stayed with Gorbachev too long," he said in 1992. "I would say the transition has been peaceful—not without some bumps in the road, but the transition has been peaceful. And the coup failed. And I think that we handled it about right."[51]

V. OBAMA: "IT DIDN'T WORK."

Barack Obama's first insight into foreign policy decision-making came as an undergraduate at Columbia University in the early 1980s, when as a senior he took a yearlong course on international relations. He considered Ernest May's uses of history and probed Irving Janis's perils of "groupthink." He studied presidential decision-making in the 1961 Bay of Pigs, the 1962 Cuban Missile Crisis, the 1965 military escalation in Vietnam, and the 1973 Yom Kippur War. He learned that in moments of crisis, the best decision-makers followed a few basic principles: solicit diverse views, probe situations from multiple perspectives, closely scrutinize promises of quick answers and easy solutions, and always consider the worst-case scenarios. Until then, this was the most serious coursework Obama had ever tackled. On his final paper, he earned an "A."[52]

Sitting in the White House three decades later, Obama benefitted from not just reading books by great scholars, but also inviting them to Washington for private tutorials. Recalling his discussions with esteemed presidential historians like Doris Kearns Goodwin and David McCullough, Obama told his aides that "they made the point that the most important thing a president can do on foreign policy is avoid a costly error." They warned him to heed the examples of Johnson and Vietnam, Jimmy Carter and the failed Desert One hostage rescue mission in Iran, and Bush 43 and the Iraq War. The lesson, he concluded, was a simple one: "don't do stupid shit."[53]

Many of Obama's top advisors reinforced this insight, often citing the examples of Eisenhower and Bush. Obama's first Defense Secretary, Robert Gates, had been one of Bush's closest White House aides during the end of the Cold War, and during the Obama administration he gave a speech at the Eisenhower Library in which he praised Ike's restraint as wise recognition that the US "did not have unlimited political, economic and military resources." Similarly, Hillary Clinton recalled Eisenhower's example as "you've got to be careful. You have to be thoughtful. You can't rush in." And Chuck Hagel, one of Gates' successors at the Pentagon, who was also a lifelong Eisenhower admirer, sent copies of historian David Nichols' book *Eisenhower 1956* to Obama and other senior officials to show how Ike's handling of Hungary and Suez was a good model for the crises they faced. The two toughest were Libya and Syria.[54]

WHEN OBAMA CONSIDERED HIS FOREIGN POLICY STRATEGY, it is safe to say he was not thinking of a country like Libya. Wanting to shift emphasis from the two conflicts he inherited to a long-game approach to meet challenges like China and climate change, Obama was not looking to start new wars. He wanted to maintain US influence in the Middle East, but at a more affordable and sustainable price. He contemplated using military force to achieve a finite set of regional goals: to fight Al Qaeda; to prevent the use or spread of weapons of mass destruction, most notably the threat of Iran's nuclear weapons program; and to protect Israel. Not to help a revolution in Libya.

So when he walked the few steps from the Oval Office to the Roosevelt Room one late afternoon in March 2011, nine days into a massive US-led bombing campaign against Libya, Obama knew he had some explaining to do.

Gathered around the big wooden table was a handful of leading foreign policy commentators and columnists, the kind of folks who pass judgment and, for better or worse, shape the narrative around how to think about a president's foreign policy decisions. That evening, Obama would travel across town to Fort McNair, home of the National Defense University, to deliver a nationally televised speech intended to outline what the military efforts against Libya had achieved thus far, and where they were going. This off-the-record session was a kind of warm-up, in which the president could preview and expand on his reasoning for action.

"We didn't have the luxury of planning Libya a month in advance," Obama said with a tinge of defensiveness. He wanted to preempt those who believed his initial response to events, when a slaughter of hundreds of thousands of Libyan civilians seemed imminent, was too slow. Now the military effort was underway and going well, with US airpower making quick work of Libya's ill-matched forces and fulfilling the primary mission to protect civilians from a massacre.

Like Bush in Iraq in 1991, the United States worked with its partners to mobilize a broad diplomatic and military international coalition, forged a UN mandate to act, and established a no-fly zone in less than a month after the unrest began in Libya. NATO was poised to take over command of the mission. International support poured in to bolster the Libyan opposition. At that point, it looked like Obama's plan—to respond to the crisis without getting sucked into another all-consuming Middle East conflict—was actually going to work.

Obama defined success narrowly. Noting the lessons of George W. Bush's mistakes in Iraq—which he saw as the very kind of "stupid shit" a president should avoid—he made clear overthrowing strongman Muammar Qadhafi was not the military objective. It would, however, remain a political goal—and he expected this process to be "messy."

He explained the United States would not be solely responsible for what came next. Instead, the Libyan people and the international community, especially the Europeans, were expected to step up. The overall approach, Obama said, in echoes of Ike's desire to navigate between the unattainable and the unacceptable in Dien Bien Phu, was to find a course between those "hyperrealists" who argued that Libya was not worth it and those who believed the United States should go all in, pursue regime change, and own the problem.

Predictably, the foreign policy grandees wondered whether these actions added up to some new kind of doctrine or a broader framework for future interventions. Obama rebuffed the idea, saying that beyond matters of self-defense, the United States was always better off taking its time and rallying partners to act together. Moreover, he argued, just because the United States was acting in Libya did not necessarily mean it should act the same elsewhere, warning against a "cookie-cutter approach" to crisis management.

With his words and body language, Obama reflected the stress of the moment. For the previous two months, the unexpected events of the Arab Spring whipsawed his administration. As the Middle East order unspooled, Obama wondered if this was analogous to the collapse of communism, when democracy bloomed, or situations like Hungary in 1956, Tiananmen Square in 1989, or postwar Iraq in 1991, when hopes for freedom were brutally crushed. Obama found it hard to handle the velocity of events, especially when weighed against the other crushing demands at home and abroad.

"We're living at a moment in which more consequential change is happening on the world stage than at any point in my lifetime, and that's combined with a media environment that is more demanding than ever before," Obama observed that March afternoon in the Roosevelt Room. Yet the challenge was to establish an approach to serve a larger strategy— one in which, he said, America could "describe [how] what's going on leads to a better story rather than a worse story."

Unfortunately, Obama would later concede, Libya's legacy—especially when considered alongside the inferno that soon engulfed Syria—made the case for a "better story" very tough to argue.[55]

"Do we have an answer for the day after?" The question vexed Obama, seen here in the White House Situation Room deliberating over Libya in 2011.
(Official White House Photo by Pete Souza. Courtesy of the Barack Obama Presidential Library)

CONSIDERING THE TRAGEDY LIBYA WOULD BECOME, it is hard to remember that the campaign appeared to be a success when it ended and Qadhafi met his brutal demise in the fall of 2011, found on the run and killed by a raging mob. After all, the immediate humanitarian crisis was averted, and for awhile Libya looked relatively stable. The United States contributed its unique capabilities to the effort—such as precision strikes, intelligence, and aerial refueling—while allies took the lead and conducted nearly 90 percent of the over ten thousand airstrikes. The entire campaign cost just over $1 billion, roughly equivalent to what the United States spent per week in Iraq or Afghanistan. NATO proved adept in organizing and coordinating the operation, and the world seemed poised to give the Libyan people the political and economic assistance they deserved.

In almost every way, this seemed different than Iraq in 2003, a conflict that divided the nation and the world. And unlike Eisenhower and Dien Bien Phu in 1954, but like Bush and Iraq in 1991, Obama had the vigorous support of key European allies (who had made clear they would act even if the United States did not), regional partners who had called for intervention, UN backing, and for at least a moment, congressional support. Although Obama remained attentive to the risks—which was why he tried so hard to push allies to do more and limit US involvement—there were plenty of reasons to think this could be successful.

Nevertheless, by the end of his presidency, Obama summed up his Libya policy bluntly. "It didn't work," he said. "Libya is a mess."[56]

Why did this happen? In retrospect, it is tempting to think any intervention in Libya was ill-considered and fruitless, and the United States should have stayed out altogether. Some scholars argue that the threat to civilians in February 2011 was overblown, based on a fundamental misreading of Qadhafi's behavior and a gross misunderstanding of the conflict itself. There's no question the United States lacked expertise on Libya at the time, and to a certain extent, American officials were flying blind. Yet almost everyone who watched the situation unfurl—such as European allies and regional partners, journalists on the ground, intelligence analysts, the NGO community—believed a massive slaughter was imminent. Instead of asking why the United States would act, everyone asked why not.

Still, intervention was a tough call—51 to 49, Obama said at the time—with the president admitting to his team that he was "as worried as anyone about getting sucked into another war." But they did not feel they had the luxury to wait and see if Qadhafi was bluffing. Therefore Obama tried to thread the needle. He crafted a response in which the US military would do a lot of the upfront work in an air campaign with the objective of stopping an imminent attack on civilians, and then turn most of the responsibility over to NATO allies and partners for the long-term mission of protecting them—maintaining a no-fly zone and, presumably, helping rebuild a post-Qadhafi Libya—with Washington playing more of a role behind the scenes.[57]

For six months, the air campaign achieved its core goal to protect civilians. Yet the definition of success proved frustratingly elusive. Just a few days of bombing arguably had addressed the immediate threat. The enduring danger persisted, however, with Qadhafi still in power. While Obama publicly stressed he would not go beyond a well-defined goal, and that broadening the military mission to include regime change would be a mistake, that is exactly what happened. The United States never clearly outlined when the principal objective—to protect civilians from danger—would be achieved. When it grounded Libya's air force? When it decimated the Libyan army? When it neutered Qadhafi's regime? Ultimately, the administration got caught in a strategic tautology of its own making: the mission remained to protect civilians, but that could not be achieved so long as Qadhafi remained in power. Despite the best of intentions, the whole experience demonstrated the inexorable pull of mission creep.[58]

Once Qadhafi departed the scene, the question then became what the United States would do to help Libya recover. Obama still did not want postwar Libya to become a massive US-led reconstruction project like Iraq or Afghanistan, diverting the United States from its larger strategic interests. Instead, the effort followed the same kind of "unique capabilities" logic, with the United States offering assistance in areas where it mattered most and it could make a meaningful difference—such as counterterrorism training and securing Libya's substantial weapons stockpiles. For everything else, others would carry the burden.

Driven by Obama's determination to keep American responsibilities commensurate with what he considered the minimal interests at stake, the small footprint approach also suited Libyan desires. Fiercely independent, they did not want their nation rebuilt by outsiders. The fact that the Libyans simultaneously wanted the United States to do more while also doing things their own way presented a conundrum the Obama administration could never solve.

ALTHOUGH OBAMA HIMSELF CONSIDERED the handling of postwar Libya as one of his greatest regrets and publicly said "our coalition could have and should have done more to fill a vacuum left behind," the reasons were more complicated. There was plenty of planning for the day after—for months, US officials worked with their international counterparts and the Libyan opposition to prepare. They earnestly tried to apply the hard lessons learned from post-conflict efforts in Iraq and Afghanistan. But with a limited number of American officials on the ground—and without a military presence to provide security, logistics, and organizational support, without a US Congress willing to fund significant assistance efforts, and without a Libyan leadership that welcomed such help—there were substantial limits to what outsiders could accomplish. "It wasn't so much a lack of 'planning' that doomed the effort," former White House official Philip Gordon argues. It was "Libyan nationalism, Libyan dysfunction, intervention fatigue, U.S. domestic political opposition, the agenda of outside rivals, and an unwillingness among Western powers to bear the costs and risks of sending forces to the Middle East. Those obstacles could not just be wished away."[59]

Libya's mixed lessons had a profound impact on Obama. By intervening, the United States prevented a massacre almost everyone saw as imminent while maintaining a limited role rightsized to its interests. Yet in the conduct of the air campaign, the Obama administration and its allies failed to prevent mission creep. And in the war's aftermath, they failed to do enough to bring stability.

Several years after the intervention, Libya remained in a state of perpetual turmoil. Obama said that while he did not regret getting involved, he greatly underestimated the challenges that followed. To him, the key conclusion was the "need to come in full force if you're going to do this." The Libya experience, Obama explained, offered a lesson he would apply every time the question of military intervention arose: "Do we have an answer [for] the day after?' "[60]

This dilemma would prove especially difficult when Obama faced the most vexing foreign crisis of his presidency: Syria.

VI. OBAMA: THE MORAL MORASS OF SYRIA

When the conflict in Syria erupted in the latter half of 2011, occurring at the same time the Libya campaign wound down, it presented all of the same problems: a humanitarian catastrophe, a ruthless dictator, a massive refugee crisis, violent extremists, multiple countries competing for influence by pumping money and weapons into the conflict, and the specter of weapons of mass destruction. Yet in every instance, these problems were exponentially worse. When Obama considered what to do in Syria, the lessons of Libya—alongside those from Iraq and Afghanistan—loomed large in his mind.

This background mattered. "A president does not make decisions in a vacuum," Obama later explained. "He does not have a blank slate," especially given America's recent history in the Middle East. As he saw it, being a "thoughtful president" meant using caution when "making a renewed commitment in the exact same region of the world with some of the exact same dynamics and the same probability of an unsatisfactory outcome." Obama well understood the costs of inaction. He maintained faith in the good that can come when the United States takes risks and asserts its leadership. He also remained acutely aware of how easy it could be for the United States to forget the lessons of the past and lose its way, undermining its overall foreign policy strategy.[61]

Considered in the broader context of US interests, Obama viewed Syria as an urgent priority but not a particularly important one. As troubling as the conflict became, and however wrenching its ramifications, it did not warrant completely diverting the United States away from other challenges. Obama wanted to maintain American influence in the Middle East, but not at any price. He believed the United States had been preoccupied with the region for too long at the expense of addressing challenges like a rising China, climate change, possible pandemics or a more just global economic order. Other than the possibility of preventing the spread of weapons of mass destruction, Obama could never reconcile how more American involvement in Syria, especially militarily, would have better enabled the US ability to handle these more important goals. Because of this, he designed a policy aimed not at solving the problem, but containing the crisis and mitigating its most dangerous consequences. He wanted to do the most good with the least harm.

Perhaps the fundamental flaw came in his policy's inception—with the decision that Syria's president, Bashar al-Assad, needed to go. Obama came to this conclusion early in the crisis, just as the Libyan conflict reached its climax in August 2011 (the announcement about Assad came a few days before rebel forces overran Libyan's capital and two months before Qadhafi was captured and killed). At the time, Assad's departure seemed more likely than not, and the policy goal seemed self-evident. Obama remained cautious and tried to keep the United States at arm's length, publicly stating that the Syrian people must choose their leaders and the United States "cannot and will not impose a transition." While Obama wanted to get rid of Assad, he did not want the United States to be on the hook to do it no matter what.[62]

Eisenhower once described this quandary as the "tyranny of the weak," in which the United States has to live grudgingly with weaker, abhorrent leaders doing terrible things because the military option to teach them a lesson or remove them from office, while tempting, is too costly. Because the United States needs to be selective using military power, often the only recourse in dealing with such leaders, Ike said, is to "put up with it."[63]

Yet like Eisenhower and Hungary, or Bush and Saddam, Obama's declaration about Assad set high expectations for what the United States would do. At a political level, they all signed on to regime change, and the nuance of what the United States would or would not do was lost. This underscores a dilemma: although the United States has the most diverse set of diplomatic and economic policy tools of any nation, if a president calls for a leader to go, quite often that's interpreted to mean he is prepared to use only one instrument, military force, to make that happen.[64]

THE NOTION THAT IF THE UNITED STATES was not going to go all the way and overthrow the regime in Syria, it should have just stayed quiet, proved immensely frustrating to the president and his team. "That's a weird argument to me," Obama would later say. It was hard to understand, he continued, how the United States could sustainably exercise its moral authority if calling out a brutal dictator meant "you are obliged to invade the country and install a government you prefer." Yet even he knew this was a bit of a false choice. The United States possessed a range of military tools it could deploy to dial up the pressure against the Assad regime, far short of an all-out invasion—it could set up a no-fly zone, bomb Syria's runways to ground Assad's air force, or launch a precision strike to take out a favorite palace. It could cripple Syria's command and control and provide training and assistance to opposition forces (something the administration eventually tried, without much success). It was never a question of capability, but rather of uncertainty about what would happen next.

When weighing what to do in Syria, Obama would question whether the proposed idea would actually work. "We have to be able to distinguish between these problems analytically," he would say, "so that we're not using pliers when we need a hammer." He worried about efficacy and escalation. "Would a military intervention have an impact?" he would ask. "How would it affect our ability to support troops who are still in Afghanistan? What would be the aftermath of our involvement on the ground? Could it trigger even worse violence or the use of chemical weapons? What offers the best prospect of a stable post-Assad Syria?" The answers proved frustratingly elusive.[65]

Moreover, Obama's recent experience in Libya fundamentally influenced his reluctance to use American military power as a way to gain leverage over Assad and shape the direction of the Syrian civil war. Compared to Syria, Libya seemed an easier task—its military was far weaker, and the intervention enjoyed broad international support, including UN Security Council authorization, as well as significant allied participation. None of that applied to Syria. Therefore deeper intervention, Obama warned, increased the "possibility that we would have made the situation worse rather than better on the ground," and US involvement would have meant "we would have the fourth war in a Muslim country in the span of a decade." Obama worried that those few allies who pledged to work alongside the United States were unlikely and unable to live up to their commitments. He felt that he was pushed to intervene in Libya at the urging of the British and French, whom he wrongly assumed would play a larger role in the postwar reconstruction. He could expect even less of their help in Syria.[66]

At home, Obama predicted that no matter how much Members of Congress howled about US inaction, they would not provide any support for the use of force. The Libya experience left him cynically wondering whether "the American people are ever going to support this kind of thing." In Libya, Obama said, "we saved thousands of lives, we didn't have a single casualty, and we took out a dictator who killed hundreds of Americans. And at home, it was a negative." Given this, he believed that if intervention in Syria went badly, Congress would likely try to impeach him, much like Bush's concerns if the United States acted beyond its 1991 Gulf War mandate. These facts definitely shaped Obama's lack of enthusiasm for deeply engaging in Syria. He knew that no matter how many promises were made, if the United States acted, it would do so alone—and he, alone, would be accountable.[67]

THE RISKS OF ACTING—making a bad situation worse, or getting mired in another major war in the Middle East—were profound. These concerns also help explain the thinking behind the most iconic moment of Obama's Syria policy, if not his overall foreign policy: the "red line" over the use of chemical weapons.

It is hard to overstate the impact of Syria's massive undeclared chemical weapons arsenal on Obama's calculations. For the first three years of this crisis, until the bulk of the vast stockpile was removed in the summer of 2014, it was the most urgent issue—and the one that Obama believed ranked at the very top of US national interests. Estimated to be over thir-teen hundred metric tons spread out over as many as forty-five sites in a country three times the size of Virginia, Syria's chemical weapons pro-gram was the world's third largest. Yet since Assad remained committed to propagating the fiction that he did not have such weapons and there-fore never officially declared having them, the Obama team was aware of what it didn't know (such as the exact number of weapons, their location, and their level of security) and thus had to plan for the worst. That was why Obama said publicly if such weapons were used or left unprotected, it would cross the threshold of risk—a red line—that would change his cal-culation about intervention.[68]

When Obama considered any of the options to use force in Syria, he worried most about two risks related to chemical weapons: escalation and loss of control. Obama recognized the danger that Assad might retaliate against any US strike with chemical weapons, but ultimately believed the Syrian leader would be deterred. However, Obama never got a reassuring explanation about what would happen to the tons of chem-ical weapons the United States could not destroy—any planned strikes would only hit a fraction of Assad's arsenal because it was secretive and widely dispersed—and how, in the wake of an attack, they could fall into the hands of others, especially terrorists.

Nevertheless, after Syria used chemical weapons in August 2013, killing nearly fifteen hundred civilians, Obama was prepared to strike, ordered the military to stand ready, and walked right up to the brink. After an inel-egant turnabout to seek congressional support, Obama—like Eisenhower in Vietnam and Bush in Iraq—faced stiff resistance. Although many members of Congress had criticized Obama's inaction and called for some-thing "tougher," when the spotlight turned to them, very few were ready to share accountability for whatever came next in Syria. Instead, they cast dire warnings about American involvement in a morass, expressing many of the same concerns Obama shared.

Yet Moscow and Damascus took Obama seriously, resulting in an un-expected achievement. The credible threat of force caused the Russians to pressure Assad to come clean on his massive chemical weapons stockpiles he always denied having, agree to give them up, and allow an international coalition to remove and destroy thirteen hundred tons, all in the midst of civil war. To put this in context, the size of Syria's chemical weapons arsenal was as much as *ten times* more than the CIA wrongly estimated Saddam Hussein to have in Iraq in 2003. In Syria, the United States avoided war to deal with the arsenal of weapons of mass destruction that did exist; in Iraq, it went to war to deal with the threat that did not.[69]

But this success proved partial at best. While the international coalition removed and destroyed the declared chemical weapons stockpiles in 2014, Assad's forces manufactured homemade bombs with civilian industrial chemicals like chlorine—which were not covered by the 2013 agreement, but still illegal. Moreover, as proved by attacks a few years later, they retained some small number of chemical weapons (something the Obama administration suspected but could not prove). This certainly diminished the accomplishment—for which the Organization for the Prohibition of Chemical Weapons, or OPCW, was awarded the Nobel Peace Prize—but it did not erase it.

From the perspective of the US national interest, the red line episode was Obama's only meaningful success in Syria. Syria's chemical weapons arsenal was a cornerstone of its regional influence and a significant threat, especially as instability spread. After the summer of 2014, Assad was weaker and had a far less formidable chemical weapons arsenal. While the threat of retaliation always existed, the risks of intervention were easier to reconcile than a year before. Since Syria no longer had a vast chemical weapons program, there was little danger of any US military action worsening matters by sparking a proliferation nightmare. With most of the stockpiles removed, the Obama administration found itself better able to manage the risks of military force when it launched its air campaign to combat ISIL in 2014–16. And the reduced risks of escalation and loss of control enhanced future US presidents' ability to conduct strikes in Syria.

With remarkable serendipity, in September 2014, just weeks after the OPCW completed its work to remove Syria's declared chemical weapons, the ISIL crisis exploded and Obama ordered an intensive air campaign over Syria and Iraq that lasted until the end of his presidency—conducting well over ten thousand airstrikes. When combined with a small presence of US special operations forces on the ground in Syria training and assisting an anti-ISIL force of Kurdish fighters, this military effort brought ISIL to its knees and was the basic strategy pursued by the next administration.

Once again, the effort was focused on crushing ISIL, not confronting Assad. After the Libya experience, Obama was even more intent on keeping the United States off the glide path toward deeper intervention. He acknowledged to aides that Syria was a "shit show" that continually racked his brain and conscience. He explained he did not have an ideological predisposition to inaction, but could never answer in practical terms what the United States could do. "Was there something that we hadn't thought of?" he recalled asking himself. "Was there some more that [an] Eisenhower might have figured out?"[70]

Other military options were available—practical ones that stood a chance to change Assad's calculus and, maybe, alleviate Syria's suffering. But Obama never found them compelling enough to risk overextending the United States for a project he thought it could not deliver on. Moreover, key advisers, including his senior military commanders, warned against such a move.

Obama grew impatient whenever aides would recommend certain courses of action (such as creating "safe zones" in Syria) without answering much larger questions (such as how they would be enforced and be legally justifiable). "It is very difficult to imagine a scenario where our involvement in Syria would have led to a better outcome, short of us being willing to undertake an effort in size and scope similar to what we did in Iraq," he said. "And when I hear people suggesting that somehow if we had just financed and armed the opposition earlier, that somehow Assad would be gone by now and we'd have a peaceful transition, it's magical thinking."[71]

TWO CONCEPTS HELP EXPLAIN HOW OBAMA wrestled with the Syria crisis: "traps" and "reliance interest." The president and his top advisers frequently thought in terms of traps and talked openly about avoiding them, always keeping a wary eye on what actions would lead to and the unanticipated ways they could make things worse. What Obama once derisively dubbed the "Washington playbook"—his shorthand for the received foreign policy establishment wisdom that relied too much on militarized responses—he described as "a trap that can lead to bad decisions." When Obama surveyed options for escalating the use of force in the Middle East in the context of broader US interests, he saw one giant trap.[72]

This followed a certain tragic logic. Obama was deeply skeptical that US military actions against Assad could stay limited. As he wrote before his election as president, he saw how a US military incursion in the region could spiral: a use of force "which in turn spurs on insurgencies based on religious and nationalist pride, which in turn necessitates a lengthy and difficult U.S. occupation, which in turn leads to an escalating death toll on the part of U.S. troops and the local civilian population. All of this fans anti-American sentiment among Muslims, increases the pool of potential terrorist recruits, and prompts the American public to question not only the war but also those policies that project us onto the Islamic world in the first place."[73]

Obama could not find a way to transcend this reasoning. No matter how compelling a single action may seem at the time—like a targeted air strike, special operations raid, arming an opposition group, or cyberattack— Obama focused on the fact that it might lead to something worse and bind the United States to the outcome. "Then what?" he'd always ask. Like Eisenhower in Vietnam and Bush with postwar Iraq, Obama's approach to Libya and Syria wasn't all or nothing. They each sought to make a difference without falling into a larger trap. In this sense, Obama didn't want to undo the Eisenhower Doctrine in the Middle East, he wanted to return to its original "constructive" intent.[74]

These presidents also had to avoid traps set by expectations of their own making. Obama often warned of creating a "reliance interest," which is a legal term describing how one party can be damaged if it acts in anticipation that another party will also act as promised (as a former law professor, Obama often fell back on legal concepts when thinking through problems). In other words, he understood the danger in overpromising, yet underdelivering—the United States had to keep expectations of what it might do in check. While Obama proved willing to gamble, he did not bluff; he worried about what would happen if it got called.

As Libya and Syria proved, just because Obama successfully avoided some traps did not mean he could dodge all of them. There were no clear paths. Too much caution risked humanitarian disaster; too much forcefulness risked an all-encompassing intervention. In both cases, Obama's decision to call for the departure of strongman leaders seemed to be morally right, but it arguably created a reliance interest in that regime opponents, and much of the world, thought the United States would do whatever it takes to make it happen, incentivizing people to rise up with the expectation the cavalry would eventually come. In the end, as Ben Rhodes observes about the "moral morass" of Syria, America's "inaction was a tragedy, and our intervention would only compound the tragedy."[75]

* * *

Reflecting on how Eisenhower, Bush, and Obama managed these six crises, one sees how hard it can be to stick to a strategy, juggle competing goals, and manage expectations. These crises illuminate the challenges a president faces when wrestling with both the potential and limits of American power; they also show the perils of marrying maximalist ends with minimalist means. In each instance, these presidents struggled to craft the right formula to make a difference without making the same mistakes of the past or jeopardizing what they considered larger US interests. In their efforts to wrest some control over events, they remained keenly focused on not compounding their problems.[76]

To do so, they had to weigh questions of intervention and nonintervention, figure out how to get the most out of allies and international institutions, and ponder what would come next. They had to measure the bounds of their domestic support and make trade-offs among their priorities. In key instances, these presidents had to swallow the implications of their own rhetoric—such as Eisenhower's warnings of falling dominoes or pledging to free captive nations, Bush saying Saddam must go, and Obama calling for regime change in Libya and Syria. No matter how hard they tried to clarify the limited meaning of such declarations, the fine print was lost.

These moments were instrumental in shaping perceptions of their leadership. They also became key factors in the political debate over foreign policy, especially questions of whether the United States should be doing "more" and what actions constituted being "strong" or "weak." At the time, many observers considered their responses underwhelming and feckless; consequentially, they were seen less as chess masters dictating outcomes than as pawns having to submit to them. In several key cases, however—notably, whether to intervene in Vietnam and Iraq, and how to handle the collapse of the Soviet Union—history rendered a more sympathetic judgment. One day, the same may be said about limiting US involvement in Syria. What contemporaries often perceive as weakness is later remembered as wisdom.

Politics

One evening in early February 1951, America's most celebrated man in uniform invited the presumptive Republican nominee for president to the Pentagon for a secret meeting to make an unusual offer.

Sitting down with Robert A. Taft, Dwight D. Eisenhower proposed a political truce: if the Ohio Senator would back the bipartisan concept of collective security and support a strong NATO, then the General would publicly vow not to run for president in 1952. Demonstrating the seriousness of this proposition, Eisenhower kept a draft announcement in his pocket.

Taft refused, instead choosing to carry on his fight against Ike's brand of American leadership. After their meeting concluded, Ike called his assistants into his office and tore up the draft statement in front of them. Given Taft's intransigence, Eisenhower explained it "would be silly for me to throw away whatever political influence I might possess."[1]

At the time, no one knew if Eisenhower might run as a Republican or Democrat—in 1948, he had rebuffed overtures from both parties to lead their ticket. But Taft, then known as "Mr. Republican" and one of the most respected politicians in Washington, already campaigned for the White House twice before. He was the voice of American unilateralism— or what Ike called isolationism—by opposing the Marshall Plan, voting against the establishment of NATO, and speaking out against a robust American role in Europe (he did, however, advocate for more aggressive actions against China). Taft did not stand alone. Herbert Hoover, who was then the only living former president and still a figure of considerable authority, also championed these causes, appearing on national television and testifying before Congress to argue forcefully against US military aid, troop commitments abroad, and NATO. Dusting off the pre-war idea of "Fortress America," these Republican elders appealed to many weary Americans who justifiably asked: why us, and why now?

In this debate, Eisenhower was an unusual yet influential figure. Although he retired from the army, President Truman asked him to leave his post as president of Columbia University and take charge as NATO's first military commander (Taft opposed this too). Created in April 1949, the nascent alliance was still taking shape, and it fell to Ike to create a command structure, prod European nations to rebuild their militaries, and galvanize public support for deploying American troops to keep peace on the continent. With his unique credibility and stature, it also became Eisenhower's task to push back against the formidable wave of Republican opposition and advocate for what he described as the "enlightened self-interest" of American leadership in the alliance.

His journey began in January 1951 with a three-week tour to Europe to meet with key leaders and assess the situation. Then he traveled to Washington to make his case in dramatic fashion. On February 1, he appeared before both houses of Congress for the first time since the end of World War II, while the press recorded his words to be printed verbatim in the next day's newspapers.

Standing before a full auditorium in the Library of Congress, Eisenhower made an impassioned plea for US leadership and sending a robust military presence to Europe. He implored Congress to remember the "strength of America" and what it could achieve "when we bind that up heart and soul in material ways with our friends overseas." Eisenhower was not blind to the war-wariness among large swaths of the American public or the skepticism about overseas commitments. He therefore made clear this was not America's problem alone. The Europeans needed to step up as well, he said, so the United States was not "merely an Atlas to carry the load on its shoulder."

Eisenhower labored over the speech for days—"few speeches have given me so much trouble," he recalled—and his stirring words conveyed a sense of confidence and conviction about American leadership. He later summarized his message in a half-hour televised address to the nation. With this, he effectively neutralized the rising opposition to NATO. James Reston wrote in the *New York Times* that Eisenhower's performance "transcend[ed] that of the Secretary of State or president," in which his "combination of knowledge, experience and achievement" made it hard for "even the most cynical congressman [to] dismiss him with a wisecrack." In an editorial praising Eisenhower's message, the *Times* observed "faith in America is the principal inspiration prompting other nations to do their best to match our own exertions."[2]

This episode came at a pivotal moment in the political debate about America's global role. Six years after the end of the Second World War, Eisenhower argued the country had arrived at a "decade of decision," asking "what nation is more capable, more ready, of providing this leadership than the United States?" In retrospect, Ike was certainly right: if he had faltered and Taft prevailed, it is hard to see how NATO—which was then a new, fragile foundation of America's postwar defense—would have sustained enough political support to survive.

Eisenhower understood the seductive pull of isolationist views promoted by GOP leaders like Taft and Hoover. "God knows I'd personally like to get out of Europe and I'd like to see [the] U.S. able to sit at home and ignore the rest of the world!" Ike lamented in his diary in March 1951. "What a pleasing prospect—until you look at the ultimate consequences—destruction." Within a year of the speech, and with so much at stake, he declared himself a Republican and announced his campaign for president. "I'm running because Taft is an isolationist," Eisenhower said. "His election would be a disaster."[3]

FORTY YEARS LATER, the Eisenhower-Taft battle lines resurfaced when political operative–turned-conservative pundit Pat Buchanan rose to challenge the incumbent president, George H. W. Bush, during his 1992 campaign for reelection.

With the Soviet Union gone, Buchanan transformed from staunch Cold Warrior to fiery champion of isolationism. Raised in Washington, DC, he spent a career as a political staffer before climbing to prominence as a pioneer of talk radio and the kinds of cable news shout-fests that dominate twenty-first century politics. The paid provocateur was a long-standing thorn in Bush's side—his bombastic style never fit with the buttoned-up Bush team. For Buchanan, politics was less about appealing to better angels than it was about exploiting grievance and insecurity. So as the 1992 campaign began, he could not resist the temptation to aim his ire toward the man he derided, with a devious wink, as "King George." Buchanan's argument was simple: with the Soviet Union consigned to the ash heap of failed empires, it was time for America to come home.[4]

For decades anticommunism united conservative elites and the GOP's grassroots; but absent the Soviet menace, these old rivalries burst into the open. Buchanan drew a connection to another time when moderate internationalists—like Bush—scoffed at those who argued that America needed to trim its commitments abroad. He explicitly harkened back to the foreign policy of his proclaimed boyhood heroes, Robert Taft and Joe McCarthy. Like Taft, Buchanan believed that the United States could sit at home and ignore the rest of the world; and like McCarthy, he understood the power of anger, conspiracy, and fear.

Buchanan heaped scorn on Bush's idea of a "gauzy" new world order, dismissing the president as an "Ivy League globalist" and proudly identifying himself as a working-class nationalist. For him, the postwar economic success of a democratic Germany and Japan weren't proud American achievements, they were threats. Pledging to "take the country back" and "make America great again," Buchanan called for "a new nationalism, a new patriotism, a new foreign policy that puts America first, and, not only first, but second and third as well."[5]

This revamped America-first agenda was a hodgepodge of nativist and isolationist causes—things like building a two-hundred-mile "Buchanan Fence" on the US-Mexico border, restricting immigration to "Englishmen," and ridiculing democracy promotion as "messianic globaloney." Tribe, race, and sovereignty were at the core of his nationalist conservatism. Barely concealing his prejudice, Buchanan criticized Bush's policy during the Gulf War as being promoted by Israel's "amen corner."[6]

Bush watched Buchanan's rise warily. As early as the summer of 1990, White House staffers shared with him news clippings from right-wing publications reporting rumors of the pundit's interest in the presidential race. Bush always kept a close eye on his right flank, and Buchanan was the latest of the right-wing agitators he faced over his political career. Yet the president never really took this threat very seriously, dismissing Buchanan as another one of the "wackos" more interested in rabble-rousing than becoming a worthy presidential contender.[7]

Therefore, it was a big surprise when, in late 1991, Buchanan's vanity campaign started to gain traction and his poll numbers rocketed upward in critical primary states like New Hampshire, where he drew the support of one out of every three Republicans. Bush tracked Buchanan's efforts to enlist conservatives to attack him and woo away supporters with personal appeals and exaggerated claims (such as that Bush was "wedded" to the UN and only desired to fly "all over the world shoveling out foreign aid"). Eventually Bush grew tired of the "mean and ugly" attacks and decided to hit back by cutting a television ad criticizing Buchanan's opposition to the Gulf War.[8]

Ultimately, Buchanan never got close to seizing the nomination. Unlike Eisenhower and Taft in 1952, Bush did not have to fight him all the way to the convention floor. The pundit's strong primary showing nevertheless wounded Bush, and Buchanan carried on as a conservative icon (having been endorsed by a then rising star of right-wing talk radio, Rush Limbaugh). Buchanan's sudden rise sent shockwaves throughout the 1992 race, and when combined with the success of the populist-nationalist third-party candidate Ross Perot, his story foreshadowed post–Cold War conservatism's crack-up over US global engagement that erupted twenty-five years later.

BY 2015, THE POLITICS OF FOREIGN POLICY morphed into a Buchanan fever dream, full of outrage, anxiety, and bombast. Hope seemed in short supply. Conspiracy and anger seemed in abundance. Americans—deeply shaken by the rise of the ISIL in the Middle East and a wave of major terrorist attacks in Paris and San Bernardino—wondered if the Obama administration had the right strategy to keep people safe.

For the gaggle of Republicans running for president, it was another chance to brand a Democrat in the White House as weak and promise something tougher. The surprising GOP presidential front-runner at the time, Donald Trump, said the United States should not only kill terrorists, but also target their families. He warned of Muslim hordes crossing borders, recalling recent images of millions of migrants from the Middle East flowing into Europe. More than anyone, Trump tapped into the anger and exhaustion of the moment, articulating a foreign policy that was equal parts isolationist and militaristic. Some saw him as a curiosity—a flashier, richer, spray-tanned Buchanan—who did not reflect the heart of the party.[9]

Obama did not see Trump as an aberration, but as a culmination of many years of a Republican strategy of fearmongering and sowing division. While optimistic calls for unity and aspirations of hope propelled his own political rise, Obama found himself at the center of the breakdown of American politics. For years, millions of Americans were fed a steady diet of false allegations about Obama's un-Americanness—from Rush Limbaugh's ridicule of "Osama Obama" to the racist "birther" fabrication. At the time, these seemed easy to dismiss as trivial assaults from the fringe—just like accusations leveled at Eisenhower and Bush for being closeted communists and wooly-headed globalists. Obama saw something more consequential—and ominous—at work. Donald Trump saw opportunity.

Obama worried about the conditions that gave rise to this moment. He warned of the decline of civility and the splintering of the political debate, seeing how both were fueled by a high-speed, ravenous media. "The spin, the amplification of conflict, the indiscriminate search for scandal and miscues," Obama wrote prior to his first run for the White House, "the cumulative impact of all this is to erode any agreed-upon standards for judging the truth." He spent his years in office trying to work against this by practicing a politics he often described as "on the level"—that is, a vigorous give-and-take based on a common set of facts and fundamental honesty. Later, he resigned himself to the fact that for most conservatives, no crackpot idea or act of political opportunism seemed out of bounds.[10]

Buchanan once observed that the "exaggerated metaphor is really the staple of American political language." When attacking Obama, this discourse devolved from hyperbole to outright lies. Critics assaulted the president's domestic achievements this way, such as by claiming healthcare reform would institute "death panels" to kill the elderly. But such falsehoods were used to slam his foreign policy as well, whether by denying the basic science behind global threats like climate change, accusing him of secretly forging an alliance with Iran, or paying off the Ayatollah with piles of cash.[11]

With the coincidence of the spike in terrorist threats occurring just as the 2016 campaign heated up, the sense of paranoia reached a new level. Obama saw a symbiotic relationship between the ISIL propaganda of beheadings and attacks, 24-hour cable news coverage, and Republican political discourse. All three fed on the other, whipping everyone into hysteria.

Despite his frustrations with this doom loop, especially his perception of the media's role in perpetuating it, Obama realized he sometimes could seem out of step with the public's concerns about ISIL. He would recite for his aides statistics showing that people had a far greater chance getting injured by slipping in the bathtub than getting hurt in a terrorist attack.

But he was self-aware enough to know he needed to be more intentional about speaking to people's anxieties without worsening them. In December 2015, Obama talked about terrorism every day, making symbolic visits to the Pentagon and the National Counterterrorism Center for briefings, and speaking to the American people in a prime-time address from the Oval Office. It was nevertheless impossible to break through the media's noise, amplified by the Fox News bullhorn, which depicted the world as a raging inferno that demanded more bombs and tough talk.

Considering this political landscape, Obama was not the least surprised to find that a year before the election to choose his successor, the GOP's leading presidential aspirant was someone who proved to be a master at gaudy entertainment—a person who would say and do anything to divide people and exploit fear for political advantage. It seemed fitting, if not a bit sad, that this modern-day demagogue ended up humiliating the presumptive GOP front-runner in the process—George H. W. Bush's second son, Jeb, the one many considered most like his father.[12]

ONE OF THE GREAT MYTHS OF AMERICAN FOREIGN POLICY is that politics stops at the water's edge. It is a story we tell to reassure ourselves that there can be some kind of pure US interest that can be conceived and pursued without consideration of partisanship or other priorities. Yet in American democracy, foreign policy and domestic politics are inextricably linked. National security decisions are not handed down from the Almighty— they are the result of a political process. In turn, decisions about how the United States should act abroad, and what it is should stand and fight for, fundamentally shapes politics.[13]

Although they traveled very different routes to reach the same destination, Eisenhower, Bush, and Obama shared an approach to the politics of foreign policy. They were all first-class politicians who innovated how the game was played. They summoned the cunning and ruthlessness requisite to reach the nation's highest office. And they shared a similar philosophy for how to govern.

Because their Middle Way brand of foreign policy often defied the prevailing political trends, it elicited many of the same criticisms. Moreover, they all faced a type of antagonist that shared a common ancestry—from Taft and McCarthy, to Buchanan and Perot, to Trump.

Seen this way, these three presidents are the principal actors on one side of a long-running political debate about America's global role. By briefly retracing their respective political journeys on foreign policy, as well as by revisiting a few of the critical episodes and fights they waged, we can take measure of how they succeeded—and failed—to shape the politics of their moment. This is essential to understanding their foreign policy choices, assessing their successes and failures, and evaluating their legacies.

I. EISENHOWER: THE POLITICS OF FEAR

Eisenhower was always something of a political enigma. Although he long resisted entering the partisan arena, Ike displayed considerable political skills—a person could not climb the ladder of the peacetime army and successfully work for such leaders as Douglas MacArthur and George Marshall, or deal with the likes of FDR and Churchill during World War II, without a sophisticated understanding of politics. His wartime image made him the most popular man in America and perhaps the most famous in the world. Moreover, Ike proved a master of the new era of politics—as the first president of the television age, he became the first modern celebrity politician. Yet Ike was a reluctant political warrior; he never cared much for partisan battles, nor did he have an affinity for ideology.[14]

For several years, Ike resisted shedding his uniform to enter the arena. Among the reasons, he explained to friends, was the difficulty in bridging the gap between "clear judgments based solely on moral grounds" and the "practical solutions" required for progress. While Ike became loyal to the GOP brand, he aspired for foreign policy to rise above petty partisanship. By doing so, he hoped to establish a new consensus in which both the political left and right had a similar stake in upholding the postwar order.[15]

As the first Republican president elected since Hoover in 1928, Eisenhower's victory in 1952 set the terms for the politics of foreign policy during the Cold War. He showed how the GOP simultaneously could champion strong internationalism and paint the Democrats as weak. He vanquished Robert Taft in a bitterly fought nomination process, and then he won the general election in a landslide. Translating this into governing, Ike pursued a straightforward goal: to navigate strategy between the extremes of isolationism and cynical hysteria (as personified by Taft and McCarthy) and incompetence (as Ike perceived Truman and Adlai Stevenson) to put US foreign policy on sustainable footing.

This task proved tough. After two decades out of power, Republicans grew unaccustomed to the sober realities of responsibility. Many found it easier to wallow in negativism than to promote a positive, forward-looking agenda. The pull of isolationism remained strong. After the trauma of losing five elections in a row, a lot of Republicans almost seemed nostalgic for the pre–World War II years of the 1920s and 30s. Although Taft died of cancer in July 1953, his ideas lived on, and Ike felt constantly harassed by what he called the certain "reactionary fringe" of the party "that hates and despises everything for which I stand."[16]

Democrats, meanwhile, were deeply shaken by the way politics turned on them. After triumphantly leading the country through World War II and the early years of the Cold War, they suddenly found themselves tainted, with some of their most revered figures, like former Secretary of State Dean Acheson, even accused of being communist sympathizers. As a result, while most Democrats backed Ike's policies (like support for NATO, expansion of alliances in Asia, and more spending on foreign assistance), they had every political incentive to outflank him to reclaim the mantle of "strength."

BUT THE POLITICS OF THE EISENHOWER ERA possessed a more pernicious element: the manipulation of fear. Ike governed at a time when genuine anxieties pulsed through the country—when Americans worried about nuclear holocaust, falling behind the Soviets, losing China to Mao, and of communist enemies plotting from within. Eisenhower's instinct, however, was to counsel patience and offer reassurance; he believed calming people's nerves to be one of his essential tasks.[17]

Beyond allaying public apprehensions, Ike came under tremendous pressure to attack the most toxic fear-peddler of the era—Joe McCarthy. The senator from Wisconsin did not invent red-baiting, but he mastered its dark arts. Observers at the time described him as a political speculator who found his gusher. Through personalized witch-hunts, McCarthy tapped into the idea that if things weren't going America's way in the world, it wasn't because events were beyond Washington's power. It was because of treason and conspiracy; failures required scapegoats. The fact McCarthy tried was not so shocking. It was that he proved so successful.[18]

McCarthy's demagoguery and ability to drive the media cycle repulsed Eisenhower, who dismissed him as a "pimple on the path of progress." Yet Ike was not insulated from the fears McCarthy stoked. He caved-in to him when politically expedient—most shamefully when he refused to defend his friend and mentor George Marshall from the Senator's attacks on the 1952 campaign trail (a fact that Eisenhower would go on to elide). Once in office, Ike and his team worried about McCarthy's impact both on domestic life and the country's international stature. They fretted over the damage done to the country's image, assessing that foreign leaders believed they were witnessing the rise of "an American fascism" and wondered if "this country is either unsure of itself or has no genuine attachment to some of the fundamental values of a democratic society."[19]

Nevertheless, few Republican politicians were ready to confront McCarthy directly (one exception being Senator Prescott Bush, who condemned his colleague's methods and later pushed to censure him). Instead of launching a frontal assault against McCarthy, Ike waged a Washington-style guerrilla campaign of legal maneuver and carefully timed press leaks to undermine him. As for his public stance, Eisenhower believed that one of the most important lessons from his wartime experiences was to avoid indulging in "hateful or hypercritical remarks." He therefore refused even to utter the senator's name, convinced a direct attack would only elevate McCarthy by giving him more of the attention he so desperately craved.[20]

McCarthy was a symptom, rather than the cause of America's malady. While Eisenhower could not, or would not, take on the abusive senator directly, he could still speak to the public's fears, offering what he described as "chins-up" reassurance. This is exactly what he set out to do when addressing the nation on the evening of April 5, 1954. While less acclaimed than his 1961 farewell address, it is in many ways just as important.[21]

The speech came less than a month after the television broadcaster Edward R. Murrow's famous takedown of McCarthy at the end of the *See It Now* broadcast (a moment dramatized in the 2005 George Clooney movie *Good Night and Good Luck*). Eisenhower explained to his press secretary that he needed to "take [the] Red play away from McCarthy and put it back on [a] decent level." To do this, the president tried something new: speaking informally, without a prepared text, live on national television from a specially designed White House studio. In the mid-1950s, this format amounted to Ike's version of Twitter.[22]

Eisenhower did not aspire to stretch toward rhetorical greatness. He wanted to speak "off-the-cuff" with a "simple talk." As usual, he prepared carefully, spending the weekend at Camp David revising six pages of typed notes he used as an outline. The result was a thirty-seven-hundred-word analysis of the challenges at home and abroad and his assessment of America's strengths to deal with them—a speech he described to an old friend that day as "an undertaking of considerable magnitude."[23]

That was clear from Eisenhower's opening words, when he looked straight in the camera and asked the audience to survey the country's "strengths, its problems, its apprehensions, and its future." Ike said he understood why people were worried, as "we see threats coming from all angles, internal and external, and we wonder what's going to happen to us individually and as a nation." In less than four decades, he noted, the US arsenal went from "mere musket and little cannon" to a hydrogen bomb capable of killing tens of thousands in an instant, reflecting "how much more we have developed scientifically than we are capable of handling emotionally and intellectually."

Eisenhower walked viewers through a litany of fears, which he carefully listed in his notes: from the Kremlin's aggressive intentions to the dangers of nuclear war, from the threat of communist infiltration into American schools and unions to the misuse of "intemperate investigative methods" to malign innocent people (which was the closest he came to calling out McCarthy), to the return of economic depression. Acknowledging these threats, Ike urged that "we look at them clearly, face to face, without fear, like honest, straightforward Americans, so we do not develop the jitters or any other kind of panic, that we do not fall prey to hysterical thinking."

Then Eisenhower soothed these concerns one-by-one, asking his fellow Americans to "think about the counterbalancing factors to set over against the threat itself." He stressed the strengths of alliances, the Kremlin's awareness that initiating war would be suicidal, and the exaggerated fear of the internal danger of communism. Notably, he also explained that the "great bulwark" against communist influence was the FBI, which was doing a "magnificent job."

Most of all, Eisenhower reprised his core theme of rejuvenating the country's "spiritual strength," which he said was "just as great in its requirements as it has ever been in our whole history." This meant a steadfast commitment to the values reflected in the Bill of Rights. It meant a clear-eyed recognition that none of these concerns "has an easy answer, and many . . . have no answers at all." And it meant, Eisenhower urged, that these problems must be approached with the same pragmatic, can-do spirit of the average American family gathered around the dinner table discussing their plans, "saying this is what we can do, [and] this is what we will do."

"This is what we can do, and this is what we will do." Eisenhower tries to calm the nation's fears in his televised address on April 5, 1954.

(Courtesy of Dwight D. Eisenhower Library)

Normally wooden and halting when reading a speech, many commentators admired Ike's reassuring, conversational style—which was aided by tutorials from Oscar-nominated actor Robert Montgomery, who joined the White House staff to help the president prepare for such performances. Leaning against his desk, relaxed, arms crossed, as if he were delivering a televised fireside chat, Eisenhower attained what the *New York Times* TV critic raved was "television's most desired quality—naturalness."[24]

The "fear" speech served its purpose. Beyond good television, Ike hoped his message would bolster support for what he described as his "one objective": to "give America a chance, once more, to live under moderate government and to begin the restoration of respect for the qualities that have made this country what it is." Slowly, he succeeded. Ike's subtle tactics allowed McCarthy to self-destruct, although not without significant cost: the senator's witch-hunts destroyed many reputations and ruined careers. They also hurt Eisenhower's standing and undermined his efforts to rally countries alongside the US. For example, Ike's aides concluded that some of the impact of his generally acclaimed April 1953 "chance for peace" speech was lost by the "almost simultaneous reaction of mingled ridicule and dismay provoked by [McCarthy]" among allies abroad.[25]

Moreover, Eisenhower could not fully extinguish the fires McCarthy fueled. The Wisconsin senator's nativist, pessimistic, cruel, fear-based legacy distorted the political debate about national security for decades—whether it was Democrats, who feared labels of weakness, or Republicans, who were susceptible to what historian Richard Hofstadter called the paranoid style. "McCarthy's carnival-like four-year spree of accusations, charges, and threats touched something deep in the American body politic," David Halberstam observed, "something that lasted long after his own recklessness, carelessness, and boozing ended his career in shame." Eisenhower labored for the rest of his presidency against a torrent of criticisms that the United States was falling behind in the arms race, losing geopolitical ground to Moscow, or facing threats from within. He may have dismissed McCarthyism as "McCarthy-wasm," but fear remained a potent force. The basic McCarthy vision—that America's ills were the result of a vast conspiracy of government and media elites in harness with foreign enemies—became hard-wired into political discourse.[26]

EISENHOWER WON TWO ELECTIONS with ease and remained widely popular—according to Gallup polls, he was the most admired person in America for the decade after 1951, with an average approval rating of 65 percent. But he never stopped having to battle against isolationism and fear. Republican Party stalwarts assailed his calls for collective security and dismissed his support for foreign assistance as "do-gooderism." The question for Republicans, Ike stated privately, was whether they would be seduced by McCarthy and the "ludicrous partnership" between red-baiters and "old guarders" like Taft, or stand behind his "middle-of-the-road" philosophy.[27]

Ike thought the party needed to reinvent itself for the post–New Deal, Cold War era—transforming into what he eventually called "Modern Republicanism." Primarily concerned with domestic affairs, this idea also embodied the core elements of Eisenhower's foreign policy: a rejection of isolationism; bipartisanship; collective security; alliances; open trade; and using all the tools of American power, not just military. As Ike put it, all this required "unity in spiritual values."[28]

While these were recurring themes in Eisenhower's speeches and correspondence for years, he believed they were best distilled in a 1956 best-selling book by one of his aides, Arthur Larson, entitled *A Republican Looks at His Party*. Eisenhower read the book while recovering from abdominal surgery and publicly endorsed it. Subsequently, Ike asked Larson to come by to discuss his ideas and then later enlisted him to become a White House speechwriter.

The "awesome responsibility" of America's global role, Larson wrote, should have a "sobering effect on all political discussion . . . we cannot be wrong or out of date . . . or our institutions and freedoms may be lost forever." Larson therefore described the imperative to pursue policies aimed toward an "authentic American center." Most Americans, Larson observed, were looking for a way forward after several decades of national emergency defined by economic depression, one hot global war and an intensifying cold one. They did not want to line up on one side or another. Therefore, Larson argued, "the man who holds the center holds a position of almost unbeatable strength." He characterizeded politics as a pragmatic art, emphasizing the importance of common sense, empathy, and balance.[29]

Eisenhower believed his own political rise reflected this approach, declaring after his 1956 reelection that Modern Republicanism had proven its worth. Despite his electoral success and enduring popularity, however, he had a hard time getting fellow Republican leaders to emulate him. Conservative intellectuals heaped scorn on the idea, conceding it may have brought economic prosperity, but left America unprepared to fight the Soviets.

National Review founder William F. Buckley led the attack on Eisenhower, claiming that Ike's brand of middle-of-the-road politics was "politically, intellectually, and morally repugnant." Citing the examples of Hungary and Suez, Buckley asserted that Eisenhower possessed a "deficient understanding" of the communist threat. For Buckley and other influential critics, Ike's careful pragmatism was nothing more than "an approach designed not to solve problems, but to refuse, essentially, that problems exist; and so, to ignore them." In significant ways, the modern conservative movement began as a reaction to Eisenhower's policies and politics.[30]

Eisenhower not only lost support in the pages of stuffy, small circulation opinion magazines. GOP congressional leaders also kept their distance from Modern Republicanism. They resisted Ike's efforts to increase foreign aid and remained skeptical of his plans to negotiate with the Soviets. His popularity could not convert into a lasting electoral coalition, as the GOP lost congressional seats in the electoral contests of 1954, 1956, and 1958. Ike conceded that among his greatest failures was not getting his fellow Republicans to think "constructively and dynamically" about the key problems of the moment and agree on a "common basic philosophy." Or, as Larson later reflected, Eisenhower's ambitions were thwarted by "a reluctant party that seemed subconsciously to prefer the more congenial role of heckling from the safety of the wings."[31]

ULTIMATELY, THE POLITICS OF FEAR consumed Ike's presidency, most acutely when the Soviets launched a 184-pound aluminum satellite into space. Once Sputnik left the earth's atmosphere in October 1957, Eisenhower lost control of the narrative. It is hard to overstate the national anxiety Sputnik unleashed—people could see it traveling across the night sky, and television networks interrupted their programming to broadcast the distinctive beeps the satellite transmitted. Americans worried the enemy might own the heavens, with the potential for raining nuclear-tipped missiles in a matter of minutes. Seen as a technological Pearl Harbor, Sputnik made it much harder to believe the country could afford a patient, steady, balanced approach to the Cold War struggle. Influential newspaper columnists like Joseph Alsop—nourished by a steady stream of leaks from the intelligence community and Pentagon—seized on Ike's "flaccid" leadership and claimed that the United States faced a "missile gap" with the Soviets.[32]

Ike dismissed these claims as "nothing more than imaginative creations of irresponsibility." Publicly, he responded with his customary calm, delivering earnest speeches to reassure the public and contextualize Moscow's accomplishment (because, as he knew from highly sensitive intelligence, it did not fundamentally alter the strategic balance). He also launched a series of policy initiatives, rushing America's own satellite into orbit, reforming the Pentagon, boosting the defense budget, and creating institutions like NASA.[33]

While Eisenhower sympathized with the public's concern, he was troubled about its impact on the country's larger strategic goals. He warned his advisers not to succumb to a "Sputnik complex" which insatiably demanded the United States "do everything yesterday." Their task, he reminded them in the last days of his presidency, was to "think about the country as a whole, the economy, and the other demands on the budget"— themes he would return to in his farewell address.[34]

For Democrats eager to seize the mantle of strength, they now had their opportunity, and it was time for some payback. Flipping the script on Eisenhower, they asserted that his obsession with budget discipline and limits on military spending left the nation's defenses dangerously under-resourced. After Sputnik, Democratic Senator Henry "Scoop" Jackson of Washington called for a "National Week of Shame and Danger," and Ike's approval rating plunged by over twenty points. Lyndon Johnson declared the Soviets could now bomb the US like "kids dropping rocks onto cars over freeway overpasses." Dean Acheson decried Eisenhower as complacent and miserly, claiming the president had misled the country about the extent of the Soviet threat. Seeking revenge for their trouncing in 1952, Democrats merged all their grievances against Eisenhower into a single theme the American people could understand. Once Ike's unique strength, national security now became his core vulnerability.[35]

As the sun set on Eisenhower's tenure, he worried about America's future, believing something was chronically wrong with the country's sense of self. "We have too much thought of bombs and machines and gadgets as the arsenal of national and cultural strength," he wrote to an aide in late 1958. Pessimism ran too deep, he thought, concluding that the "great problem is to get people—our own people and our friends—to think objectively and with a sense of inspiration and uplift."

Five years after he tried to appeal to the higher power of America's spiritual strength in his "chance for peace" speech, Ike privately acknowledged "we don't seem to have accomplished much." He struggled to find the right words to translate his lofty aspirations into practical policy, saying he wanted the country to be "generous without surrendering." Ike would spend his final months in office trying to make his case as a "tribune of the people," and while he remained proud of his achievements, he was frustrated by this unfinished business.[36]

THE POLITICAL LEGACY of Eisenhower's foreign policy is mixed. Impelled to enter the political arena to forestall the slide toward Fortress America, he defeated Taft, secured an internationalist posture, and mobilized enough domestic support to put the country on a sustainable path to wage the Cold War. Nevertheless, the public's mood about the future remained pessimistic. By the end of Eisenhower's presidency, the United States seemed to be declining, and influential commentators (such as a young Henry

Kissinger, then making his name) claimed its global position was deteriorating to the point of irrelevance.[37]

Since Eisenhower never fully tamed the power of fear, he failed to build a new kind of politics. For eight years, Ike was whipsawed from three directions—two wings of the Republican Party, and the Democrats. One side of the GOP constituted the "ludicrous partnership" between the old-guard isolationists and McCarthyite demagogues. The other wing, a growing movement of new conservatives, embraced a more militant, aggressive anticommunism and rejected Ike's moderation. And from the other side of the aisle, Ike faced Democrats who were deeply stung by charges of weakness for "losing" China and betraying Eastern Europe at Yalta. They were now determined to act "tough" and pursue a foreign policy that would, as Ike's successor would say, project vigor.

While Eisenhower's efforts to forge a lasting, centrist Modern Republicanism never realized the potential he once hoped for, it did propel his personal electoral success. And importantly, it set an example for future generations of politicians, especially George H. W. Bush.

II. BUSH: THE POLITICS OF "MORE" VS. THE POLITICS OF "LESS"

Bush contended with the right wing of his party from the outset of his political career. His first brush came in 1952, when he raised money and organized for Eisenhower against Robert Taft in Texas. A few years later, as the rookie Harris County GOP chair in Houston, Bush tussled with angry adherents of the John Birch Society, a grassroots faction of conservatives who trafficked in conspiracy. Believing that communists infiltrated every aspect of American life, their founder even made wild accusations about Eisenhower's role in Marxist-led plots, claiming to have evidence of Ike "consciously serving the communist conspiracy for all his adult life."[38]

By the early 1960s, the Birchers had grown into a potent political force on the right, with tens of thousands members nationwide. Home to the

organization's second-largest chapter in the country, Harris County's
Birchers hounded Bush, mocking his East Coast elitism and claiming his
father was part of a vast "one world" scheme to turn America into a so-
cialist police state. While Bush thought these folks were crazy, they could
not be ignored by an aspiring GOP politician in early 1960s Texas. Instead
of first purging them, Bush attempted to use his charm to garner their
support. Failing, he soon regretted even trying—condemning the "mean,
negative, super-patriotic" Birchers as a "nut fringe" that bequeathed to
Republicans the "unfortunate image of irresponsibility."³⁹

These early experiences were critically important in shaping Bush's aver-
sion to right-wing politics and establishing his commitment to moderation. After Barry Goldwater's landslide defeat in 1964, Bush believed the
Republican Party's conservatism needed to be "sensitive and dynamic, not
scared and reactionary." He lamented the influence of those right-wing
"militants" and "primitives" who wanted to "bomb the UN" and "scared
the hell out of the plain average non-issue conscious man on the street."

Asked to write a 1964 election postmortem for a special issue of the
National Review (which included a contribution by another rising GOP
star, Ronald Reagan), Bush argued for a conservative outlook based on
"moral fiber, prudence, love of country, the enlightened self-interest of the
United States, strength in foreign policy and freedom of the individual."
Bush's conservatism, like Eisenhower's, reflected a disposition more than
an ideology. To him, leadership ought to be "practical and positive,"
seeking to realize an America that was kinder and gentler.⁴⁰

While Bush remained true to this approach—as the famed presidential campaign chronicler Theodore H. White once reported, Bush was re-
liably "somewhat to the center of center"—he faced a constant barrage
of criticism from conservatives who never quite believed he was one of
them. These voices grew louder as he ascended the political ladder and
the GOP moved further right, dismissing Bush as a "lapdog." Before his
presidency, Bush rebutted such charges by pointing to his voting record
in Congress and invoking his loyal service as vice president to the patron saint of modern conservatism, Ronald Reagan. Although he often
decried the "ugliness" of politics, he embraced bare-knuckled tactics and

used hired guns like Lee Atwater and Roger Ailes (who stepped aside from a formal role in Bush's inner circle to pursue a new media/entertainment venture that eventually became Fox News). Yet Bush never credibly fit the mold of conservative firebrand. Nor did he really want to.[41]

Once in the White House, this disposition served Bush well as he managed crises and steered the Cold War to an end. He seemed ideally suited to the national mood at the time, which yearned for reassurance and sought a steady hand amid the tumult. According to one scholarly analysis of public attitudes, Americans' political outlook in the early 1990s resembled those during the Eisenhower years. But when public preferences shifted—becoming more impatient, uncertain, and worried about the future—Bush found himself ill-suited for the turbulent politics that were unleashed. In the final weeks of his ill-fated 1992 reelection campaign, Bush tried to outline an agenda for "American renewal," but to no avail. The forces arrayed against him were too strong.[42]

Ironically, Bush's own leadership style enabled those very forces that ended up making him a one-term president. His moderation itself became a catalyst for change, as both the political right and left demanded something different.

From the right, Bush's pursuit of prudent internationalism came under attack from neoconservative voices who never trusted him in the first place and believed he was too timid when events demanded action. Meanwhile, others within the GOP argued that the president cared too much about the world and adhered to a dangerous globalism.

From the left, Democrats lambasted Bush for not doing enough to stand up for democracy and human rights around the world, an accusation of weakness he found particularly galling. They also assailed him for being too much of a "foreign policy president," preferring geopolitics to domestic affairs—a charge he privately conceded was "absolutely true." Democrats, though, understood a larger truth. If not for Bush's able stewardship bringing the Cold War to a peaceful conclusion—and if, as a consequence, the world had been not transformed, but left in turmoil—it is unlikely someone with such little foreign policy experience as Bill Clinton would have been elected president in 1992.[43]

As the politics of foreign policy unfolded during the Bush years, the critiques coalesced around two basic arguments: that Bush did too little to assert US leadership in the world, reflecting his lack of confidence about the possibilities for American power; or that he did too much, subverting the national interest to a larger global cause when it should have been focused more at home.

One sees the former critique among those who believed that Bush was too wedded to the status quo and failed to hasten the Soviet empire's collapse. The story of the US response to the struggles for independence within two Soviet Republics, Lithuania and Ukraine, helps illustrate how the politics of foreign policy began to shift during the Bush era, marking the battlelines for the next several decades.

CRITICS RIPPED BUSH FOR FAILING to support the democracy movement in Lithuania as it gained momentum in the spring of 1990. Championing independence for the Baltic "captive nations" was a staple of American politics since Eisenhower's 1952 campaign ("Remember Estonia, Latvia and Lithuania!" Ike once declared before a joint session of Congress). Therefore, many on the right and left asked, when the Baltics were on the cusp of freedom, why did Bush appear so ambivalent?

His caution stemmed from both tactical and strategic considerations. He wanted to keep a positive relationship with Gorbachev, hoping to thread the needle between encouraging greater autonomy for the Soviet Republic while not provoking a crackdown by Kremlin hardliners. More broadly, Bush saw Gorbachev as the kind of partner who could steer the Cold War to a peaceful end—he thus wanted to encourage the Soviet leader to do the right thing. The result was a classic Bush play: supporting democracy publicly while stressing caution and working behind the scenes to discourage Gorbachev from using violence.

Critics thought Bush had it exactly backward. They saw his strategy as a betrayal like Yalta, when critics charged FDR with selling out Eastern Europe to Stalin at the end of World War II. Instead of throwing Gorbachev a lifeline, they believed the United States should push harder to end Soviet occupation in places like Lithuania and actively seek the USSR's disunion.

While few argued the United States should threaten war, prominent conservatives believed Bush needed to stop sending mixed signals and embrace the Baltic leaders. Pundits worried the president's "sweet talk and body English" could give Gorbachev the impression that "military force can work." Members of Congress from both parties called for immediate recognition of Lithuanian independence.[44]

Bush knew his prudence exacted a political cost. He felt pressure to act, and was inclined to do so. But he could never shake his worries about risks. "Everybody wants us to do 'more,'" Bush dictated to his diary in March 1990, "though nobody is quite clear what that means." He worried that if the United States did what many critics demanded and simply recognized Lithuania's independence, the result could be disastrous, and he would be left holding the bag.

"They're hitting me as a wimp unwilling to move," Bush lamented, "but the big thing is to get through this so the Soviets and Lithuanians get into negotiations and handle it without bloodshed or force." If the situation escalated like Hungary in 1956 and the Soviet military acted, "there is not a damn thing the United States can do about it and you'd have blood on your hands for encouraging her and enticing the Lithuanians to bite off more than they can chew . . . I don't want to see Lithuania ground under the same boot that ground the children of Hungary into the dirt in 1956 by saying 'go to the barricades' . . . we have to find a better way."[45]

Bush eventually clarified to Gorbachev that the United States could not sit "idly by" as a crackdown loomed. If the Soviets acted, Bush warned, he would not be able to advance issues the Soviet leaders valued, like enhanced trade. These calibrated threats, delivered privately in letters and meetings, worked for a time. But in January 1991, events took an ugly turn. Soviet paratroops killed over a dozen Lithuanians at a TV tower broadcasting independent news.[46]

This moment, soon known as "bloody Sunday," occurred at the same time Bush was preoccupied with the start of the Gulf War and ousting Saddam from Kuwait. Reminiscent of the attacks leveled against Eisenhower during the twin crises in Hungary and Suez, critics highlighted the contrast between Bush's willingness to stand up to aggression in the Middle East but not in Europe.

If Bush's new world order truly existed, they asked, why didn't it apply to the Baltics? Moscow's crackdown forced the president's hand. He subsequently threatened a range of steps to punish the Soviet Union economically, warning Gorbachev that if the violence continued, the United States would abandon its support for Soviet reform efforts. Desperate for American financial help, the Soviet president got the message and eventually backed off.[47]

Just a few months later, during a trip to Ukraine in August 1991, Bush took the opportunity to send a similar message of restraint. In a speech before the republic's parliament, he cautioned against a precipitous sprint toward independence from Moscow, warning about a "suicidal nationalism based on ethnic hatred." Although Bush was thinking of the alarming example of Yugoslavia—which at that moment was ripping itself apart in civil war fueled by cynical leaders stoking ethnic hatreds—his words were interpreted as once more prioritizing stability at the expense of freedom. Columnist William Safire, a reliable Bush skeptic, declared it the "Chicken Kiev speech," slamming Bush for falling prey to "policy paralysis he calls prudence." With its suggestion of timidity and missed opportunities, "Chicken Kiev" became an enduring moniker for the president's overall foreign policy—and it so angered Bush that he refused to speak to Safire for well over a decade.[48]

Bush dismissed these criticisms as foolhardy. "When the going gets tough the extremists weigh in," he wrote in a letter to Indiana Senator Richard Lugar the day after the August 1991 Soviet coup. He lamented that too often in foreign policy, opportunists "try to make political hay," as "extremes on both sides, be they 'talking heads' . . . or ultra right warriors or hand-wringing second guessers on the left want to instantly pile on." Bush explained those were the times "for steady, prudent leadership."[49]

GIVEN THAT THE SOVIET UNION IMPLODED shortly thereafter, it is tempting to consider the debate about Bush's handling of Lithuania and Ukraine as mere historical footnotes. In the weeks after the 1991 Soviet coup, Bush and his team thought their political fortunes could hardly get any better. "Do you think the American people are going to turn to a Democrat now?" Bush's eldest son, George W., cackled to journalists at the time.[50]

Yet in significant ways, Bush's handling of communism's collapse shaped the politics of foreign policy on both the political right and left.

For many neoconservatives, this was a pivotal moment. Because they believed the United States needed to act forcefully to promote democracy, they saw Bush's reluctance to push harder for independence—only to be followed by his lackluster support for the new leadership in Moscow after the Soviet Union's collapse—as betraying core American values (a similar argument was made against Bush for his most consequential domestic policy decision, to violate his "no new taxes" pledge in 1990). Seeking a more muscular foreign policy, the lessons they took from Lithuania and Ukraine—as well as Bush's handling of postwar Iraq, post-Tiananmen Square China, and the dissolution of Yugoslavia—was that weakness levied a hefty price.

Moving forward, these Republicans did not want to repeat these mistakes. In reaction to Bush, they called for an activist, values-driven approach that used all instruments of American power to promote freedom. The argument for Republicans to pursue a more "neo-Reaganite" foreign policy was a major force in the conservative debate of the 1990s—and the intellectual logic driving many of the George W. Bush administration's decisions during the early 2000s.[51]

For the same reasons, Bush's perceived weakness emboldened many liberals, especially those gravitating toward then–presidential candidate Bill Clinton. Since most of them opposed the Gulf War—all but ten Democratic senators voted against authorizing the use of force, arguing it would be another Vietnam—they were chastened after the easy victory. They needed to find a line of attack against Bush's strongest attribute.

Democrats drew two lessons from this experience: first, they concluded they should be willing to support military intervention—and the perceived political costs of the 1991 vote against the first Iraq War influenced many Democrats' support for the 2002 authorization for second Iraq

War (especially for senators like Joe Biden and John Kerry). Second, and more important, Democrats considered the Cold War's end as an opportunity to wrest foreign policy "strength" away from Republicans. Like their predecessors at the end of the 1950s, progressives sought new ways to seem tough. They targeted Bush's unwillingness to stand for democracy and human rights. They derided him for, as Clinton put it in his 1992 Democratic convention speech, "coddling tyrants from Baghdad to Beijing." Seeking to portray himself as bolder than Bush, Clinton condemned the president for being "overly cautious" about providing assistance to Russia.[52]

Because of these stances, Clinton garnered support from prominent neoconservatives who were critical of Bush and therefore willing to take a chance on a Democrat if it meant having a more robust foreign policy. Safire endorsed Clinton for president in 1992, as did several of his influential peers. In this way, the post–Cold War identity of many Democrats as liberal interventionists was forged in direct response to Bush's perceived shortcomings. They believed that, as the "indispensable nation," the United States had a unique duty to help solve the world's problems and stand up for democratic values—even if that meant using force.

YET AN OPPOSITE FEATURE OF THE BUSH-ERA POLITICS proved just as consequential: many looked at the same events and argued the United States should be doing less, not more. With the Cold War over, these individuals thought it was time for the United States to declare victory, start looking out for itself, and come home. After decades of sacrificing to fight communism, many Americans expected a "peace dividend." The fierce opposition to the Gulf War was a harbinger of this debate—"no blood for oil," became the antiwar rallying cry—and the brief moment of postwar unity proved to be illusory.

Bush worried about succumbing to the "lone trumpets of retreat." While he remained sympathetic to the argument of limits—and implemented significant cuts in the defense budget—Bush did not deviate from his belief that the United States needed to play a leading global role. "I don't think that we can be looked to for solving every problem every place in the world," he told his diary in 1991. However, he said in a classic Bushism, "I don't want to sound isolationistic."[53]

This line of reasoning got the most traction among conservatives, as Buchanan dusted off the "America First" slogan. But it also gained momentum with the independent presidential candidacy of Ross Perot.

The Texas tycoon came out of nowhere in early 1992 to lead a campaign fueled primarily by appearances on cable television call-in shows like CNN's *Larry King Live*, and innovative appeals for people to donate money and volunteer by dialing into toll-free telephone numbers (which he acquired from the Home Shopping Network). At one point, Perot topped the polls over both Bush and Clinton, earning his ticket on the stage for the fall presidential debates.

Perot never suffered from modesty. Like Eisenhower, he thought it his duty to run in 1992. Yet like McCarthy, he was prone to explain-it-all conspiracism. Perot approached foreign policy as a plain-spoken businessman, as if everything were a matter of maximizing profit and minimizing loss. He came out swinging against a free-trade agreement with Mexico—memorably asserting that it would create a "giant sucking sound" of jobs flowing south—deriding the "losers" who negotiated these agreements and calling for a tough approach toward trade with Europe and Japan. He demanded US allies pay for the stationing of American troops abroad, especially in Europe, whose purpose he dismissed as akin to using a child's "nightlight" to ward off ghosts. Although Perot projected a more folksy, somewhat sunnier outlook than Buchanan's, it too contained a strong dose of nativism, isolationism, and conspiracy. He also took Bush to task for caring too much about the world while the nation declined. It was time, Perot declared, to "make America strong again."[54]

Bush saw the menace of 1930s isolationism lurking in both these men. After initially dismissing them as sideshows, he confronted them directly. Encouraged by his closest advisers to capitalize on his strengths, Bush spoke out forcefully against the dangers of isolationism and protectionism, arguing that this kind of "America First" argument was "phony." In his January 1992 State of the Union address, Bush celebrated the end of the Cold War and acknowledged the country needed to focus more on things at home. Yet he warned of going too far and called for a robust global role. "Strength in the pursuit of peace is no vice," Bush said, in a clever twist borrowing from Barry Goldwater's most famous phrase from his 1964 convention speech that attacked the very idea of moderation, and "isolationism in the pursuit of security is no virtue."[55]

"Isolationism in the pursuit of security is no virtue." Bush on the campaign trail in 1992. (Photo by J. David Ake/AFP via Getty Images)

Bush easily defeated Buchanan in the 1992 primaries and received 20 million more general election votes than Perot. However, both opponents showed surprising resilience. This was especially true for Perot, who, despite dropping out of the race in July only to reenter in October, still earned nearly 20 percent of the 1992 popular vote in the strongest third-party showing since Teddy Roosevelt's Bull Moose Party run in 1912.

A quarter-century later, the ideas of Buchanan and Perot would not be so marginalized. Their message—as outsiders angry with Washington's professional class, skeptical of trade and tired of freeloading allies, worried about immigrants and wanting to build walls, and putting America First by returning to some mythical past to make it great again—would become a dominant force in American politics, indelibly shaping the direction of US foreign policy.[56]

III. OBAMA: THE BREAKDOWN

When Barack Obama began his campaign for president as a first-term senator with negligible foreign policy experience, one might not have expected him to say much about America's global role beyond proving a basic level of competence. Nearly two decades after the Cold War's end, the conventional wisdom still held that national security remained a political loser for Democrats.

Yet Obama's rise was inextricably tied to the shifting politics of post-9/11 foreign policy, with his upstart candidacy boosted by early opposition to one of the most damaging decisions in recent US history: the 2003 war in Iraq. This distinguished him not only from Republicans, but from his more seasoned Democratic primary opponents vying to become president in 2008.

Throughout the early 2000s, Democrats approached foreign policy from a defensive crouch. Conservative foreign policy was ascendant after the 9/11 attacks. The muscular approach of George W. Bush converged with the views of his father's staunchest critics, who advocated for the United States to be more decisive and less apologetic in wielding its power. Some thought that, like the Cold War's containment, the fight against terrorism could be the new basis for American global leadership. With the nation at war, the politics of foreign policy reverted back to its old Cold War stereotypes of hawks and doves, with Republicans again stressing the importance of being "tough," while Democrats cowered from being seen as "weak."

In this mix, Obama cut a unique profile. His generation was unburdened by the legacy of the Cold War, and his early and consistent opposition to the Iraq War made him attractive to a new cadre of liberal activists who gained considerable influence over center-left politics in the late 2000s. At the same time, he made clear he saw the world's dangers and believed the United States did not have the luxury of doing less. While Obama affirmed that the top foreign policy priorities for liberals—like withdrawing from Iraq and addressing climate change—were necessary, they were hardly sufficient for a comprehensive, let alone compelling, national security policy. "Like it or not," he wrote, "if we want to make America more secure, we're going to have to make the world more secure."[57]

Obama's opposition to the Iraq War was not knee-jerk pacifism; after all, he called for a more intense focus on the war in Afghanistan and a more vigorous campaign to fight terrorists. However, he explained such decisions should be rooted in reason and principle, not passion or politics. Obama later remembered the moment he first articulated his opposition to the Iraq War, at a 2002 peace rally in Chicago, this way: "there were all these signs that [read], 'War is not an option.' And I actually started my speech by saying, 'I disagree with those signs. Sometimes war is an option. World War II had to be fought. The Civil War is part of the reason why I can stand here on this podium. The question is, are we fighting the right wars in the right ways?'"[58]

This idea—fighting the right wars in the right ways—became the central plank of his broader critique of the political debate over foreign policy. For example, in an October 2007 campaign speech he delivered at DePaul University, on the fifth anniversary of his Chicago rally speech, Obama reprised his argument as a rebuke of what he called Washington groupthink.

"The American people weren't just failed by a president," Obama said, referring to George W. Bush. "They were failed by much of Washington. By a media that too often reported spin instead of facts [and] by a foreign policy elite that largely boarded the bandwagon for war." For Obama, the mentality that led to Iraq was the most prominent example of a systemic breakdown, the result of a distinct mindset afflicting foreign policy debates. Trying to change this mindset was one of the defining tasks of his presidency.[59]

Through his appeal to both the next generation and the establishment, Obama became a kind of political Rorschach test. He was a unifying figure for Democrats because everyone saw what they wanted. Although

Obama positioned himself as an outsider in the 2008 campaign and made his name opposing the war, his agenda reflected the mainstream of Democratic thinking at the time: responsibly managing transitions out of Iraq and Afghanistan; refocusing the fight on Al Qaeda; maintaining military strength while achieving greater balance between defense, diplomacy, and development; revitalizing core alliances, especially in Europe; leading on transnational issues like climate change, energy security, global health, and nuclear nonproliferation; and placing greater emphasis on the Asia-Pacific region. For Democrats, these ideas comprised the core of a new policy consensus: while America remained exceptional and its leadership indispensable, it needed to understand its limits, work with others, reorient toward future challenges, and recognize the power generated by legitimacy.[60]

With Democrats relatively unified, Republicans found themselves facing a very different political reality. Punctured by the failures of the Iraq War, the excesses of the terrorism fight, and the body blows of the 2008 financial crisis, the GOP was divided and uncertain. The George W. Bush years were supposed to be a restoration—to reclaim a presidency that was rightfully theirs, something that Bill Clinton could only have taken from them in 1992 because he benefitted from a bad economy and was abetted by anomalies like Pat Buchanan and Ross Perot. But instead, this era exposed deep rifts among conservatives, especially between the dwindling number of traditional internationalists and the rising populist wing.

In retrospect, the ticket opposing Obama in 2008, Arizona Senator John McCain and Alaska Governor Sarah Palin, personified this divide vividly. Even in defeat, the internationalist McCain remained an influential political figure, tapping into the conservative foreign policy tradition of Ronald Reagan. Yet it was the vice-presidential nominee Palin—a plainspoken politician famous for "going rogue" by launching spurious attacks on Obama's background and loyalties—who emerged as a folk hero. As a direct political descendant of Buchanan and Perot, she became an early indicator of the populist, nationalist, celebrity demagogic

politics that dominated conservatism in the Obama era, from the Tea
Party to Trump.[61]

REFLECTING BACK ON THE OBAMA-ERA politics of foreign policy, one sees
the same dynamics that afflicted Eisenhower and Bush: the emphasis on
doing "more," especially militarily; the impatience and addiction to action; the imperative to be "strong" and "tough"; and the manipulation of
fear. Obama mostly let these critiques wash over him. In the last years of
his presidency, however, his frustration led him to answer these critiques
more forcefully, frequently voicing his annoyance with the politicians and
foreign policy elites who promulgated them.

Two moments from 2015 highlight the acrimonious debate: Obama's
approach to Iran's nuclear program and his response to terrorism.
Considered together, they encapsulate the dysfunction and cynicism that
characterized the politics of foreign policy during his presidency.

Obama's response to the threat posed by Iran's nuclear ambitions reflected his strategic approach. His administration worked with allies to deploy
diplomatic, military and economic pressure to create the conditions that
brought Iran to the table. It then brokered a complex, multinational deal
approved by the UN Security Council to cut off Iran's pathways to develop
nuclear weapons, placing it under a strict international inspections regime.

Like Iraq in 2003, Iran was an aspiring regional hegemon with ambitions
to develop weapons of mass destruction, with one key difference: it actually possessed an ongoing WMD program. Moreover, while the United
States barreled forward to use force in Iraq, with Iran, it addressed the
threat by using all the tools available to build leverage and find a solution
without resorting to war. In essence, Obama modeled his Iran policy on
the way Bush 41 handled Iraq in the early 1990s, and in the process, he
repudiated the way Bush 43 handled Iraq after 9/11. With its emphasis
on the collective enforcement of shared rules, Obama's Iran nuclear deal
would have fit comfortably within George H. W. Bush's new world order.[62]

Nevertheless, the deal was hardly perfect. While it effectively froze the
country's nuclear program, which Obama judged to be the most urgent

priority, it did not address all aspects of Tehran's nefarious behavior. The agreement ignited a massive domestic political firestorm—as big and bitterly partisan as any since the debate over the 2003 Iraq War. Republican opponents, nourished by powerful interest groups and tens of millions of dollars in support, lined up uniformly against it. Influential foreign leaders like Israeli Prime Minister Benjamin Netanyahu got directly involved too, taking the unprecedented step of coming to Congress at the invitation of Republicans to make the case against the deal.

Obama and his team relished the opportunity to face their critics openly, responding to them with a campaign of their own (in the White House they established a communications hub they jokingly dubbed the "antiwar room"). They wanted to rebut specific criticisms of the deal, but more importantly, assail the mindset that undergirded them. They saw a direct line between the arguments against the 2015 Iran deal and those made in favor of the 2003 Iraq War.

For Obama, this debate exemplified everything he believed to be wrong with the politics of foreign policy—the dubious claims, the absolutist demands, the shameless partisanship, and especially the lack of accountability. To drive home this argument, he delivered a speech at American University in August 2015, which stands as one of Obama's most important statements about the foreign policy debate.

The problem, he explained to an audience of nearly two hundred students, was that they were "living through a time in American politics where every foreign policy decision is viewed through a partisan prism, evaluated by headline-grabbing sound bites." To answer his critics and frame the choice in the starkest of terms—between diplomacy and war—Obama returned to the arguments he made when he first ran for president. He wanted to hold his critics accountable for their past mistakes and, in words that stretched back to his 2008 campaign, to call them out explicitly:

When I ran for president eight years ago as a candidate who had opposed the decision to go to war in Iraq, I said that America didn't just have to end that war—we had to end the mindset that got us there in the first place. It was a mindset characterized by a preference for military action over diplomacy; a mindset that put a premium on unilateral U.S. action over the painstaking work of building international consensus; a mindset that exaggerated threats beyond what the intelligence supported. Leaders did not level with the American people about the costs of war, insisting that we could easily impose our will on a part of the world with a profoundly different culture and history. And, of course, those calling for war labeled themselves strong and decisive, while dismissing those who disagreed as weak—even appeasers of a malevolent adversary.

The Iran deal's critics, Obama reminded, "had no compunction with being repeatedly wrong." They were simply recycling the same arguments they once used to justify the war in Iraq. Instead of offering different solutions, the critics chose to hide behind "vague promises of toughness" and paint diplomacy as appeasement. "I know it's easy to play on people's fears, to magnify threats, to compare any attempt at diplomacy to Munich," he said. "But none of these arguments hold up. They didn't back in 2002 and 2003; they shouldn't now."

The fundamental issue came down to the perennial questions of what one meant by "strength" or how one defined being "tough." Eisenhower, too, once expressed his own bewilderment with such labels. What exactly does having a tough policy mean, he would ask. Explaining that since he was "a pragmatic sort of guy," such terms only made sense when applied to concrete problems one was trying to solve.

Similarly, Obama believed strength couldn't be measured by simply thumping one's chest and narrowing all your options while the problem festered, leaving no choice but the use of force. After all, that was the exact kind of "strong" policy toward Iran that Obama inherited in 2009, which left the United States isolated and Iran barreling ahead with its nuclear program. Strength meant using all the tools of statecraft to accomplish a goal—requiring patience, persistence, and confidence.[63]

"Worry less about being labeled weak; worry more about getting it right." Obama speaks at American University in August 2015.
(Courtesy of American University/Jeff Watts).

Like Eisenhower and Bush, Obama understood such an approach could be politically underwhelming. He told journalists at the time this fact was "built into a political lexicon that makes you sound tougher if you don't talk to somebody and . . . very loudly, wield a big stick." In concluding his American University speech, Obama conceded the pursuit of peace is not as dramatic as the pursuit of war. He acknowledged that, in the moment, tough talk was easy and often more politically rewarding. But drama was not strength. After over a decade of war in the Middle East, Obama said the United States needed to heed some basic lessons: "On the front end, ask tough questions. Subject our own assumptions to evidence and analysis. Resist the conventional wisdom and the drumbeat of war. Worry less about being labeled weak; worry more about getting it right."[64]

Obama eventually mustered enough support to keep the Iran deal alive. However consequential this proved to be, it was only a tactical success. He failed to shift the political debate fundamentally. If anything, his opponents' inability to prevent the Iran deal from taking effect merely hardened their resolve to undermine it. They told themselves that Obama did not succeed because he won on the deal's merits, but because he and his aides manipulated the public with manufactured claims. They often asserted, without any evidence, that the agreement's true intent was to upend US policy and forge allegiance with the Iranian regime.

Regardless of whether Iran complied with its end of the deal or not—and it did, according to US allies and international experts charged with overseeing the deal, for the next several years—Republican critics never cared for the facts and therefore never changed their minds. Killing the deal became their singular obsession. It was the one thing they unified around, even if they couldn't agree what should come next. In their zeal, they only proved the resilience and power of the political forces about which Obama warned.

IF THE TUSSLE OVER THE IRAN DEAL was fundamentally about the politics of strength, then the debate about Obama's approach to terrorism was about the politics of fear. As a matter of policy, Obama brought a brutal intensity to the terrorism fight, using lethal means that elicited no shortage of controversy, especially among those on the left. For example, he deployed special operations forces and used drones to kill terrorists in an unprecedented fashion. Nor was he above engaging in the occasional, and sometimes unwise, macho talk, such as after the 2011 killing of Osama bin Laden, or by initially belittling ISIL as the "jayvee team."

Obama understood the dangerous power of fear. He saw how it could be used to rally support, channeled to demonize opponents, and mobilized to rationalize the harshest response. Soon after the ISIL crisis exploded in 2014, Obama explained to aides that they needed "to reflect on what fear can do to this place." Seeing how easy—and politically expedient—it would be to succumb to fear and exploit it for advantage afforded him a greater appreciation for how the US ended up in the Iraq War. He could understand how, in the moment, leaders could bow to pressure and justify almost anything. Public anxiety and insecurity made it easy, he said, for a president to "get in that wave" and do whatever they wanted. His appreciation for how such power could be exploited left him cautious.[65]

"I believe that we have to avoid being simplistic," Obama explained, to ensure "our political debates are grounded in reality." He decried the incentives generated by the media and political punditocracy. These forces only stoked fear and rewarded "impetuous [or] manufactured responses that make good sound bites but don't produce results . . . For me to satisfy the cable news hype-fest would lead us to making worse and worse decisions over time." Because Obama believed one should not make decisions based on emotion or hysteria, in moments of crisis his instincts were to tap the brakes. "It's my job to calm folks down," he said, "not scare them."[66]

WITH THIS GOAL IN MIND, Obama stepped before the television cameras positioned in the Oval Office on a Sunday evening in early December 2015. Symbolizing the gravity of the moment, it was only the third time Obama used the historic setting to deliver a prime-time address to the nation. To a country deeply shaken by recent ISIL-inspired terrorist attacks in Paris and San Bernardino, which killed over 150 people, Obama sought to contextualize the threat, offer reassurance, and detail his administration's actions to keep the public safe.

In purpose and tone, this was Obama's own version of Eisenhower's "fear" speech delivered from the White House in April 1954. Like Ike, Obama neither denied the dangers nor belittled the magnitude of the task. He urged his fellow citizens not to give in to cynicism by thinking the cause was hopeless, depicting all Muslims as inherent enemies, or embracing facile solutions.

"Our success won't depend on tough talk, or abandoning our values, or giving into fear," Obama said. "That's what groups like ISIL are hoping for." Rather, he explained, a sustainable victory required "being strong and smart, resilient and relentless, and by drawing upon every aspect of American power." Obama detailed the military's bombing of ISIS and training of partners to fight the terrorists on the ground. He asked Congress to get more engaged in the effort, starting with a formal authorization to use force against ISIL. He called for measures like tighter gun control (since the recent attacks involved mass shootings with assault rifles) and stricter measures to prevent suspected terrorists from crossing the border.

While Obama shared Eisenhower's intent, his effort did not earn the same accolades. Obama did not enjoy Eisenhower's stature as a commanding war hero. Moreover, a lot had changed since the mid-1950s, when it was enough for a president to seem innovative by appearing on TV and speaking informally. By the mid-2010s, politics rewarded spectacle, and Obama didn't deliver. As one analyst described, it seemed the president was just going through the motions, turning "to a venue he doesn't like to discuss a subject he would rather avoid." Predictably, Obama's words did nothing to mollify his Republican opponents, who greeted his reasoned remarks with universal scorn. As the leading Republican candidate for president, Donald Trump, mocked on Twitter: "That all there is? We need a new President—FAST!"[67]

When concluding his April 1954 speech, Eisenhower made one final appeal to the bigger picture, stressing that "we must have the faith that comes from a study of our own history." Over sixty years later, Obama closed his speech with a similar message, drawing upon history to remind Americans that, fundamentally, the opposite of fear is hope.

"Let's not forget that freedom is more powerful than fear," Obama said. "We have always met challenges—whether war or depression, natural disasters or terrorist attacks—by coming together around our common ideals as one nation, as one people." For future presidents—and for citizens thinking about what we should want from a leader in these moments—Eisenhower's and Obama's efforts to calm nerves, provide perspective, and fight fear offer enduring lessons.[68]

Both Obama and Eisenhower believed they needed to level with the American people about hard truths, without resorting to simplistic sound bites. They rejected the notion that Americans can't handle complicated facts. "They're not always paying attention, and there's a lot of noise out there," Obama observed in 2016, "but when they have the time, they're not looking to be spoken down to and there's no requirement to dumb things down. They get it." At the same time, these presidents understood leaders could not do this alone. Citizens, too, needed to engage. Defining the stakes for America abroad "is not the task of one individual," Eisenhower wrote in 1957. "This is a case where all who believe . . . must do their parts, each to the extent of his ability and to the limit of his endurance."[69]

OBAMA WAS SUPPOSED TO USHER in a different kind of politics. In almost every way, he aspired to be what the writer David Remnick aptly describes as a "bridge"—a leader who could connect across the country's racial divide, between its widening political gap of left and right, across generations, and between America and the world. Because the United States faced such extraordinary challenges, Obama thought that Democrats and Republicans could come together to forge a post-9/11 Middle Way. Of course, the reality turned out to be much different.[70]

Republicans weren't interested in working constructively. Obama faced a party not only determined to win at all costs, but to contort truth in the process. He once hoped that "the fever may break" and he could find common cause with "the tradition in the Republican Party of more common sense," those like Eisenhower and Bush. Yet there seemed to be little of that tradition left in the GOP.

By the 2010s, the cleansing of any trace of "Modern Republicanism" from conservatism was nearly complete. The GOP essentially gave up on good faith compromise and effective governing. It was impossible to have a coherent, steady, and sensible foreign policy when one side of the political debate embarked on such a trajectory—fully embracing a fantasy-industrial complex in which everything is possible and nothing is true. That, too, was seeing the world "as it is." "The breakdown in American government and the dysfunction in our politics are the result of the steady radicalization of American conservatism," political analyst E. J. Dionne argued. Another factor, he added, was "Obama's failure to anticipate it and tardiness in dealing with it." While Obama was not surprised a reality television star emerged as the GOP standard-bearer, he still believed Trump not only wouldn't win in 2016, but that he couldn't.[71]

Obama accepted his share of the blame. He conceded that his inability to salve Washington's partisan dysfunction was one of his few regrets as president. "The rancor and suspicion between the parties has gotten worse instead of better," he lamented in his final State of the Union address in January 2016. In retrospect, his observation was a notable understatement.

Yet he maintained faith in the judgment of the vast majority of the American people—believing they were fundamentally optimistic, pragmatic problem-solvers committed to doing good abroad. But he acknowledged that amid so much uncertainty and anxiety about the future, political leaders were failing. Moreover, he presciently warned, things could deteriorate further. "As frustration grows," he said, "there will be voices urging us to fall back into tribes, to scapegoat fellow citizens who don't look like us, or pray like us, or vote like we do, or share the same background."[72]

Obama sensed the tremors. But the earthquake's magnitude surprised him. He often said that history never travels in a straight line, it moves in fits and starts, and it zigs and zags, taking a few steps forward and then a few back. But in the shell-shocked days after the 2016 election—an outcome that could not have been more of a repudiation of everything not only he stood for, but Eisenhower and Bush as well—Obama asked himself whether he pushed things too far and too fast, wondering if, perhaps, his presidency was ten to twenty years premature. Maybe, he lamented, people just want to fall back on their tribe.[73]

HERE IT IS IMPORTANT TO DWELL on one final point: race. Because no matter how many parallels exist between Obama and Eisenhower and Bush, the debates surrounding their presidencies are inescapably defined by this fundamental difference. And more specifically, with the first Black commander-in-chief in the White House, systemic racism deeply affected the politics of the 44th president's foreign policy.

Quite often, this racism was explicit. The poisonous right-wing "birther" conspiracy—which was vigorously promoted by the person who became the 45th president—propagated racist tropes by falsely claiming that Obama was foreign-born and illegitimately elected. Going further, conservative commentators insinuated that he was a Muslim and sympathetic to adversaries wishing to harm the United States, with some even refer-ring to him as a "terrorist leader."

Racial bias also manifested in more subtle, implicit ways, often influen-cing views in the more polite precincts of the foreign policy establishment, especially among many of those with a more conservative bent. Systemic racism has been a problem in this mostly white, and male, establishment for a long time, but its effects were more obvious with Obama in office. This can be seen in the assertions that Obama did not love his country because he was "brought up differently," or doubts expressed about his commitment to the idea of American exceptionalism, or suggestions he could not be trusted to support Israel (including accusations he used anti-Semitic dog whistles) and did not value the U.S.-Europe relationship in some instinctual way.

Racism was hardly the only factor motivating the political critiques of Obama's foreign policy—as this story shows, similar political forces aligned against Eisenhower and Bush. However, its unique, enduring impact can neither be denied nor ignored, both in terms of what transpired during Obama's presidency, and for what came after. Racism filters perceptions even in retrospect, which helps explain why it is so hard for some to see the similarity between these three presidents' approach to foreign policy.

* * *

When thinking about the political dynamics that shaped the foreign pol-icies of Eisenhower, Bush, and Obama, several common themes emerge. Each president pushed back against the forces of isolationism and America First. They wrestled with the politics of fear. They were dogged by questions about whether they were sufficiently "strong" and what it meant to be "tough." They tried hard to remain optimistic and reassure people in times of turbulence. And they all had to grapple with demagogues ped-dling ominous conspiracies and offering easy solutions.

Obama experienced the ills of a political ecosystem in which facts are denied, making it impossible to, as he put it, "have a common conversa-tion." He therefore saw how politicians who played to people's fears about the changing world could succeed, because they were "able to distill the anger and resentment and the sense of aggrievement." This was what Bush called the "jugular politics" pushed in his own time by "nuts" like the Birchers, and then Buchanan, in which "everybody loses."[74]

Eisenhower saw this too. One of the most impactful books on Ike's thinking was Eric Hoffer's 1951 *The True Believer*, which probed the psychology of mass movements and the appeal of authoritarian politics. Hoffer depicted the mental stress and burdens of democracy, arguing that "faith in a holy cause" was a "substitute for the lost faith in ourselves." Ike devoured the book, sent copies to his friends, and Hoffer was referred to as Ike's "favorite author."

Ike sensed the temptation for people to insulate themselves from the pressures and uncertainties of a free society. In a 1959 letter, Eisenhower highlighted Hoffer's observation that dictatorial systems derive adherents and energy by "freeing" their citizens "from the necessity of informing themselves and making up their own minds concerning these tremendous complex and difficult questions." Ike considered this especially problematic for national security, in which fears could be so easily exploited for political advantage. "It is indeed difficult to maintain a reasoned and accurately informed understanding of our defense situation," Eisenhower wrote, "when so many prominent officials, possessing no standing or expertise except as they themselves claim it, attempt to further their own ideas or interests by resorting to statements more distinguished by stridency than accuracy." Hoffer's warnings proved far-sighted; during the 2016 presidential campaign, when the psychology of mass movements and fanaticism returned with force, Hillary Clinton recommended her staff read his book.[75]

EISENHOWER, BUSH, AND OBAMA WERE ELECTED to arrest the decline of American power and, in the case of Eisenhower and Obama, clean up foreign policy messes their predecessors created after succumbing to overreach. Therefore, they set out to steady the ship and set a course for the long haul. They tried not to overpromise and were determined to stay out of trouble.

This measured approach initially proved politically popular, but eventually foundered under accusations of weakness and indecisiveness. In turn, forces calling for riskier, more costly, aggressive approaches—or what is described as "maximalism"—gained momentum. These presidents' political fortunes suffered as new leaders replaced them with promises to be bolder and tougher. The political incentives for maximalism are formidable—it is easy to get outflanked by opponents who argue for doing "more" of something while not having to make any trade-offs or be held accountable for the consequences.[76]

Eisenhower, Bush, and Obama had plenty of ambition and could be politically ruthless. But as a matter of governing in foreign policy, they often defied political expediency. They could be dismissive of the so-called "smart" politics recommended by elites, and were reluctant to exploit outrage or stoke fears. While they sought to do big things when necessary, they were unafraid to champion measured responses, even if it exposed them to charges that they were indecisive or out of touch. They each paid a political price for this. History's verdict, though, may be a different matter.

Finally, their experiences help show how dramatically the politics of foreign policy has shifted. While both liberals and conservatives resisted these presidents' attempts to forge a Middle Way, both sides were not equally culpable. The most consequential enemies of these presidents' foreign policy centrism came from the political right—from forces that were once insurgent outliers, but who steadily gained influence and came to define the GOP of the early 2020s. It is easy to see the ghosts of Taft, McCarthy, Buchanan, and Perot when looking at Trump's rhetoric and policies (and, of course, McCarthy and Trump shared a common lawyer and henchman, Roy Cohn). Aside from a few lonely voices, the modern Republican Party has little interest in adhering to the foreign policy legacies of leaders like Eisenhower and Bush. Most Democrats, however, gladly claim them.[77]

Legacy

I n December 2018, more than three thousand mourners packed the
Washington National Cathedral's pews to commemorate the life of
George H. W. Bush, who died at the age of ninety-four.

Bush had seen his reputation evolve and improve over time. Evicted
from the White House in 1993 after one term, he initially seemed
condemned to the dustbin of uninspiring presidents—seen as a compe-
tent commander-in-chief who presided over a major transformation of
geopolitics, yet never quite fully rose to the occasion. A quarter-century
later, Bush's legacy looked quite different. The news of his death uncorked
an outpouring of emotion and nostalgia—reflecting a renewed appreciation for the former president's accomplishments in office and for the political brand he represented.

As Bush's flag-draped casket rested at the altar of the capital's cathedral,
just as Eisenhower's had in 1969, the grieving seemed to be about more
than one man. "As bells tolled and choirs sang and flags flew at half-staff,"
journalist Peter Baker reported in the *New York Times*, "the nation's 41st
president was remembered as a 'kinder and gentler' leader whose fortitude

steered the country through a tumultuous moment in history even as his essential decency stood in contrast to the politics of insults now in vogue."[1]

To get a sense of that contrast, one needed to look no further than the front pew, where the former presidents and first ladies were seated together to pay their respects. Barack Obama sat in the middle. Two seats away on the aisle, Donald Trump rested with his arms crossed and face frozen in a scowl, looking like he would rather be anywhere else. As each eulogist extolled Bush's virtues—his courage and principles, his humility and grace, his gift of friendship, and his commitment to internationalism—the implicit rebuke to the 45th president was unmistakable.

Obama did not speak at the state funeral, but he joined in the encomiums for what Bush achieved and the kind of leadership he stood for. When news of Bush's passing first broke, Obama reprised his words from the 2011 Medal of Freedom ceremony, praising the 41st president's example and the diplomatic skill which "made possible an achievement once thought anything but—ending the Cold War without firing a shot."

Just days before Bush's death, Obama had seen his predecessor one last time. He was in Houston for a public event with James Baker, Bush's best friend and former secretary of state, where they lamented the decline of the "responsible center" in politics and defended the idea of a pragmatic, internationalist foreign policy. During his visit, Obama stopped by Bush's house to say goodbye to the person he called "my buddy 41." They spent a quiet forty-five minutes together, with Obama making a point of telling Bush how much he admired his foreign policy leadership.[2]

LESS THAN TWO YEARS LATER, in May 2020, the $150 million memorial to honor Dwight D. Eisenhower was scheduled to open to the public in Washington, DC.

Developed by renowned architect Frank Gehry, the monument located on Independence Avenue just off the National Mall was subject to a bitter fight that lasted far longer than the 34th president's two terms in office. Critics worried about its cost and size, traditionalists scoffed at its unorthodox design, and Eisenhower's descendants claimed it to be too modest, failing to evoke the glories of Ike's military and political career.

In the end, "Eisenhower Park"—which is marked by a massive steel tapestry with seven-story high columns and nine-foot bronze statues spread across four tree-filled acres—reflects a compromise between the different ways we remember Eisenhower: the everyman from Kansas and the commanding general who liberated Europe; the reluctant, novice politician beloved by the public, who modernized campaigning and tried to remake the Republican Party; and a presidency from a seemingly simpler time that nevertheless charted America's global dominance.[3]

The controversy over how Eisenhower should be memorialized is not surprising; nothing about his legacy was ever simple. Ike's political opponents on the right and left initially defined him as an ailing, unimaginative, befuddled, over-the-hill duffer who could never quite rekindle his World War II heroism. That spin prevailed for several decades. Today, however, many Americans consider Eisenhower as one of the greats. In a 1962 poll asking historians to list the finest presidents, Ike placed at 22nd. In 2018, he ranked 7th.

Yet just as the nation's permanent monument to Eisenhower readied to open officially, on a day also marking the 75th anniversary of the World War II Allied Victory in Europe, the celebration was postponed because of the lockdown forced by the 2020 coronavirus pandemic. As the country grappled with its greatest crisis since the era that made Ike a hero, the symbol of the kind of nation he represented and tried to build—and the global role it aspired for—stood ready, gleaming, yet temporarily shuttered, awaiting a new day.

"LET HISTORY BE THE JUDGE," Bush once said when asked about his legacy. How a country remembers its leaders is about more than simply recording the past; it reflects the concerns of the living and aspirations for the future. "We arouse and arrange our memories to suit our psychic needs," wrote the historian Michael Kammen, whose scholarship illuminated how public memorials, traditions, and myths (as expressed in things like funerals and monuments) shape America's ethos and sense of identity. How we think about a president's reputation—in foreign policy and otherwise—is a product of our expectations for what we want our leaders to be.[4]

What is a legacy? It is a timeless question we ask of our presidents, as well as of ourselves. It is one pondered by our greatest thinkers and artists. For the Athenian statesman Pericles, the answer is weaving oneself into the lives of others. For the writer Maya Angelou, it is making a mark on the world that can't be erased. And for the title character in the smash Broadway musical *Hamilton*, it is planting seeds in a garden one will never get to see—and understanding that someone else will write your story.

This captures a view all three presidents shared: that the journey on what Eisenhower called the "long lane of history" never ends. Like any leader, they were conscious of their image and hardly immune from criticisms of the moment. Yet they knew the ultimate judgment would come decades after leaving office. This gave them perspective; it also engendered a healthy dose of humility. "We're on this planet a pretty short time," Obama once explained, "so that we cannot remake the world entirely during this little stretch that we have . . . At the end of the day, we're part of a long-running story. We just try to get our paragraph right."[5]

How do their paragraphs look? How should we think about the foreign policy legacies of Eisenhower, Bush, and Obama?

What follows briefly traces how those legacies have evolved over the years, and what conclusions we may draw. It assesses the inheritance they bequeathed to their successors, as well as their flaws. Finally, we draw some broad lessons from their tradition of Middle Way leadership, and what it means for the future.

I. HISTORY

Eisenhower's reputation was always a contradiction. He consistently ranked as one of the most popular men in America throughout his tenure in office, and for years afterwards. At the same time, intellectuals, academics, and the political press corps remained underwhelmed. They thought of him as an amiable mediocrity; an inattentive, grandfatherly leader who lacked major achievements and left the United States adrift in the world.

The first histories of Eisenhower's presidency, along with the bestselling memoirs that used the staid 1950s as a foil to mythologize and romanticize JFK's Camelot, reflected this view. This perception started to change in the late 1960s when Ike's restraint began to look more judicious. Prominent critics like Murray Kempton and Garry Wills reconsidered Eisenhower, heralding his political "genius" and steady leadership. "He was the great tortoise upon whose back the world sat for eight years," Kempton wrote in an influential 1967 essay that foreshadowed Eisenhower revisionism. "We laughed at him; we talked wistfully about moving; and all the while we never knew the cunning beneath the shell."[6]

Quiet cunning contributed, at least in part, to Ike's enhanced legacy. As he prepared to leave the White House, Eisenhower plotted to push back against those who argued his foreign policy was feckless or out of date. For example, in the summer of 1960, he gave every member of his cabinet a private memo written by a sympathetic observer describing a way to "sell" his foreign policy as "ahead of its time" and "more promising than anything proposed by critics." Once he left Washington in 1961, Eisenhower and his lieutenants set out to tell the story of his presidency in memoirs, articles, extensive interviews, and document collections. They knew his vast archive of letters and diaries would be a historical jackpot, so they enlisted Johns Hopkins University Press to publish them in twenty-one edited volumes totaling over fourteen-thousand pages. It was not an overstatement—as one of the Eisenhower Library's top archivists later observed—to describe these efforts to shape the historical record as a war.[7]

Such a description is fitting, because Ike understood that a presidency, like a war, is waged twice: first on the battlefield (or in office), and then in memory. His perspective on the relationship between history and memory was likely shaped by his early career experiences in the 1920s writing a narrative history and guidebook to the battle monuments commemorating US military efforts in France during World War I. He got this position with the American Battle Monuments Commission, where he worked under the great General John J. Pershing, with the help of his old mentor, Fox Conner.[8]

Ike's post-presidential campaign, and the new scholarship based on the availability of Eisenhower's voluminous records, helped counter his image as an absent leader by portraying him as engaged, purposeful, and manipulative (a notable exception was the depiction of Ike by his former aide Emmet Hughes, who wrote several critical memoirs about Eisenhower, and who declared such revisionism as "a lot of bullshit"). The events that followed Ike's tenure, however, were just as important in reversing low opinions of his time in office. As the country tore itself apart over the Vietnam War and suffered through the domestic and geopolitical turmoil of the early 1970s, Eisenhower's cautious statecraft and shrewd sense of the limits of American power made him look wiser. In retrospect, his handling of Dien Bien Phu in particular was a main catalyst in the revision of earlier critiques.[9]

There is perhaps no better example of this perceptual shift than the contrast between the two editions of Richard Neustadt's landmark book, *Presidential Power*, which shaped how generations of students and experts interpreted presidential performance. When first published in 1960, the Harvard scholar's book offered an uninspiring take on Ike's leadership and became a bible of sorts for JFK and his team, for whom Neustadt served as an informal adviser. Yet when Neustadt revised it thirty years later, with the benefit of hindsight and Eisenhower's records, he reinterpreted Ike's management of Dien Bien Phu as a standout example of presidential success.[10]

"Many liberals in the 1950s derided the Eisenhower foreign policy as weak, inflexible, and unimaginative," historian Alan Brinkley observed in a 1990 essay. "But those who experienced the consequences of the more expansive and aggressive foreign policy strategies of the 1960s tend now to find virtue in Eisenhower's relative restraint." Similarly, as the US defense budget ballooned and deficits soared in the 1980s, Ike's emphasis on fiscal discipline and maintaining strategic solvency seemed wiser—and his far-sighted investments in science, education, and infrastructure were heralded for establishing the foundation for decades of innovation, prosperity, and power.[11]

When a group of historians and former administration officials gathered in Gettysburg for a retrospective symposium on Eisenhower in October 1990, a few months after congressional leaders and President

Bush celebrated Ike's achievements in Washington, the legacy of the 34th president had come full circle. Some scholars even raved that he was the best president of the second half of the twentieth century.

Ike's legacy bears its share of blemishes—from his culpability in the 1953 coup in Iran and failure to contain the nuclear arms race, to his commitment to South Vietnam and acknowledged inability to rein in the military-industrial complex. Nevertheless, his overall reputation aged favorably. Appreciation only grew for his commitment to alliances, his clear-eyed approach to negotiating with adversaries, and his support for greater foreign assistance. By the early 2020s, Ike's leadership was considered a source of inspiration and an antidote to Trumpian politics by both liberals and disaffected conservatives alike.[12]

For the scholars gathered at Gettysburg in the autumn of 1990, Eisenhower's example contrasted favorably with the performance of the man then occupying the White House. They took a dim view of George Bush. They criticized his handling of the Gulf War crisis, in particular his decision-making process and haphazard diplomacy, which they compared unfavorably to Eisenhower. Ike's descendants wrote op-eds asserting he would have been disappointed at the inability of the United States to seize the historic opportunity presented by communism's collapse. There is no small irony in how Bush got pummeled with his idol's legacy—especially because the critiques were almost identical to what was once said about Ike himself.[13]

Bush did not push back. Routed in the 1992 election—he earned just 37 percent of the popular vote, the lowest total for an incumbent president since William Howard Taft in 1912—and restrained by his penchant for modesty and conviction that former presidents should be rarely seen or heard, he retired to Houston and Kennebunkport and stayed relatively quiet. He did not write the customary major presidential memoir; instead, he co-authored an unusual yet invaluable book on his administration's foreign policy and published a single collection of selected diary entries and letters. If Eisenhower's post-presidential legacy campaign can be described as a war, it seemed Bush barely waged a skirmish.

For well over a decade after Bush left office, the conventional wisdom about him did not budge. He remained seen as someone who meant well though never quite delivered—a skilled manager respected for his energy and graciousness, but who squandered opportunities and shirked too many decisions.

Former Carter National Security Adviser Zbigniew Brzezinski, who endorsed Bush for president in 1988 (and would be an early supporter of Obama in 2008), spoke for many when he concluded that "as a global leader [Bush] did not seize the opportunity to shape the future or leave behind a compelling sense of direction." As Bush's sons stepped into the national limelight in the 1990s, he acknowledged his record could be a political liability. In a 1998 letter to George W. and Jeb, Bush said he was ready for those stories "that contrast you favorably to a father who had no vision and who was but a placeholder in the broader scheme of things." Not to worry, he reassured them, because "I am content with how historians will judge my administration."[14]

Of course, Bush did not expect, or particularly welcome, how that contrast would eventually get drawn. As much as anything else, the mistakes of Bush's eldest son forced a reexamination of his father's legacy. Many saw Bush 43's foreign policy as an explicit counterpoint to Bush 41's perceived failures. Analysts speculated about the psychological motives behind George W. Bush's desire to undo past mistakes, "finish the job" in places like Iraq, and show more spine in the defense of democracy. Neither father nor son had patience for such psychoanalysis. However, there is strong evidence these past perceptions mattered, if not for Bush 43 personally, then for many of those around him who thought they needed to redress the elder Bush's missteps. In the end, Bush 43's bad decisions definitively burnished Bush 41's legacy—including among those who once ridiculed it.[15]

In a 1987 cover story, Newsweek torched Bush for being a "wimp"—an accusation he could never quite shake, nor ever forgive. In March 2011, the month after Obama gave him the Presidential Medal of Freedom, the magazine tried to make things right with a story praising Bush's "civil tone, willingness to reach across the aisle, even his sway with Middle Eastern strongmen."

While such qualities were "once branded for vices," the article read, in words almost identical to those once written about Eisenhower, "suddenly [they] seem more like virtues in a world weary of attack politics and confronting a cascading series of global crises." These leadership qualities—when rounded out by greater appreciation for Bush's post-presidential generosity of spirit, whether he was parachuting out of airplanes on his birthday, shaving his head in solidarity with a young cancer patient, or forging such a warm, almost father-son relationship with one-time political rival Bill Clinton—left a healthy sense of a nostalgia for his presidency.[16]

Toward the end of his life, Bush admitted to his biographer that he sometimes wondered if he might amount to more than a historical asterisk, barely mentioned among more larger-than-life figures who once occupied the Oval Office. This rare moment of self-reflection—and doubt—about his place in history is revealing, because the story of Bush's legacy is one of being constantly written off, only to be resurrected and reinvented.

As the late journalist Marjorie Williams wrote in a brilliant portrait of Bush, "it is worth taking stock of how often and how radically we have changed our minds about this man, rejecting and then discovering, again and again, the same basic reality that has been there all along." And just as Eisenhower's reputation improved exponentially with the opening of his archives—providing scholars with a new perspective into his thinking and decision-making—the realities of Bush's leadership, and the strength of his record, become clearer as his papers and diaries are made available. When contemplating the state of the world at the beginning of the 2020s, Bush's "vision thing" looks pretty good after all.[17]

IN NOVEMBER 2016, JUST THREE DAYS after the presidential election, another group of scholars convened to discuss a presidential legacy. The mood, though, was more wistful than celebratory. Meeting in Princeton to offer their initial assessment of Obama's presidency, the group had prepared a conference presuming Hillary Clinton, whose own path-breaking campaign promised an extension of the Obama era, would be his successor. Instead, they found themselves asking if everything Obama stood for had been repudiated, and whether his legacy would be left in tatters.[18]

To a significant degree, every president is initially defined by what comes next. Eisenhower looked older and slower when compared to the men of action on Kennedy's "New Frontier," just as Bush appeared out of touch when contrasted with Clinton's baby-boomer "New Democrats." It is hard, however, to conjure a purer antithesis to Obama than Donald Trump.

Trump's foreign policy—indeed, his entire presidency—boiled down to one thing: undoing almost everything Obama touched. Whether pulling out of the Paris Climate Change Accord, the Trans-pacific trade pact with Asian partners, or the Iran nuclear deal, he pursued this task with special vigor and disdain. Historians could not recall another instance when the new president seemed so singularly intent on gutting his predecessor's accomplishments just for the sake of doing so, and often without any replacement in mind. All this was just an extension of the effort to delegitimize Obama entirely, which of course started well before he left the White House.[19]

Even for those who did not wish to erase the past, the first take on Obama's foreign policy legacy is that while he was a history-making leader, his presidency was underwhelming. Obama remains widely admired—respected for his temperament, thoughtfulness, and grasp of history. As the first Black president, he will always have a prominent place in the American story. Yet because so many of his foreign policy achievements proved fleeting and fragile—on Iran, climate change, Cuba, regional trade deals in Asia and Europe, and nuclear disarmament—means that, to some, his legacy looks more like the historical asterisk that George H. W. Bush feared.[20]

A stronger version of this critique, especially prominent among those on the left, is that Obama did not go far enough. According to this argument, there is a symbolic mismatch between the sweeping change his historic presidency portended and his incrementalist approach. Obama was so careful and compromising that he did not do enough to rollback the policies of his Republican predecessors, especially those involving military force and counter-terrorism. Even worse, such critics assert, he failed to bring about the fundamental change that could have thwarted Trump's rise. Since Obama's failures "inadvertently laid the basis for a powerful backlash," the scholar Andrew Bacevich argues, what he achieved in office "pales in comparison to what happened once he stepped down." In this sense, Obama's presidency is viewed as a missed opportunity, with an ironic result: instead of rescuing the US position in the world, it brought the triumphant post–Cold War era to a decisive and bitter end.[21]

Another angle on Obama's legacy, coming mainly from the right— particularly among the small band of self-proclaimed "Never Trumpers"— emphasizes continuity with his successor. This is an extension of the critique Obama faced during his presidency—that by "downsizing" (he would say "right-sizing") America's global role, he put the country on a course of isolationism and decline. Considered this way, Obama's pledge to start "nation-building at home" is considered not much different than Trump's promise to put "America First." The trends that define the Trump era—such as frustration with "free rider" allies and retreat in the Middle East—are seen as originating with Obama.

This presents a paradox. At once Obama is remembered as flouting the rules, too aggressive and eager to exercise power; or he is seen as too cautious and timid, unwilling to wield America's might. Whether he is accused of doing too much or too little, critics blame Obama for the same thing: the relative decline of US influence. These dueling perceptions of Obama are the product of many factors, from ideology and partisanship to historical amnesia and racial bias. But more generally, they also illustrate the difficulty of categorizing a Middle Way foreign policy— something that has never been easy, but is especially hard when politics are so polarized.

Like Eisenhower and Bush, any dispassionate assessment of Obama's legacy must be measured against what he inherited and what he left behind. He took office at a perilous moment of crises at home and abroad— with a global economic meltdown underway and two wars that were not going well—yet he attempted to stop the bleeding, turn things around where he could, and put policies on a sustainable course. Obama was indelibly influenced by what he inherited, and therefore determined not to leave the same kind of mess to his successor; he said he wanted to leave a "clean barn."[22]

This may seem modest—maybe too modest, and not exactly the stuff meriting a Nobel Peace Prize after less than a year in office. But it is greater than what many presidents achieve. Moreover, it reflects the "better is good" standard Obama set for himself. He explained that a president is like a relay racer (or, for those more inclined toward baseball, a middle relief pitcher), in which one inherits a situation, has a limited opportunity to make a difference, and then hand something off to a successor. "You don't start with a clean slate, and the things you start may not come to full fruition on your timetable," he once said.

That was certainly true for Obama: he did not complete his goal to fundamentally reorient US foreign policy away from its post-9/11 focus on terrorism and toward twenty-first-century challenges like Asia, climate change, and global health security. But he did chart a new direction— one that, in many ways, was validated by the disastrous consequences of his successor's missteps and failures. Like Eisenhower and Bush, Obama left the US in a stronger position to pursue its interests and lead others. Considering the domestic turmoil that followed his tenure, one wonders if his critics still think the US would have been better off with even less "nation building at home" during his presidency or greater military involvement in a places like Syria. Ultimately what mattered most, Obama reflected, is that "at the end of your presidency you can look back and say I made more right calls than not . . . and that America, as best it could in a difficult, dangerous world, was, net, a force for good."[23]

II. IMPLICATIONS

Thinking about the historical evolution of these presidents' legacies, one must ask: why was their foreign policy leadership once perceived to be so disappointing, only to, on balance, improve over time? Before we examine the broad lessons of the Middle Way approach, let's consider some of its shortcomings and implications.

First, even though they tried, these presidents did not—and in reality, could not—leave behind an entirely "clean barn." The world is too complicated for that. They each bequeathed plenty of international problems to their successors. For example, Ike might have kept the United States out of Vietnam in 1954, but he strengthened the US commitment to that country's future; and he passed on an ill-considered plan against Cuba that blew up in the Bay of Pigs. Bush stayed out of Baghdad, yet left the United States entangled in a seemingly Sisyphean effort to "contain" Iraq, and his half-intervention in Somalia and nonintervention in Bosnia in 1992 were passed on to Bill Clinton to sort out. Obama didn't allow Libya and Syria to become another Iraq, bleeding the United States dry, but both were in shambles when he left the White House. And Eisenhower and Obama were criticized for mismanaging major crises with Moscow during their last months in office: the Soviet downing of an American U-2 spy plane in May 1960, and Russia's interference in the 2016 presidential election.

In none of these instances were these presidents attempting to pass the buck or intentionally set up their successors for failure. Rather, they tried to forge a way forward while weighing difficult trade-offs and calibrating risks. They saw this as prudence. Others saw it as abdication of responsibility. Yet one must ask: Would the alternatives have delivered a better outcome? Would different policies, especially those requiring greater US military involvement and more resources, have been preferable? Would these alternatives still have allowed the United States to pursue its long-term interests as these presidents defined it? Asking these questions are essential to following the Middle Way.

These presidents expressed regret for their failure to solve certain problems. Because they were willing to acknowledge the limits of US power, and believed that some things were too difficult to "fix," they measured success by whether they could make a difference at an acceptable price. They did not want to hand off something worse. To them, better is good.

This is another reason why their foreign policy legacies seem modest at first. Americans often impatiently demand more than better; they tend to imagine their greatest presidents as heroes on horseback, sitting upright, sword held high, and acting boldly without apology. Stylistically, Ike, Bush, and Obama all had moments when they fulfilled this image (think of Ike during the Suez crisis, Bush during Iraq, or Obama after the killing of Osama bin Laden). But they believed the most important part of foreign policy leadership was the least glamorous: adeptly handling the unexpected, avoiding mistakes, patiently accumulating successes, and charting a sustainable course.

Too often, foreign policy is judged by what is considered "heroic." Years ago, the scholar Robert Divine observed that because so many of Eisenhower's achievements were "negative in nature"—meaning, he practiced restraint and avoided war—they were judged poorly by those who applied the "activist standard" that tends to dominate foreign policy debates. The same could be said about Bush and Obama. Almost all their perceived failures were when they were accused of doing too little, not too much. These three presidents believed, as historian Jon Meacham describes, that there is great merit in a foreign policy "dedicated more to steadiness than to boldness, more to reform than revolution, more to the management of complexity than the making of mass movements." This may appear unheroic, but in foreign policy, there rarely exists greater virtue.[24]

Staying out of trouble is tough to celebrate. It is hard to rally support for things that did *not* happen, to be credited with small steps or quiet competence when bold strokes hog all the attention. Even if it is the right thing to do, it is not very compelling, and easy to characterize as weakness.

Which brings us to a third complicating factor of these presidents' Middle Way foreign policy legacy: they failed to build a strong domestic constituency for their approach.

Being president means making your case, packaging your agenda, and bringing people along. Each of these presidents tried—after all, they were highly skilled politicians and, in the case of Ike and Obama, popular global icons—but they did not accomplish their goals. Governing was their strength. Their nuance, patience, and compromise, however, fared poorly when making the political sale at home. They found it hard to harmonize with the dyspeptic and hyperpolarized politics of their eras, especially on the right.

Each of them suffered deep political loss: Eisenhower failed to remake the Republican Party, Bush lost reelection, and Obama got stymied by

GOP opposition and was followed by a right-wing populist demagogue. These failures had lasting implications. Subsequent administrations felt compelled to appear "strong," and the American public grew accustomed to promises of quick fixes and simplistic, binary choices. At first glance, this does not make an attractive case for the immediate political rewards of the Middle Way.[25]

HISTORY, HOWEVER, TELLS A DIFFERENT STORY. In retrospect, Middle Way leadership was essential to pursuing US interests and managing complex international change—whether it was the superpower rivalry in the 1950s, the end of the Cold War in the early 1990s, or the geopolitical disruptions of the 2010s. Considering how we now celebrate and memorialize presidents like Eisenhower and Bush—and how we will likely remember Obama—there should be broad appreciation of, and political support for, their brand of foreign policy.

This is especially important to remember as we confront the profound geopolitical uncertainty of the 2020s, marked by the return of nationalism, protectionism, economic distress, and great power competition. Eisenhower, Bush, and Obama each believed in maintaining America's unique strength, and they were all ardent champions of the country's vital leadership role. They sought to recalibrate foreign policy to sustain America's influence across the three most strategically important regions—adjusting its efforts in Europe, Asia, and the Middle East—while at the same time leading the charge to address new global challenges.

Just as they understood the United States could not do everything itself, they realized influence could not rely on military and economic muscle alone. Values mattered too, and for leadership to be effective, it needed to be seen as legitimate and to galvanize others to act. They believed the United States was always better off with capable partners, strong alliances, and effective international institutions. To strengthen America's middle class, they promoted a stable, open political economy rooted in a free and fair trading system. And they embraced the importance of forging strong domestic support for robust American engagement, seeking to maintain strategic solvency by keeping resources in balance, while at the same time pursuing critical investments at home so America could compete in the future.

Perhaps most important, they each prioritized the importance of what Eisenhower called the country's "spiritual strength," recognizing that America's internal health—not only its economic well-being, but protecting free speech and welcoming dissent, nurturing creativity and innovation, promoting opportunity and prosperity, strengthening service and community, and striving for a more inclusive, just society to render a more perfect union—is an essential attribute of its geopolitical advantage.[26]

In their own imperfect ways, these presidents championed the expansion of rights for citizens—for example, Eisenhower and school integration, Bush and disabled Americans, and Obama and gay marriage—and sought to foster a broad and vibrant civil society. All this, they were convinced, contributed to America's exceptionalism—which they saw not as an immutable fact or self-regulating machine, but as something requiring constant effort.

This is what Bush meant when he called for building a "kinder and gentler" nation and a tradition of service through "a thousand points of light," and why Obama extolled America's resilience and its capacity for self-correction and renewal. Like Eisenhower, they understood that a successful foreign policy begins at home, rooted in a common set of ideas and ideals, enabling America to engender confidence, inspire, and set an example. "It is essential in the world struggle that the world know something about our good intentions, latent strength, [and] respect for the rights of others," Ike wrote in his diary in 1950. "But the truth must be nailed, bannerlike to a staff, and we must do that by convincing the whole world that our announced intentions of peace are the truth."[27]

These beliefs, and this style of leadership, are not lost relics; they are an enduring reflection of America's national character. At moments when many rightly call for reinventing US foreign policy to make it more relevant for the twenty-first century, we would be wise to heed these lessons from history—because in essence, the kind of leadership required is not necessarily so new. Looking ahead, leaders must be confident enough to embrace this Middle Way —and citizens need to remember how it reflects some of the best parts of the American past, set their expectations accordingly, and reward leaders who follow the tradition.[28]

Therefore, let us conclude by examining a few broad lessons to glean from these presidents' leadership, which can serve as a guide for the future.

III. LESSONS

Recognize the Limits of Power

Eisenhower, Bush, and Obama aimed to enhance America's power abroad and use it to pursue the national interest. They viewed the United States as an indispensable force for good with an obligation to lead. At the same time, they recognized that despite America's superior power, it could not solve every problem—it, too, had limits on what it could do.

Because the United States possesses tremendous capabilities and spends so much more than any other country to project its influence, it is tempting to think trade-offs are not necessary, events can be fully controlled, and everything has a solution. Yet these presidents teach us that it is best to approach policymaking with humility and with the awareness that the United States often gets in the most trouble abroad when it tries to do too much, not too little.

For them, restraint was not a dirty word. Instead, they saw it as one of the most important but least appreciated qualities in a commander-in-chief. Since statecraft is about making choices—after all, doing more of everything is not a strategy—they understood that deciding what *not* to do is as important as what one does. Of course, restraint did not always apply to every circumstance, and each of these presidents chose to act when he thought US interests so warranted. Neither does restraint equal inaction. Policy choices rarely boil down to a binary choice of doing something or doing nothing.[29]

As the Protestant theologian, historian, and philosopher Reinhold Niebuhr once observed, Americans need "a sense of modesty about the virtue, wisdom and power available to us for the resolution of [history's] perplexities." The traits these presidents displayed—to maintain humility and eschew hubris; to acknowledge imperfections; to understand that the exercise of power, however just, can bring tragedy; and to recognize that one's idealism is never as virtuous as one thinks—fit squarely in the Niebuhr tradition. These presidents sought to steer between those he describes who would "renounce the responsibilities of power for the sake of preserving the purity of our soul," and those who would deny "any ambiguity of good and evil in our actions by the frantic insistence that any measure in a good cause must be unequivocally virtuous." In this way, Niebuhr should be seen as the Middle Way's prophet.[30]

Niebuhr was one of the towering intellectuals of the mid-twentieth century—George Kennan once described him as "undoubtedly the greatest moral philosopher of our age"—and his warnings of the "illusion of American omnipotence" still resonate. Although perhaps best remembered as the author of the Serenity Prayer, he was a shrewd critic of American innocence and its addiction to power. Yet this self-awareness of flaws and limits did not mean the United States should withdraw or appease. He made the case for American active leadership that was sober, realistic, and morally grounded.[31]

These three presidents did not engage such ideas the same way. Eisenhower and Niebuhr worked at Columbia University at the same time yet rarely crossed paths. Bush apparently did not reflect upon Niebuhr at all. In contrast, Obama studied his work and drew on his teachings explicitly. Whether conscious of it or not, they all reflected the Niebuhrian approach to world affairs; they pursued foreign policy as "a method of finding proximate solutions to insoluble problems."[32]

This recalls lessons from an entirely different discipline: medicine. These presidents practiced "Hippocratic diplomacy" because their dilemmas, in fundamental ways, were very similar to those faced by doctors. They had to handle complex, chronic problems, navigate uncertainties, and act upon imperfect information, all while grappling with finite capabilities and weighing the consequences of intervention. As the surgeon Atul Gawande explains, physicians must recognize limits without illusion and proceed with care. "Sometimes we can offer a cure, sometimes a salve, sometimes not even that," he writes. "But whatever we can offer, our interventions, and the risks and sacrifices they entail, are justified only if they serve the larger aims." The same can be said about an effective foreign policy.[33]

Like doctors, foreign policy professionals are trained to solve problems—and leaders are rewarded for their ability to fix things. Because of this, both can fall prey to "commission bias," or the tendency to favor action over inaction. To acknowledge limits, therefore, runs counter to their common ethos. What Gawande writes about clinicians applies to foreign policy practitioners: "nothing is more threatening to who you think you are than a patient with a problem you cannot solve."[34]

Appreciate the Value of Incremental Change

These presidents wanted to do big things. They were willing to take significant risks. They proved ready to take bold actions, often acting with—as Obama liked to quote Dr. Martin Luther King, Jr.—"the fierce urgency of now." At the same time, they appreciated that the most consequential changes are often incremental. "Perfection is not quickly reached," Eisenhower explained in a 1960 letter. "Just as a tree does not instantly reach full stature when it is planted as a seedling, progress must be attained by steps, some of them at times discouragingly small." Obama sometimes referred to his achievements as a "starter home," because while they were better than what came before, they were just a first step and over time would require improvements.[35]

Since the public usually wants visible progress or demands immediate results—especially as information hastens and attention spans shorten—it can be hard for presidents to get credit for incremental change. Nevertheless, it is a vital part of their job. For a president to get anything done, as Bush once put it, they must be "steady and prudent and able." Or, as Obama said in a 2015 interview, "sometimes your job is just to make stuff work."[36]

Over a century ago, one of the most astute observers of Washington, Henry Adams, himself the direct descendant of two presidents, argued that the American chief executive "resembles the commander of a ship at sea. He must have a helm to grasp, a course to steer, a port to seek." This metaphor aptly describes how these three presidents saw themselves—and they each described their circumstances, and the value of incrementalism, in similar terms.[37]

A president's task, Obama explained, is "to make incremental improvements or try to steer the ocean liner two degrees north or south so that ten years from now, suddenly we're in a very different place." Yet as Obama experienced, this kind of slow, steady, sensible pace of progress requires patience and persistence that is often in short supply. "At the moment people may feel like we needed a fifty-degree turn," he said, but the danger is capsizing. "If I turn fifty degrees, the whole ship turns. And you can't turn fifty degrees . . . progress is never instantaneous, it is always partial [and] always happens in fits and starts."[38]

In a 1957 letter, Eisenhower used a similar image to describe his own decisions: "Possibly I am something like a ship which, buffeted and pounded by wind and wave, is still afloat and manages in spite of frequent tacks and turnings to stay generally along its plotted course and continues to make some, even if slow and painful, headway."[39]

And for Bush, who perhaps felt most at ease when aboard his Fountain speedboat, *Fidelity*, off the rocky coast of Maine, such nautical metaphors offered lessons for America's role in the world. He warned against a "foreign policy [that] seems like a tiny sail boat adrift on a violent sea, tossed in one direction or another by every gust of wind." If that happened, he warned, "neither friend nor foe can look upon us for steady, reliable leadership," with the result being their "beginning to pursue their own course, independent of American interests."[40]

Therefore, a president needs a clear vision of America's global goals, a strategy for how to achieve them, an understanding of the steps required, and the patience and persistence to stick with them. This means appreciating our presidents for living for more than the moment, and giving credit for the steady, persistent, often quiet skill required to get things done. Late-night comics may have mocked Bush's determination to "stay the course," just as critics dismissed Obama's admonition to hit "singles

and doubles." But in fundamental ways, their commitment to incrementalism proved wise.

Social science has long-established incrementalism—or what is sometimes referred to as "muddling through"—as an essential method for
bringing about major change and avoiding mistakes. And once again, it
is useful to draw lessons from the medical profession. Although we often
herald physicians for sweeping, heroic acts to cure problems (like major
surgical interventions and vaccines), often it's the small steps (like primary care and masks) that make a big difference over time. As Gawande
argues, "success is not about the episodic, momentary victories, though
they do play a role. It is about the longer view of incremental steps that
produce sustained progress." Valuing prudent, patient approaches means,
Gawande writes, "discovering the heroism of the incremental."[41]

To make this possible, we must rethink the expectations we place on a
president. "One of the things you learn," Obama observed, is that "as powerful as this office is, you have limited bandwidth." And things seem to be
only getting worse. In many ways, the weight of the job has grown heavier;
the incentives for quick results greater; the measure for success impossible
to meet. More is being demanded than ever can be delivered, and presidential retraint is too often seen as a liability rather than a virtue.[42]

This has a particularly distorting effect on foreign policy. Because
challenges tend to be escalated, threats hyped, and remedies oversold, the
incentives American presidents face often lead to trouble. Therefore, it is
important to recognize that short-term thinking, bombast, and clever eye-
catching moves may garner the most attention and make the social media
swarms momentarily happy, but they distract from the long, slow, tough
incremental work often required to achieve lasting results over the long
term.[43]

Reward Strategic Foresight

Strategic foresight is a prerequisite of successful incremental change.
We need our foreign policy leaders to be clear-eyed about the future,

imagining what is possible and planning for it. Of course, this is very hard to do. Especially in times of uncertainty, there are powerful inducements to seek refuge in the more predictable short term and act in the moment with little regard for future interests. There are also significant obstacles to making tough choices today to address challenges that will arrive on a distant tomorrow. Consequently, we must appreciate the significant psychological, social, and structural impediments to focusing on long-term goals—let alone achieving them.[44]

"One of the most important necessities of the office is vision," Eisenhower wrote in 1968. A president must "be able to look down the road of the future and see the needs of the nation. Coupled with this is the courage to implement this vision with the necessary hard decisions, despite almost sure criticism—often actual vilification—from the press, the opposition party, and even from within the incumbent's own party."[45]

In their own ways, Eisenhower, Bush, and Obama each practiced strategic foresight. They tried to think ahead, invest in imagination, and maintain the necessary discipline and perserverance to make long-term decisions. In this way, they were like Wall Street value investors, focused on future payoffs and paying less attention to the noise of market fluctuations. They understood this approach entailed possibly taking some short-term hits, but saw the larger benefit—even if it was not appreciated until after they departed office. "I will make smarter political decisions than a lot of guys who are pros," Eisenhower once said, "because they have gotten used to the narrow quick advantage, rather than taking a look at the longer range."[46]

This required a healthy degree of patience, which is key to a successful foreign policy. Policies need time to work, and leaders must stick to the painstaking, often unglamorous work required to get results. It is therefore fitting that Bush's favorite baseball player was Lou Gehrig, the great Yankee first baseman celebrated for showing up every day, being exceptionally good at his job, putting in the hard work, and being humble enough to await history's recognition. Turning to another sport, Obama once compared his circumstance to being like an NFL quarterback dropping back for a pass: "you can't be distracted by what's around you, you've got to be looking downfield." To extend the metaphor, while the play needs time to develop, one must also act before the defense closes in and you get sacked. Thus while we need leaders to focus on the long term—and should reward them for doing so—we also must recognize that often the essence of leadership is knowing when to call an audible and change the play.[47]

Maintain Tragic Optimism

The greatest statesmen think with tragic optimism. We should want our presidents to be idealistic and determined to use American power to improve the world, so long as they are tempered by a sense of tragedy. Again, maintaining a tragic sensibility is not succumbing to pessimism. It means mixing sobriety and optimism—combining the knowledge that while hardship is inevitable, and some problems are beyond our grasp to solve, there is much the United States can do if it remains creative, hopeful, and forward-looking.[48]

To reflect on how this outlook shaped the presidencies of Eisenhower, Bush, and Obama, consider their final messages to the American people. How they chose to say goodbye says a lot about their concept of leadership and vision for America's global role—and for the hard work that each thought remained.

When Eisenhower addressed the nation for the last time from the White House in January 1961—in a televised speech most famous for its warning about the influence of the military-industrial complex—he conveyed the sensibility of tragic optimism that he worried was disappearing from modern life. He wanted to warn of the consequences if this was lost.

Eisenhower spoke that evening as "one who has witnessed the horror and lingering sadness of war," who believed that while he brought the world closer to peace, America still faced dangers of "indefinite duration." He urged his fellow citizens to remain confident but eschew arrogance, reminding them that global leadership depends not simply on the aggregate of US power, but how that power is used. Americans, he argued, should always remain true to their principles while being "confident but humble." After a decade of peace and prosperity, he was proud of the success the United States achieved, yet he counseled that "we should take nothing for granted."

Looking out at the world, Eisenhower projected an outlook to help Americans navigate between the impulses of hubris, complacency, and resignation. This perspective reflected his unique experience, the kind he worried would be lost to the next generation.[49]

Three decades later, Bush evoked Eisenhower's tragic optimism in two speeches as he prepared to leave the White House. After an unexpectedly dramatic four years and reelection defeat, he wanted to send a final message to the American people about their country's global role and his perspective on leadership.

Speaking in December 1992 at Texas A&M (the location of his future presidential library), Bush described the Cold War's peaceful end as a testament to how "dreams were made real." He celebrated the opportunity to build a wider democratic peace. But he warned against "voices sounding the retreat," arguing that "the alternative to American leadership is not more security for our citizens but less, not the flourishing of American principles but their isolation." He described American leadership as "indispensable"—sounding a theme that would define US foreign policy for the next three decades.

Destiny, Bush said, is a matter of choice, not chance, because "we can either shape our times, or we can let the times shape us," and because "we can never safely assume that our future will be an improvement over the past." In exercising its power abroad, the United States needed to be "hard nosed" about its interests but agile in how it pursued them. It must recognize, he said, that "there can be no single or simple set of guidelines for foreign policy."[50]

A few weeks later, in January 1993, Bush further elaborated on these themes when he stood before four thousand West Point cadets gathered in—appropriately enough—Eisenhower Hall located on the bucolic New York campus. Bush sought to offer a rationale for his use of military power (which at the time he had done more often than any president since Lyndon B. Johnson), but he advised against using any rigid formula.

"Anyone looking for scientific certitude is in for a disappointment," he cautioned. Yet Bush acknowledged how tempting the use of force can be. "Sometimes the decision not to use force, to stay our hand," he said, is "just as difficult as the decision to send our soldiers in battle."

Bush repeated his warning that while the United States could not be the world's policeman, neither should it succumb to the folly of isolation. He described the multifaceted nature of leadership—political and diplomatic, economic and military, moral and spiritual—and stressed it could not simply be asserted. Leadership "must be demonstrated," he said. "Leadership requires formulating worthy goals, persuading others of their virtue, and contributing one's share of the common effort and then some. Leadership takes time. It takes patience. It takes work."[51]

These themes were resonant in Obama's January 2017 farewell address. Obama returned to his hometown, Chicago, for the occasion, where a rapturous crowd of eighteen thousand cheered him on at an event overflowing with nostalgia for his historic election-night victory speech eight years earlier, and a brooding sense of the turbulence to come.

Few of those watching needed a reminder that tragedy still existed. If anything, in the wake of the 2016 election, most needed a pep talk. Obama did his best, explaining that with so many corners of the globe gripped by fear, "we must guard against a weakening of the values that make us who we are." He called for "practical problem-solving," warned against quick fixes, and acknowledged that progress is always uneven.

Nevertheless, Obama said he was leaving office more hopeful than when he entered. Because of America's unique attributes, he said, "the future should be ours." Yet just as Ike advised Americans to take nothing for granted, and Bush reminded them that destiny is a choice, Obama warned his fellow citizens that success was not inevitable. America's potential "will only be realized if our democracy works," he stressed. "Only if our politics better reflects the decency of our people; only if all of us, regardless of our affiliation or particular interests, help restore the sense of common purpose that we so badly need right now." In other words, for America to realize its potential, it needs leaders with the tragic optimism of the Middle Way.[52]

Embrace Moderation as a Virtue

Moderation, compromise, and civility are the essential virtues of a functioning democracy. They are also the key ingredients of sound foreign policy leadership.

Because global politics are so complex, and because so many problems defy easy solutions, leaders must balance competing interests, maintain a sense of proportion, and combine ambition with humility. In his book on the character of leadership, columnist David Brooks argues that we should want statesmen who are "passionate about [their] ends but deliberate about the proper means to realize them." We need them to understand, Brooks writes, "the damage leaders do when they get things wrong is greater than the benefits they create when they get things right. Therefore caution is the proper attitude, an awareness of limits the foundation of wisdom."[53]

It is easy to ridicule this as wishy-washy and selling-out—to think that suspicion of absolutes is somehow weak, and that pure and authentic leadership only resides on the extremes. However, as Bush wrote to a friend in 1964, we should recognize "this mean humorless philosophy which says everybody should agree on everything is not good . . . when the word moderation becomes a dirty word we have some soul searching to do."[54]

Just as decisive leadership requires fortitude, it takes backbone to acknowledge that not every problem has a simple fix. Having the right idea is important, but that is not enough; one must have the ability to get things done, informed by the understanding that progress is often partial and compromise is inevitable. These presidents understood that policymaking is always messy—it is a product of weighing risks and making trade-offs among competing interests. "If you are doing big, hard things," Obama observes, "then there is going to be some hair on it—there's going to be some aspects of it that aren't clean and neat and immediately elicit applause from everybody."[55]

The ability to get things done, however imperfect that can be, is a key ingredient of global influence. After Obama left office, he reflected that one of the things that surprised him most about being president is how even America's adversaries looked to the country to "solve problems and keep things moving." Yet the challenge, as he experienced acutely, is that when Washington becomes so dysfunctional and unable to accomplish anything, it "undermines one of our greatest assets."[56]

Eisenhower understood this too. He stressed the importance of "maintaining a respectable image of American life before the world" and that "among the qualities that the American government must exhibit is dignity." Eisenhower, like Bush and Obama, believed that America's strength abroad relied not only on its example of power, but the power of its example. "In war and peace," Ike wrote in 1960, "I've had no respect for the desk-pounder, and have despised the loud and slick talker. If my own ideas and practices have sprung from weakness, I do not know. But they were and are deliberate, or, rather, natural to me. They are not accidental."[57]

* * *

Eisenhower, as a founding father of the Middle Way, deserves the final word. During the last weeks of 1968, as the seventy-eight-year-old former president lay ailing in Ward Eight at Walter Reed Army Hospital in Washington, he wanted to make one last plea for his style of leadership. Writing an article for *Reader's Digest*, he set out to cobble together an optimistic outlook during a time of profound political turbulence.[58]

The titles of the various drafts, which can be found today in the archives of the Eisenhower Presidential Library in Abilene, Kansas, help illustrate the point. The first draft began as "The Way of Common Sense," with the penultimate draft entitled "The Middle Way Is the Best Way." Yet the published version, which appeared in print shortly after his death in March 1969, is a better reflection of those divisive times, and perhaps our own: "We Must Avoid the Perils of Extremism."

Ike expressed his worries about the "emergence of a new extremism in our land," but he refused to be pessimistic about America's future. "The effect of these voices," he wrote, "few in number but strong in decibels, is to create the impression that our country no longer heeds the rule of reason and tolerance."

Applying the themes he first articulated publicly two decades earlier in his St. Louis speech to the turmoil of the late 1960s, Eisenhower saw the problem at both ends of the political spectrum. The left "wants to socialize everything," while the right "wants to turn back the clock a half-century." He urged leaders to pursue a "strategy of common sense," navigating a course "great enough to accommodate all reasonable citizens, from the moderate conservative to the moderate liberal." These are the people, he reminded, "who get things done." The Middle Way is not the approach of some "fence sitter," he argued. "It often takes more courage to occupy the Center than any other position in the political arena, for you are then subject to attack from both flanks."

A healthy democratic process, in foreign policy and otherwise, requires a willingness to engage in good faith give-and-take about a shared set of facts. Compromise, Eisenhower wrote, "is a highly useful tool in the arsenal of achievement, in some cases the only tool that will do the job. If there are to be solutions, a president must work with others, [and] bend a little this way or that within the limits of his basic principles." Although never spoken, these words were, in a way, Ike's last.

In moments of such extreme polarization and geopolitical upheaval—and when the world looks to the United States for enlightened leadership but questions whether it can deliver—the argument for decency, bipartisanship, and pragmatic problem-solving is compelling. This approach is hardly the stuff of frenzied passion and instant gratification. That's the point. Especially in these moments, such steady and thoughtful leadership of the kind exemplified by Eisenhower, Bush, and Obama—those with the courage to follow the Middle Way—can be the path to redemption.

ACKNOWLEDGMENTS

This is a book about the past, but it is very much a product of its time. The process started in the months leading up to the 2016 presidential election, when I began to consider what Barack Obama's foreign policy legacy might be. Comparing him to other presidents, I became struck by the shared outlook and approach with what seemed two unlikely predecessors, Dwight D. Eisenhower and George H. W. Bush. Digging further, I found these three presidents not only had similar perspectives on American leadership and the conduct of foreign policy, but they also became embattled with many of the same critiques and political forces aligned against them, revealing something about not only their own eras, but current debates about America in the world. In a way, spending the last few years reexamining this history and rethinking these leaders also became a kind of intellectual refuge, sheltering me from the severe turbulence of the current moment—and providing a reminder of what may be possible again someday.

Throughout this journey of research and writing, I have accumulated more debts than I can possibly repay. This starts with the scholars upon whose shoulders this book stands, many of whom kindly took time to offer me their insights and ideas. My conversations with David Eisenhower, William Ewald, Walter McDougall, David Nichols, and Will Hitchcock shaped my thinking about Eisenhower and set me in the right direction, and I am especially grateful to Will for helping me get the most out of the impressive archives at the Eisenhower Library in Abilene, Kansas.

Jeff Engel's encouragement and wise counsel about all things Bush proved indispensable, and his tips about research at the Bush Library in College Station, Texas were invaluable. I also thank Jeff for providing me the audio recordings of fascinating interviews he conducted with Bush about his time in China in the 1970s. James Graham Wilson also generously shared his massive archive of declassified documents from the Bush Library. Unfortunately, it will still be years until we see any of Obama's presidential records, which I am confident will prove to be a historical goldmine, but I benefitted greatly from the advice and insights of two who know Obama and his foreign policy best, Denis McDonough and Ben Rhodes.

I could not have written this book without institutional support from two wonderful organizations. First and foremost, the German Marshall Fund of the United States, which has been my happy home for over five years. One could not ask for a more talented group of colleagues and friends on both sides of the Atlantic. I am forever grateful to Karen Donfried, who encouraged this project from the very beginning and made sure it remained a priority among all the other urgent matters involved with helping to manage an institution as exciting and dynamic as GMF. Karen also gave the manuscript a very careful read and, thanks to her keen insights, made it much better.

My GMF colleagues Steven Keil and Sophie Arts helped keep things running, and a group of superb GMF interns, including Helen Simpson, Robert McWilliams, and Elliot Smith, tracked down numerous facts and articles. The multi-talented Itai Barsade was an essential partner at every stage of this effort, assisting with the research, brainstorming about ideas, editing drafts, hunting for photos, providing counsel, managing my time, keeping me on task, and lifting my morale when I needed it. I am grateful for all his help and friendship.

The University of Pennsylvania's Perry World House provided crucial intellectual and research support, including by hosting a lively workshop just as the book was taking shape. During the past several years I have learned so much and drawn inspiration from Perry World House's wonderful student fellows and faculty. Bill Burke-White, Mike Horowitz, and John Gans have been steadfast allies and friends, and I especially thank John for many, many hours of conversations about this book, for giving it such a close edit, and for offering an abundance of astute suggestions to make it better. I also received terrific research assistance from two very talented Penn/Perry World House students: Lauren Kahn helped get this project out of the gate, and Conor Donnan helped bring it across the finish line.

Writing can often be a slog, but I find archival research to be a true joy. For all their advice and assistance navigating their research collections, I am grateful to David Holbrook and Tim Rives at the Dwight D. Eisenhower Library; Douglas Campbell and Cody D. McMillian of the George H. W. Bush Library; and the staffs at Princeton's Seeley G. Mudd Manuscript Library and the Manuscript Division of the Library of Congress. For help finding photos, I thank Mary Burtzloff of the Eisenhower Library and Mary Finch at the Bush Library.

During the past few years I have had the opportunity to test-drive some of these ideas in short essays and reviews, which helped refine my thinking and provide raw materials for portions of this book. Here I especially thank Jacob Heilbrunn of the *National Interest*, Kevin Baron of *Defense One*, and Brian Rosenwald and Nicole Hemmer, who coedit the *Washington Post*'s fantastic "Made by History" series.

As always, I am indebted to numerous colleagues, old friends and mentors who took time out of their very busy schedules to read—and in some cases, reread—drafts of this book, providing so many smart comments, pushing me further, and saving me from many errors (although of course, any remaining mistakes are my own). In addition to those mentioned above, I thank Hal Brands, Bill Burns, Matan Chorev, Jim Goldgeier, Phil Gordon, and James Graham Wilson. Seth Center not only read a draft, but hosted a fun lunch discussion to discuss its main ideas and give it a thorough critique. My friend Kurt Campbell deserves a special shout-out both for his feedback and for allowing me to use his Iron Bell Run Farm as a retreat during a critical stage of the drafting.

Three scholars deserve special mention for the many ways they assisted along the way—talking through ideas, sharing insights, offering guidance, and providing incisive comments on a draft manuscript. They are a source of inspiration, and I feel very fortunate to call them mentors and friends. Richard Immerman, one of the greatest scholars of Eisenhower and U.S. diplomatic history, was full of wisdom and kindness. For many years I have learned so much from Melvyn Leffler, another giant of diplomatic history, and his enthusiasm and support for this book proved vital. And Robert Jervis, a titan of many fields and my teacher for a quarter-century, once again helped me from beginning to end, asking the tough questions, sending along article citations and research tips, and providing overall encouragement.

My agent, Larry Weissman, helped me translate this idea into a book, and I am grateful to him for sticking with it and bringing me to the terrific team at Oxford University Press. Dave McBride has been an encouraging editor, Holly Mitchell made sure things ran smoothly, and Cheryl Merritt skillfully managed the book's production.

Finally, and most important, thanks to my family for putting up with my many distractions and absences while writing this book, especially during the last few months when we found ourselves all stuck at home virtually going to school and work. Lucas and Aerin are the joys of my life—they always made things fun and kept me grounded. And this book is dedicated to Heather, because none of this would have been possible without her love and support.

Washington, D.C.
September 2020

NOTES

ABBREVIATIONS

AP   Joseph and Stewart Alsop Papers, Library of Congress, Washington, DC
APP   The American Presidency Project, UC Santa Barbara
ATB   *All the Best, George Bush* by George H. W. Bush, Scribner, 2013
AWF   Ann Whitman File, Eisenhower Library, Abilene, Kansas
AWT   *A World Transformed* by George Bush and Brent Scowcroft, Knopf, 1998.
EJHP   Emmet John Hughes Papers, Mudd Library, Princeton University
EL   Dwight D. Eisenhower Library, Abilene, Kansas
FRUS   Foreign Relations of the United States, Department of State
GHWBL   George H. W. Bush Library, College Station, Texas
JABP   James A. Baker III Papers, Mudd Library, Princeton University
PDDE   Papers of Dwight David Eisenhower, Johns Hopkins University Press

PREFACE

1. Bush Press Conference, March 22, 1990. APP; William Safire, "The Grave Consequence," *New York Times*, April 2, 1990; Francis X. Clines, "Lithuanian Police Guard Parliament as Pressure Rises," *New York Times*, March 28, 1990.
2. Helen Dewar, "Soldier, Peacemaker, President," *Washington Post*, March 28, 1990; *Congressional Record*, March 27, 1990, pp. 5435–5442; Bush remarks at a luncheon commemorating the Dwight D. Eisenhower Centennial, March 27, 1990, APP; GHWB Presidential Records, Daily Files, March 27, 1990, GHWBL.
3. Bush letter to Obama, ATB, p. 874.
4. Obama news conference, February 15, 2011, APP; Obama remarks on presenting the Presidential Medal of Freedom, February 15, 2011, APP; Perry Bacon Jr., "Presidential Medal of Freedom Given to Former President George H. W. Bush, 14 Others," *Washington Post*, February 15, 2011; Todd Gillman, "Obama Honors Former President George H. W. Bush with Medal of Freedom," *Dallas News*, February 16, 2011.

INTRODUCTION

1. Gelb, *Power Rules*, 279–280.
2. Text of General Eisenhower's address before Bar Association, reprinted in the *New York Times*, September 6, 1949; William M. Blair, "Eisenhower Urges 'Middle Road' Way," *New York Times*, September 6, 1949.
3. Eisenhower letter to Bradford Grethen Chynoweth, July 1, 1954, PDDE, vol. 15, pp. 1185. See also Susan Eisenhower, *How Ike Led*, 121–141.
4. Quoted in Kabaservice, *Rule and Ruin*, 412.
5. Bush letter to Eisenhower, July 21, 1964, DDE Post-Presidential Papers 1964, Signature Files, Box 3, EL; Eisenhower letter to Bush, January 16, 1965, DDE Post-Presidential Papers 1965, Principal File, Box 22, EL; Eisenhower letter to Bush, September 13, 1966, DDE Post-Presidential Papers 1965, Principal File, Box 3, EL.
6. William J. Eaton, "Stars Are Born, George Murphy Directing," *Miami Herald*, January 25, 1968.
7. George Bush for President announcement speech, May 1, 1979, available at http://www.4president.org; Bush speech at Republican National Convention, August 17, 1980; George Bush remarks and question-and-answer session at Luncheon for White House Journalists, March 31, 1989, APP.
8. Jack Nelson, "Regard for Eisenhower Sheds Light on Bush Style," *Los Angeles Times*, September 11, 1988; David Broder, "He's Like Ike," *Los Angeles Times*, September 13, 1989.
9. Chait, *Audacity*, 237; David Swerdlick, "Barack Obama, Conservative," *Washington Post*, November 22, 2019; Philip Wallach and Justus Myers, "The Conservative Governing Disposition," *National Affairs* (Summer 2014); E. J. Dionne, "Obama Foreign Policy Looks Like Bush 41," *Washington Post*, November 28, 2008; Blake Hounshell, "George H. W. Obama?" *Foreign Policy*, April 14, 2010; Fareed Zakaria, "On Foreign Policy, Why Barack Is Like Ike," *Time*, December 19, 2012; Peter Beinart, "He's Like Ike," *Atlantic*, May 29, 2014; James Traub, "Obama's Not Carter—He's Eisenhower," *Foreign Policy*, March 2014; David Ignatius, "Obama Can Be Like Ike," *Washington Post*, January 9, 2013; Nye, *Presidential Leadership*, 146–151.
10. Barack Obama, "Commencement Address at the United States Military Academy in West Point, New York," May 28, 2014, APP.
11. David Brooks, "Obama Admires Bush," *New York Times*, May 16, 2008; Meacham, *Destiny and Power*, 599–600; Obama interview at James A. Baker III Institute, Rice University, November 27, 2018; also see Chollet, *The Long Game*, 206–208.
12. Quoted in Bill Scher, "The Fiercest Democratic Debate in 2020 Is about Barack Obama," *Politico*, July 29, 2019.
13. Barack Obama, "Address to the Nation on the Drawdown of United States Military Personnel in Afghanistan," June 22, 2011, APP.
14. See Ewald, *Eisenhower the President*, 170.
15. Michael Duffy, "The Incredible Shrinking President," *Time*, June 29, 1992.
16. Engel, *When the World Seemed New*, 6.
17. Quoted in Nichols, *Eisenhower 1956*, 96.

18. Jeffrey Goldberg, "A Senior White House Official Defines the Trump Doctrine: 'We're America, Bitch,'" *Atlantic*, June 18, 2018.
19. Eisenhower speech before American Bar Association, September 6, 1949.
20. Bush self-typed memo to Peggy Noonan, July 15, 1988, ATB, p. 391.
21. Obama address to the 71st session of the United Nations General Assembly, September 20, 2016, APP.

CHAPTER 1

1. Eisenhower letter to Gabriel Stilian, August 23, 1951, PDDE, vol. 12, pp. 488–490. I thank Richard Immerman for pointing out this letter to me; see also Arthur Larson, *Eisenhower: The President Nobody Knew* (Charles Scribner's Sons, 1968), 96–97.
2. Richard Immerman, "Confessions of an Eisenhower Revisionist: An Agonizing Reappraisal," *Diplomatic History* (Summer 1990): 328.
3. Kissinger, *White House Years*, 54; Alexander L. George, "The Operational Code: A Neglected Approach to the Study of Political Leaders and Decision-Making," *International Studies Quarterly* (June 1969); William Inboden, "Statecraft, Decision-Making, and the Varieties of Historical Experience: A Taxonomy," *Journal of Strategic Studies* (2014): 307.
4. George, "The Operational Code"; Gawande, *The Checklist Manifesto*; Gaddis, *On Grand Strategy*, 102–103.
5. See Jervis, *Perception and Misperception*, 217–287.
6. Eisenhower letter to Swede Hazlett, July 19, 1947, PDDE, vol. 8, p. 1837.
7. Eisenhower letter to Lucius Du Bignon Clay, February 9, 1952, PDDE, vol. 13, p. 963; Eisenhower diary entry for January 22, 1952, Ferrell, ed., *The Eisenhower Diaries*, 210; Immerman, "Confessions of an Eisenhower Revisionist," 325.
8. Eisenhower letter to George Arthur Sloan, March 20, 1952, PDDE, vol. 13, pp. 1097–1104; Greenstein, *The Hidden-Hand Presidency*, 46–47.
9. Eisenhower diary entry for March 5, 1951, PDDE, vol. 12, p. 91; Eisenhower letter to J. E. Theophilus, August 9, 1954, AWF, Name Series, Box 25, DDE Philosophies Folder, EL; Eisenhower letter to Edward John Bermingham, February 8, 1951, PDDE, vol. 12, p. 38.
10. Nixon, *Six Crises*, 168–169; Eisenhower letter to Swede Hazlett, November 18, 1957, PDDE, vol. 18, p. 578.
11. Bush and Scowcroft, AWT, p. 16; Naftali, *George H. W. Bush*, 12, 16–17.
12. George Bush address before the Philadelphia World Affairs Council, June 6, 1979, Campaign Background Book, Box 128, Folder 1, JABP.
13. George Bush address at University of Houston Commencement, August 13, 1977, Box 20, Folder 4, JABP.
14. On Bush's views on Vietnam, see George Bush letter to Richard Mack, April 14, 1968, GHWB Collection, Personal Papers, Congressional File, General, GHWBL; Engel, *When the World Seemed New*, 45.
15. Naftali, *George H. W. Bush*, 15; Bush, *41: A Portrait of My Father*, 72–73; George Bush speech at Dallas Council on World Affairs and the Dallas United Nations Association, May 28, 1971, Presidential Daily Files, March 8, 1989, GHWBL.

16. Jeffrey Engel interview with George H. W. Bush, July 8, 2005, author's files; Bush diary entry for January 25, 1971, ATB, p. 137.

17. Rhodes, *The World as It Is*, 47–48.

18. Rhodes, *The World as It Is*, 49; Obama, *Audacity of Hope*, 303–314; Obama interview at Baker Institute, November 27, 2018.

19. Jeffrey Goldberg, "The Obama Doctrine," *Atlantic* (April 2016); Garrow, *Rising Star*, 230–233; Michael Fullilove, "The World's Community Organizer," Brookings Institution, September 18, 2010; quoted in Fred Kaplan, "The Realist," *Politico Magazine* (March/April 2014).

20. Obama, *Audacity of Hope*, 303; Goldberg, "The Obama Doctrine."

21. Goldberg, "The Obama Doctrine"; Obama, *Dreams from My Father*, 347–349.

22. Eisenhower, *At Ease*, 185; see Eisenhower letter to Fox Conner, July 4, 1942, *PDDE*, vol. 1, pp. 369–370.

23. Eisenhower, *At Ease*, 187.

24. See Eisenhower, *At Ease*, 187; Susan Eisenhower, *How Ike Led*, 163; Smith, *Eisenhower in War and Peace*, 64–66; Galambos, *Eisenhower: Becoming Leader*, 49–52; Newton, *Eisenhower: White House Years*, 31–32.

25. Engel, ed., *The China Diary*, 160.

26. Engel, *The China Diary*, 286; Jeffrey Engel interview with George Bush, July 8, 2005.

27. Engel, *The China Diary*, 357.

28. Engel interview with Bush.

29. Engel, *The China Diary*, 404–405.

30. Obama, *Dreams from My Father*, 32–37; Remnick, *The Bridge*, 58–62.

31. Rhodes, *The World as It Is*, 165.

32. Obama, *Dreams from My Father*, 45–46; Garrow, *Rising Star*, 74.

33. Obama, *Audacity of Hope*, 280; Obama, *Dreams from My Father*, 47.

34. Garrow, *Rising Star*, 73–74; "Remarks by the President at the University of Indonesia, November 10, 2010," APP.

35. Halberstam, *The Fifties*, 214–215.

36. Hoganson, *The Heartland*.

37. Kaplan, *Earning the Rockies*, 173.

38. Eisenhower, *At Ease*, 37; Timothy Rives, "Eisenhower, the Frontier, and the New Deal," *Prologue* (Fall 2015); Eisenhower and Eisenhower, *Going Home to Glory*, 191; Halberstam, *The Fifties*, 245; Goodpaster quoted in Melanson, "Foundations of Eisenhower's Foreign Policy," in Melanson and Mayers, *Reevaluating Eisenhower*, 49; Eisenhower quote from Middle Way Draft, Ben Hibbs Papers, 1961–69, Article Drafts, Box 2, EL.

39. Cramer, *Being Poppy*, 59–69; Walt Harrington, "Born to Run: On the Privilege of Being George Bush," *Washington Post Magazine*, September 28, 1986; Bush, *41*, 47–52.

40. Obama, *Dreams from My Father*, 13; President Obama and Marilynne Robinson, "A Conversation in Iowa," *New York Review of Books*, November 5, 2015.

41. Kaplan, *Earning the Rockies*, 171. For the best recent critique of Western expansion and American foreign policy, see Grandin, *The End of the Myth*.

42. Hoffman, *Gulliver's Troubles*, 143–175; Zoellick, *America in the World*, 8-10.

43. Kloppenberg, *Reading Obama*, 83, 261; Alan Brinkley, "The Philosopher President," *Democracy* (Winter 2011).

44. See, for example, Eisenhower letter to C. D. Jackson, March 26, 1952, PDDE, vol. 19, p. 800.

45. Engel, *When the World Seemed New*, 24; Eisenhower letter to Swede Hazlett, October 16, 1952, AWF Name Series, Hazlett, EL; Meacham, *Destiny and Power*, xxii; Ryan Lizza, "The Consequentialist," *New Yorker*, May 2, 2011; Obama interview with Ta-Nehisi Coates, *Atlantic*, December 21, 2016; David Remnick, "Going the Distance."

46. Engel, *When the World Seemed New*, 36; Eisenhower letter to Lucille Dawson Eisenhower, May 6, 1960, PDDE, vol. 20, p. 1940.

47. Reinhold Niebuhr, *The World Crisis and American Responsibility* (Association Press, 1958), 81. See James Q. Wilson, *On Character*; Dickerson, *The Hardest Job in the World*, 380–384. Empathy is also essential for historians trying to understand past decision-making; see Gaddis, *The Landscape of History*, 124.

48. Bush letter to his family, July 23, 1974; ATB, p. 185; Obama quote from Annie Linskey and Matt Viser, "Obama and Biden, together again to troll Trump," *Washington Post*, July 22, 2020

49. Nye, *Do Morals Matter?*, 62; Bush speech at Greenwich Country Day School Reunion, May 29, 1997, ATB, p. 605.

50. See Brands and Edel, *The Lessons of Tragedy*; Morgenthau, *Scientific Man Versus Power Politics*.

51. Eisenhower, *At Ease*, pp. 181–182; Michael Beschloss, "D-Day Wasn't the First Time Eisenhower Felt as If He Had Lost a Son," *New York Times*, June 11, 2014; Meacham, *Destiny and Power*, 101; Cramer, *Being Poppy*, 69–76; Bush, *41*, 56–57; Gail Sheehy, "Is George Bush Too Nice to Be President?" *Vanity Fair* (February 1987); Susan Eisenhower, *How Ike Led*, 240.

52. Obama, *Dreams from My Father*, x–xi, xiv; *The Audacity of Hope*, 233

53. Obama, *Audacity of Hope*, 322; Meacham, *Destiny and Power*, 101; Eisenhower letter to Edgar N. Eisenhower, PDDE, vol. 17, 2443–2444.

54. Goldberg, "The Obama Doctrine."

CHAPTER 2

1. Description of these meetings from Gates, *Duty*, 280–282; Geithner, *Stress Test*, 262–266; and Baker, *Obama*, 21–25.

2. See Hughes, *The Ordeal of Power*, 49–52; Charles J. V. Murphy, "The Eisenhower Shift," *Fortune* (January 1956); Dulles's handwritten notes on *Helena* meetings, John Foster Dulles Papers, 1951–59, Subject Series, Box 8, EL; Hughes's notes on preparation of the State of the Union message, Hughes Diary, February 2, 1953, EJHP; Eisenhower State of the Union speech, February 2, 1953, APP; Hitchcock, *The Age of Eisenhower*, 92; and Bowie and Immerman, *Waging Peace*, 84–86.

3. For background, see Bush and Scowcroft, AWT, pp. 19–21; Baker III, *Politics of Diplomacy*, 40–41; Engel, *When the World Seemed New*, 69–73; Brands, *Making the Unipolar Moment*, 276–279; Steven Roberts, "In Foreign Policy, the Bush Era Is Here," *New York Times*, November 20, 1988; Zoellick, *America in the World*, 425–426.

4. Eisenhower letter to General Albert Wedemeyer, May 2, 1947, PDDE, vol. 8, p. 1680.

5. Hal Brands, *What Good Is Grand Strategy?* , 3; Gaddis, *On Grand Strategy*, 21; Francis J. Gavin and James B. Steinberg, "Foreign Policy Needs a Road Map," *Foreign Affairs* (July/August 2020); and Nina Silove, "Beyond the Buzzword: Three Meanings of 'Grand Strategy,'" *Security Studies*, vol. 27, 2018.

6. Fred Greenstein and Richard Immerman, "Effective National Security Advising: Recovering the Eisenhower Legacy," *Political Science Quarterly* (September 2000): 335–345; Greenstein, *The Hidden-Hand Presidency*, 124–138; Susan Eisenhower, *How Ike Led*, 150–152.

7. Discussion at the 132nd Meeting of the NSC, February 18, 1953, AWF, NSC Series, EL.

8. Discussion at the 134th Meeting of the NSC, February 25, 1953, AWF, NSC Series, EL.

9. See Gaddis, *Strategies of Containment*, 130–133; Hogan, *A Cross of Iron*, 374; Charles J.V. Murphy, "The Eisenhower Shift, Part III," *Fortune* (March 1956); Discussion at the 163rd Meeting of the NSC, September 24, 1953, AWF, NSC Series, EL; see also Discussion at the 270th Meeting of the NSC, Camp David, Maryland, December 8, 1955, AWF, NSC Series, EL.

10. See Emmet John Hughes Diary, March 16, 1953, EJHP; Hughes, *The Ordeal of Power*, 100–115; Newton, *Eisenhower*, 130–132; Thomas, *Ike's Bluff*, 57–66; Susan Eisenhower, *How Ike Led*, 167–169; Ledbetter, *Unwarranted Influence*, 65–72. The definitive accounts of the events and process behind this speech are Bowie and Immerman, *Waging Peace*, 109–122, and Leffler, *For the Soul of Mankind*, 84–122.

11. Richard Rovere, "Letter from Washington," *New Yorker*, May 2, 1953.

12. Ewald, *Eisenhower the President*, 227.

13. For a full discussion of Eisenhower's emphasis on aligning resources with goals, see Bowie and Immerman, *Waging Peace*, 96–108; and Hogan, *A Cross of Iron*, 366–418.

14. On this point, I am grateful to Hitchcock, *The Age of Eisenhower*, 99.

15. Bowie and Immerman, *Waging Peace*, 245–246; Discussion at 172nd Meeting of the NSC, November 23, 1953, AWF, NSC Series, EL.

16. See Basic National Security Policy, NSC 162/2, October 30, 1953, FRUS 1952–1954, vol. 2, pp. 577–597; Leffler, *Safeguarding Democratic Capitalism*, 311–312.

17. See Thomas, *Ike's Bluff*, 98–114; H. W. Brands, "The Age of Vulnerability: Eisenhower and the National Insecurity State," *American Historical Review* (October 1989); Bowie and Immerman, *Waging Peace*, 189–198; Gaddis, *Strategies of Containment*, 145–149, 163–174.

18. Gaddis, *Strategies of Containment*, 157–159; Bowie and Immerman, *Waging Peace*, 254–256.

19. Bowie and Immerman, *Waging Peace*, 251–254; Gaddis, *Strategies of Containment*, 149–152; Eisenhower Diary, AWF, DDE Diary Series, December 1956 Miscellaneous (4).

20. Hitchcock, *The Age of Eisenhower*, 148–175; Gaddis, *Strategies of Containment*, 155–157.

21. William Stueck, "Reassessing U.S. Strategy in the Aftermath of the Korean War," *Orbis* (Fall 2009); Hitchcock, *The Age of Eisenhower*, 107; Bowie and Immerman, *Waging Peace*, 3–5; Gaddis, *Strategies of Containment*, 174; Divine, *Eisenhower and the Cold War*, 33–34.

22. Eisenhower memorandum to Secretary of State Dulles, September 8, 1953, FRUS 1952–1954, vol. 2, pp. 460–463.

23. Eisenhower letter to Alfred Maximilian Gruenther, May 4, 1953, PDDE, vol. 14, p. 203.

24. Discussion at the 270th meeting of the National Security Council, December 8, 1955, Camp David, Maryland, AWF, NSC Series, EL; Greenstein, *The Hidden-Hand Presidency*, 96–99.

25. James Reston, "An Inquiry into Foreign Policy," *New York Times*, January 16, 1955; Gaddis, *Strategies of Containment*, 159–161.

26. Engel, *When the World Seemed New*, 44–70.

27. Bush conversation with Canadian Prime Minister Brian Mulroney, May 4, 1989, Author's Files; Zoellick, *America in the World*, 426, 439.

28. For example, the May 15, 1989, cover of *Time* magazine blared "Waiting for Washington: The U.S. Dithers While Moscow Woos Europe."

29. See Bush's self-typed notes on Hamtramck speech, April 15, 1989, GHWB Presidential Records, Daily Files, April 16, 1989, GHWBL; National Security Directive 23, "U.S. Relations with the Soviet Union," September 22, 1989, Author's Files; For Gorbachev as a surfer, see Bush conversation with NATO Secretary General Manfred Woerner, April 12, 1989, Author's Files.

30. Memorandum of conversation between Bush and Gorbachev, July 17, 1991, Brent Scowcroft Collection, Memcons/Telcons, January–December 1991, GHWBL; Soviet transcript of Malta Summit, December 3, 1990, National Security Archive Electronic Briefing Book, no. 298, doc. 10, AWT, pp. 164–165.

31. See Hal Brands, "Choosing Primacy: U.S. Strategy and Global Order at the Dawn of the Post–Cold War Era," *Texas National Security Review* (Spring 2018).

32. Bush's self-typed notes to speechwriters, March 14, 1992, ATB, p. 551.

33. AWT, p. 60; Engel, *When the World Seemed New*, pp. 76–77.

34. Bush telephone conversation with Prime Minister Margaret Thatcher, January 27, 1990, Author's Files.

35. Bush Diary entry, February 24, 1990, ATB, pp. 460–461; Jeffrey Engel, "Bush, Germany, and the Power of Time: How History Makes History," *Diplomatic History* 37, no. 4 (2013), 662.

36. Bush Diary entry, September 7, 1990, ATB, p. 478–479.

37. AWT, pp. 353, 364, 370.

38. See Scowcroft handwritten notes for speech at CFR/Economic Club Detroit, 9/11/91, Brent Scowcroft Collection, Memcons/Telcons, January–December 1991, GHWBL. For an excellent discussion of the new world order's conceptual journey, see Bartholomew Sparrow, *The Strategist*, 479–487.

39. See Engel, *When the World Seemed New*, 479; Brands, "Choosing Primacy."

40. Quoted in Rhodes, *The World as It Is*, 372; Remnick, "Going the Distance."

41. Clinton memo to Obama, "Year-End Report," February 17, 2010, draft shown to author.

42. Obama press conference, Trinidad and Tobago, April 19, 2009, APP; Obama interview with Fareed Zakaria of *Time* magazine, January 19, 2012, APP.

43. Senator Obama interview with Fareed Zakaria, CNN, July 13, 2008.

44. Quote from Lizza, "The Consequentialist." This section draws on Chollet, *The Long Game*, 51–88; Hal Brands, "Barack Obama and the Dilemmas of Grand Strategy," *The Washington Quarterly* (Winter 2017); Hal Brands, "Breaking Down Obama's Grand Strategy," *National Interest* (July 2015); Michael Clarke and Anthony Ricketts, "Did Obama Have a Grand Strategy?" *Journal of Strategic Studies* 40 (2017); and Milne, *Worldmaking*, 457–513.

45. Obama interview with Zakaria, January 19, 2012.

46. Chollet, *The Long Game*, 217–218.

47. Chollet, *The Long Game*, 65–66.

48. Quoted in Goldberg, "The Obama Doctrine"; Clinton, *Hard Choices*, 230; and Chollet, *The Long Game*, 65.

49. Quotes from Karen DeYoung, "A Renewed Relationship with Cuba Was One of the Administration's Signature Achievements," in *Obama's Legacy* (Diversion Books, 2016), 138; remarks at a Young Obama Town Hall Meeting and a Question-and-Answer Session in Mona, Jamaica, April 9, 2015, APP; Rhodes, *The World as It Is*, 15.

50. Obama Inauguration Address, January 21, 2009, APP; Bush Inauguration Address, January 20, 1989, APP.

51. Quoted in Obama interview with Doris Kearns Goodwin, "The Ultimate Exit Interview," *Vanity Fair* (November 2016); also see Derek Chollet, "The Long Game versus the Long War," in *Obama's Legacy*, 64.

52. Quoted in Goldberg, "The Obama Doctrine."

53. This draws on Rhodes, *The World as It Is*, 78–82; Power, *The Education of an Idealist*, 261–265.

54. Obama speech at West Point, December 1, 2009, APP; Obama interview with Steve Kroft of *60 Minutes* (CBS), December 13, 2009, APP.

55. On the shortcomings of retrenchment and restraint as analytical concepts, see Michael J. Mazaar, "Rethinking Restraint: Why It Fails In Practice," *Washington Quarterly* (Summer 2020).

56. On the difference in strategic contexts, see Burns, *The Back Channel*, 292.

57. Eisenhower letter to John Foster Dulles, June 20, 1952, PDDE, vol. 13, p. 1254.

58. Fact Sheet on "New World Order," 1992 Presidential Campaign, Bush Administration Record and Bush-Quayle 1992 Issues Office Fact Sheets, Robert Teeter Collection, GHWBL; Dennis Ross to James Baker, "Foreign Policy in the Second Bush Administration: An Overview," April 30, 1992, William Burns Memo Archive, Carnegie Endowment for International Peace.

59. Obama remarks at Young Southeast Asian Leaders Town Hall, University of Malaysia, April 27, 2014, APP; Kimmage, *The Abandonment of the West*, 134–140, 276–291.

60. See Mira Rapp-Hooper, *Shields of the Republic*.

61. See Chollet, *The Long Game*, 216.

62. See Jervis, *Perception and Misperception in International Politics*, 128–142.

63. Remarks by President Obama on the Defense Strategic Review, January 5, 2012, APP.

64. See Lawrence Korb, Laura Conley, and Alex Rothman, "A Historical Perspective on Defense Budgets," Center for American Progress, July 6, 2011; Nicole Lewis, "Fact Checker: Trump's claim that 'they just keep cutting the military,'" *Washington Post*, December 5, 2017; Bush State of the Union Speech, January 28, 1992, APP; Bush notes on the State of the Union, GHWB Presidential Records, Daily Files, January 16, 1992, GHWBL; Bush State of the Union Speech, January 28, 1992, APP; Bush notes on the State of the Union, GHWB Presidential Records, Daily Files, January 16, 1992, GHWBL.

65. Leffler, *Safeguarding Democratic Capitalism*, 311–316.

66. John Newhouse, *War and Peace in the Nuclear Age* (Knopf, 1989), 106, 138: Andrew Goodpaster memorandum of Eisenhower meeting with Dr. George Kistiakowsky, November 25, 1960, Author's Files; Bundy, *Danger and Survival*, 346.

67. See Bush Diary, November 4, 1986, ATB, p. 352; Bush notes to speechwriters, March 14, 1992, ATB, p. 551; Bush comment, AWT, pp. 546–547; Bush remarks at the US Coast Guard Academy Commencement, May 24, 1989, APP.

68. Remnick, *The Bridge*, 116–117; Kaplan, *The Bomb*, 244; Gardiner Harris, "At Hiroshima Memorial, Obama Says Nuclear Arms Require 'Moral Revolution,'" *New York Times*, May 27, 2016; Obama interview with NHK World-Japan, May 22, 2016.

69. Eisenhower letter to Frank Altschul, October 25, 1957, Box 5, Folder 7, EJHP; Obama quote from Remnick, "Going the Distance."

70. Eisenhower letter to Swede Hazlett, August 3, 1956, AWF Name Series, EL.

71. Stephen Sestanovich, "The Long History of Leading from Behind," *Atlantic* (January/February 2016); Leffler, *Safeguarding Democratic Capitalism*, 312.

72. Lippmann, *U.S. Foreign Policy*, 3, 9.

CHAPTER 3

1. See Eisenhower news conference, April 29, 1954, APP; James Reston, "President Charts Policy of Caution in Indochina War," *New York Times*, April 30, 1954; Eisenhower letter to Dulles, May 1, 1954, PDDE, vol. 15, p. 1051.

2. See Bush Diary entry, February 28, 1991, AWT; Bush question-and-answer session with reporters in Hobe Sound, Florida, April 3, 1991, APP; exchange with reporters on Aid to Iraqi Refugees, April 11, 1991, APP. For a representative critique of Bush's weakness, see A. M. Rosenthal, "The War Goes On," *New York Times*, April 12, 1991; Gore quoted in Alfonsi, *Circle in the Sand*, 231; Maureen Dowd, "Bush Stands Firm on Military Policy in Iraqi Civil War," *New York Times*, April 14, 1991.

3. See Rhodes, *The World as It Is*, 277–278; Landler, *Alter Egos*, xi–xiv; Obama news conference with President Benigno Aquino III of the Philippines in Manila, Philippines, April 28, 2014, APP.

4. Mike Berardino, "Mike Tyson Explains One of His Most Famous Quotes," *South Florida Sun Sentinel*, November 9, 2012.

5. See Gaddis, *George F. Kennan*, 276–277.

6. Burns, *The Back Channel*, 296.

7. Eisenhower farewell address, January 17, 1961, APP.

8. See Memorandum of Meeting at the White House Between President Truman and General Eisenhower, November 18, 1952, AWF, Name Series, Box 33, EL. This section draws on Hitchcock, *The Age of Eisenhower*, 176–201; Burke and Greenstein, *How President's Test Reality*; Logevall, *Embers of War*; and Richard Immerman, "Between the Unattainable and the Unacceptable: Eisenhower and Dien Bien Phu," in Melanson and Mayers, *Reevaluating Eisenhower*.

9. Memorandum of Discussion at the 192nd Meeting of the NSC, April 6, 1954, FRUS, 1952–54, vol XIII, part 1; Halberstam, *The Fifties*, 401–402.

10. See Memorandum of Discussion at the 190th Meeting of the NSC, March 25, 1954, FRUS 1952–54, vol XIII, part 1; and George Herring and Richard Immerman, "Eisenhower, Dulles, and Dien Bien Phu: 'The Day We Didn't Go to War Revisited,'" *Journal of American History* (September 1984): 352.

11. Memorandum of Discussion of the 194th Meeting of the NSC, April 29, 1954, FRUS 1952–54, vol XIII, part 2.

12. "Hagerty Diary, April 29, 1954," FRUS 1952–54, vol XIII, part 2; Eisenhower letter to Swede Hazlett, October 23, 1954, AWF Name Series, Hazlett, EL.

13. Hitchcock, *The Age of Eisenhower*, 200; Newton, *Eisenhower*, 159; Halberstam, *The Fifties*, 405.

14. Halberstam, *The Fifties*, 410; Gelb and Betts, *The Irony of Vietnam*, 67–68.

15. See Eisenhower, "Address in Convention Hall, Philadelphia, Pennsylvania," November 1, 1956, APP; Emmet Hughes Diary, October 30, 1956, EJHP; Hitchcock, *The Age of Eisenhower*, 324–326; Nichols, *Eisenhower 1956*, 225–228; Russell Baker, "President Calls Stevenson Plans Way to 'Disaster,'" *New York Times*, November 2, 1956.

16. Nichols, *Eisenhower 1956*, 284–285; Newton, *Eisenhower*, 223–233.

17. Memorandum of Discussion at the 303rd Meeting of the NSC, November 8, 1956, 9–11:25 a.m., FRUS 1955–1957, Eastern Europe, vol. XXV; Hitchcock, *The Age of Eisenhower*, 328–329.

18. Walter Lippmann, "Hungary—The Longer View," *New York Herald Tribune*, November 29, 1956.

19. "Memorandum of Telephone Conversation with the President, November 9, 1956," FRUS 1955–1957, Eastern Europe, vol. XXV; Laszlo Borhi, "Rollback, Liberation, Containment, or Inaction: U.S. Policy and Eastern Europe in the 1950s," *Journal of Cold War Studies* (Fall 1999); Charles Gati, *Failed Illusions: Moscow, Washington, Budapest, and the 1956 Hungarian Revolt* (Stanford University Press, 2008), 74–80.

20. Eisenhower phone call with Dulles, AWF, DDE Diary Series, September 1956 Phone Calls, EL.

21. Eisenhower letter to Swede Hazlett, November 2, 1956, AWF, DDE Series, Box 20, EL; Eisenhower letter to Lewis Williams Douglas, November 3, 1956, PDDE, vol. 17, p. 2360; Thomas, *Ike's Bluff*, 219.

22. Memorandum of Conference with the President, October 29, 1956, 7:15pm, AWF, DDE Diary Series, Box 19, EL.

23. See Memorandum of Discussion at the 302nd Meeting of the NSC, November 1, 1956, 9 a.m.; and Memorandum by the President, November 1, 1956, FRUS,

1955–1957, Suez Crisis, July 26–December 31, 1956, vol. XVI; Hitchcock, *The Age of Eisenhower*, 330–331.

24. Eisenhower letter to Eli Ginzberg, November 5, 1956, PDDE, vol. 17, p. 2365; Eisenhower phone call with Herbert Hoover Jr., November 13, 1956, AWF, DDE Diary Series, Box 19, EL; Eisenhower Memorandum, November 8, 1956, PDDE, vol. 17, pp. 2373–2375; Hitchcock, *The Age of Eisenhower*, 338; Nichols, *Eisenhower 1956*, 249–257.

25. Notes on Presidential-Bipartisan Congressional Leadership Meeting, January 1, 1957, FRUS 1955–1957, Near East Region, Iran, Iraq, vol. XII; Nichols, *Eisenhower 1956*, 264–268; Newton, *Eisenhower*, 258–259; Matthew Waxman, "Remembering Eisenhower's Middle East Force Resolution," *Lawfare*, March 9, 2019.

26. See James Reston, "Mideast Setback Alarms U.S. Aides," *New York Times*, November 13, 1956; letter from Joseph Alsop to Chip Bohlen, December 28, 1956, General Correspondence, Box 13, December 1956, AP.

27. Bush letter to Henry Catto, December 1, 1986, ATB, p. 355.

28. See Jeffrey A. Engel, "When George Bush Believed the Cold War Ended," in *41: Inside the Presidency of George H. W. Bush*, 120.

29. Meacham, *Destiny and Power*, 392; Bush and Scowcroft, AWT, p. xiii; Bush Diary, November 8, 1989, ATB, p. 442.

30. Bush and Scowcroft, AWT, p. 488; memorandum of telephone conversation with Chancellor Kohl of Germany, April 16, 1991, Author's Files.

31. Meacham, *Destiny and Power*, 465; the President's News Conference on the Persian Gulf Conflict, March 1, 1991, APP; Scowcroft to Bush, "Ending the Gulf War," February 27, 1991, Richard Haass Files, Working File, Iraq—February 1991 [3], GHWBL; memorandum of conversation with German Foreign Minister Hans-Dietrich Genscher, March 1, 1991, Author's Files.

32. Bush and Scowcroft, AWT, 489.

33. Meacham, *Destiny and Power*, 467; William Safire, "Bush's Bay of Pigs," *New York Times*, April 4, 1991.

34. Baker, *The Politics of Diplomacy*, 430–433.

35. Gates, *Exercise of Power*, 202–203.

36. Michael Wines, "Parade Unfurls Symbols of Patriotism in the Capital," *New York Times*, June 9, 1991.

37. See Alfonsi, *Circle in the Sand*, 284–289, 308; Bush and Scowcroft, AWT, p. 489; Jonathan Rauch, "Why Bush (Senior) Didn't Blow It In The Gulf War," *Atlantic*, October 1, 2001; Mann, *The Great Rift*, 142.

38. Memorandum of conversation with Prime Minister Brian Mulroney of Canada, August 19, 1991, Author's Files.

39. Bush and Scowcroft, AWT, p. 9.

40. Bush and Scowcroft, AWT, pp. 502–503.

41. Bush Diary, October 12, 1990, AWT, p. 381; Engel, *When the World Seemed New*, 271.

42. Bush and Scowcroft, AWT, p. 524; Engel, *When the World Seemed New*, 461; Telcon with Lech Walesa, president of Poland, August 19, 1991, Author's Files; Telcon with President Boris Yeltsin of the Republic of Russia, USSR, August 20, 1991, Author's

Files; Bush, "The President's News Conference in Kennebunkport, Maine, on the Attempted Coup in the Soviet Union," August 21, 1991, APP.

43. See Bush and Scowcroft, AWT, pp. 521, 526

44. See Bush and Scowcroft, AWT, p. 542; Meacham, *Destiny and Power*, 488; Mann, *The Great Rift*, 152–154.

45. See Talbott, *The Russia Hand*, 24; memorandum of conversation: NATO Summit, November 7, 1991, Author's Files.

46. See Beschloss and Talbott, *At the Highest Levels*, 445–446; Gates, *Exercise of Power*, 252; and Goldgeier and McFaul, *Power and Purpose*, 45–46.

47. Bush, " Address to the Nation on the Commonwealth of Independent States," December 25, 1991, APP.

48. See Marvin Kalb, *The Nixon Memo: Political Respectability, Russia, and the Press* (University of Chicago Press, 1994); Kalb's book contains the Nixon memo as an appendix.

49. See Bush letter to Richard Nixon, March 5, 1992, ATB, p. 549; Bush news conference, March 11, 1992, APP; Goldgeier and McFaul, *Power and Purpose*, 80; and memorandum to James Baker from Andrew Carpendale, April 23, 1992, Baker Papers, Box 111, Folder 3, April 1992, JABP.

50. Beschloss and Talbott, *At the Highest Levels*, xii.

51. Richard Brookhiser, "A Visit with George Bush," *Atlantic*, August 1992.

52. Kloppenberg, *Reading Obama*, 147–148; Garrow, *Rising Star*, 146–147.

53. Rhodes, *The World as It Is*, 277.

54. Robert Gates speech at Eisenhower Library, May 8, 2010, Department of Defense; Interview of Obama and Clinton on *60 Minutes*, January 28, 2013, APP; David Ignatius, "What Suez crisis can remind us about US power," *Washington Post*, January 25, 2013.

55. See Rhodes, *The World as It Is*, 110–111, 120–121; Chollet, *The Long Game*, 102–103; Obama speech at National Defense University, March 28, 2011, APP.

56. Goldberg, "The Obama Doctrine."

57. Chollet, *The Long Game*, 103–104; see also Chivvis, *Toppling Qaddafi*, 53–68.

58. Chollet, *The Long Game*, 104–105; Dexter Filkins, "The Moral Logic of Humanitarian Intervention," *New Yorker*, September 8, 2019.

59. Obama remarks to the UN General Assembly, September 28, 2015, APP; Gordon, *Losing the Long Game*, 211–212.

60. Quoted in Thomas Friedman, "Obama on the World," *New York Times*, August 8, 2014.

61. Goldberg, "The Obama Doctrine"; and Chollet, *The Long Game*, 137–138.

62. See statement by President Obama on the situation in Syria, August 18, 2011, APP.

63. Larson, *Eisenhower*, 91.

64. For more on this argument, see Gordon, *Losing the Long Game*.

65. Remnick, "Going the Distance"; Franklin Foer and Chris Hughes, "Barack Obama Is Not Pleased," *New Republic*, January 27, 2013.

66. Jeffrey Goldberg, "Obama to Israel—Time Is Running Out," *Atlantic*, March 2, 2014.

67. Rhodes, *The World as It Is*, 239.

68. See Chollet, *The Long Game*, 1–26; Power, *The Education of an Idealist*, 359–371.
69. This draws on Derek Chollet, "Easy There, Blob. With Obama, We Faced a Different Syria," *Defense One*, April 9, 2017. For the most thorough account of the red line episode and its aftermath, see Warrick, *Red Line*.
70. Power, *The Education of an Idealist*, 508; Goodwin, "The Ultimate Exit Interview."
71. Remnick, "Going the Distance"; Burns, *The Back Channel*, 333.
72. Goldberg, "The Obama Doctrine."
73. Obama, *The Audacity of Hope*, 308.
74. See Jeffrey Frank, "Eisenhower 1954, Obama 2013," *New Yorker*, September 3, 2013.
75. Rhodes, *The World as It Is*, 339.
76. Burns, *The Back Channel*, 296, 322–323.

CHAPTER 4

1. Eisenhower, *At Ease*, 371–372; Hitchcock, *The Age of Eisenhower*, 51–52; Greenstein, *The Hidden-Hand Presidency*, 48–49; William Hitchcock, "How the GOP Embraced the World—And Then Turned Away," *Politico Magazine*, July 13, 2018; Greene, *I Like Ike*, 9, 34.
2. Text of Eisenhower speech from *New York Times*, February 2, 1951; James Reston, "Eisenhower Magic Wins Over Capitol Hill Suspicion," *New York Times*, February 2, 1951; "Eisenhower's First Report," *New York Times* [Editorial], February 2, 1951; Eisenhower, *At Ease*, 368–369.
3. Eisenhower Diary, March 5, 1951, DDEP, vol. 12, p. 91; Greene, *I Like Ike*, 34; W. H. Lawrence, "Eisenhower Is Gaining as GOP's Man in '52," *New York Times*, January 28, 1951.
4. See Goldman et al., *Quest for the Presidency 1992*, 318–340; and Kornacki, *The Red and Blue*, 145–161.
5. Patrick J. Buchanan, "America First—and Second, and Third," *National Interest* (Spring 1990): 79, 82. See also Chollet and Goldgeier, *America Between the Wars*, 23–25.
6. Patrick Buchanan, "Crackup of the Conservatives," *Washington Times*, May 1, 1991; Fitzgerald, *Way Out There in the Blue*, 75–76; John Judis, "The Conservative Crackup," *American Prospect* (Fall 1990); Frum, *Dead Right*, 131–140; Kimmage, *The Abandonment of the West*, 293–296.
7. For example, Bush took note of the lead item in the June 2, 1990, issue of *Human Events* mentioning Buchanan's interest in the 1992 campaign; see GHWB Presidential Records, Daily Files, June 3, 1990, GHWBL.
8. See memorandum to Bush from Ronald Kaufman, attaching a Buchanan letter to supporters, GHWB Presidential Records, Daily Files, December 17, 1991; and Bush notes from phone call with William Bennett, "Former Drug Czar Attacks Buchanan," GHWB Presidential Records, Daily Files, January 18, 1992, GHWBL; and Bush Diary entry, February 16, 1991, ATB, p. 548.
9. Peter Baker and Gardiner Harris, "Under Fire from GOP, Obama Defends Response to Terror Attacks," *New York Times*, December 17, 2015.
10. Obama, *The Audacity of Hope*, 126.
11. See Joe Klein, "Yes He Did," *Foreign Affairs* (July/August 2017): 135.

12. See David Ignatius, "In Fighting the Islamic State, Obama Is a Tortoise and the GOP Is Harebrained," *Washington Post*, December 16, 2015; Rhodes, *The World as It Is*, 341.

13. Zelizer, *Arsenal of Democracy*, 507.

14. See Blake, *Liking Ike*; Greenberg, *Republic of Spin*, 276–316.

15. Letter to Edward Mead Earle, September 2, 1952, AWF, Name Series, Box 8, EL.

16. Eisenhower letter to William Edward Robinson, March 12, 1954, PDDE, vol. 15, pp. 949–951; also see Dueck, *Age of Iron*, 61–62.

17. Jeffrey Frank, "Ike's Advice: How to Avoid a Multiplicity of Fears," *New Yorker*, November 18, 2015.

18. Halberstam, *The Fifties*, 52–53.

19. Nichols, *Ike and McCarthy*, 54. For the administration's study of the impact of McCarthyism on US foreign policy, see "Reported Decline in US Prestige Abroad," Special Report Prepared by the Psychological Strategy Board, September 11, 1953, FRUS 1952-1954, Vol I, Part 2.

20. See Greenstein, *The Hidden-Hand Presidency*, 155–228; Susan Eisenhower, *How Ike Led*, 189-193; letter to Governor George Craig, March 26, 1954, AWF, DDE Diary Series, Box 6, EL.

21. Meacham, *The Soul of America*, 200.

22. Quoted in Nichols, *Ike and McCarthy*, 221.

23. Letter to Alfred Gruenther, April 5, 1954, PDDE, vol. 15, pp. 1006–1007.

24. Jack Gould, "Television in Review," *New York Times*, April 6, 1954.

25. Letter to Milton Katz, April 8, 1954, AWF, DDE Diary Series, Box 6, EL; "Reported Decline in US Prestige Abroad," September 1953.

26. Halberstam, *The Fifties*, 52; Andersen, *Fantasyland*, 164-165

27. Hitchcock, *The Age of Eisenhower*, 244; Zelizer, *Arsenal of Democracy*, 129; letter to George N. Craig, AWF, DDE Diary Series, Box 6, EL.

28. Letter to Meade Alcorn, August 30, 1957, AWF, DDE Diary Series, Box 26, EL; Eisenhower memorandum for the record, November 14, 1956, WHCF, Official File, Box 602, EL.

29. Larson, *A Republican Looks at His Party*, 7–8, 19, 175; see also Dionne, *Why the Right Went Wrong*, 462–463.

30. Nash, *The Conservative Intellectual Movement*, 259–260; Willmoore Kendall, "Case Dismissed," *National Review*, July 25, 1956; Judis, *William F. Buckley Jr.*, 133, 148–150; Dueck, *Age of Iron*, 70.

31. Letter to Milton Eisenhower, September 17, 1955, AWF Name Series, Milton Eisenhower, EL; Hitchcock, *The Age of Eisenhower*, 303–304; Ewald, *Eisenhower the President*, 289–290; Kabaservice, *Rule and Ruin*, 14–18; Larson, *Eisenhower*, 53.

32. Hitchcock, *The Age of Eisenhower*, 376–382; Newton, *Eisenhower*, 253–255; Thomas, *Ike's Bluff*, 308–316; Susan Eisenhower, *How Ike Led*, 269-271; 287-288.

33. Bundy, *Danger and Survival*, 338.

34. The 470th Meeting of the NSC, December 20, 1960, AWF, NSC Series, EL.

35. Ewald, *Eisenhower the President*, 284–285; Halberstam, *The Fifties*, 700–701; Newhouse, *War and Peace in the Nuclear Age*, 117–118; Susan Eisenhower, *How Ike Led*, 274-276; Douglas Brinkley, *Dean Acheson: The Cold War Years, 1953–71* (Yale University Press, 1992), 58–64.

36. Eisenhower letter to Emmet John Hughes, November 20, 1958, PDDE, vol. 19, pp. 1210–1211; Hughes notes from Meeting with the President, December 10, 1958, Box 5, Folder 6, Diary 1953–57, EJHP; Hughes, *The Ordeal of Power*, 275–282.

37. See Henry Kissinger, *The Necessity of Choice* (Harper & Brothers, 1960), 1.

38. Andersen, *Fantasyland*, 214.

39. The best account of Bush and the Birchers is in Michael Nelson, "George Bush: Texan Conservative," in *41: Inside the Presidency of George H. W. Bush*, 32–38.

40. Alan L. Otten, "Conservative Horse Race," *Wall Street Journal*, September 21, 1966; George Bush, "The Republican Party and the Conservative Movement," *National Review*, December 1, 1964; Rowland Evans and Robert Novak, "The GOP's Southern Star," *Washington Post*, November 1, 1970; and Hugh Heclo, "George Bush and American Conservatism," in *41: Inside the Presidency of George H. W. Bush*.

41. Theodore H. White, *America in Search of Itself: The Making of the President, 1956–1980* (Harper and Row, 1982), 238; and Robert Bartley, "Bush Is Hounded for Reaffirming Ties with Right," *Wall Street Journal*, January 16, 1986.

42. This is according to James A. Stimson's "Policy Mood Index," University of North Carolina. See Meacham, *Destiny and Power*, 392.

43. Bush Diary, October 6, 1990, ATB, p. 480.

44. Beschloss and Talbott, *At the Highest Levels*, 198.

45. Bush Diary, March 28, 1990, ATB, p. 466; see also Bush comment, AWT, p. 228.

46. Bush self-typed letter to Gorbachev, April 26, 1990, GHWB Presidential Records, Daily Files, April 29, 1990, GHWBL.

47. Engel, *When the World Seemed New*, 431–433; Bush letter to Gorbachev, January 24, 1991, ATB, pp. 507–509.

48. Engel, *When the World Seemed New*, 450–451; William Safire, "After the Fall," *New York Times*, August 29, 1991; and William Safire, "Putin's Chicken Kiev," *New York Times*, December 6, 2004.

49. Bush letter to Richard Lugar, August 20, 1991, ATB, p. 535.

50. Talbott, *The Russia Hand*, 25.

51. See William Kristol and Robert Kagan, "Toward a Neo-Reaganite Foreign Policy," *Foreign Affairs*, July/August 1996.

52. Talbott, *The Russia Hand*, 31.

53. Bush Diary, July 2, 1991, ATB, p. 527.

54. See Goldman et al., *Quest for the Presidency 1992*, 413–423; Andersen, *Fantasyland*, 351-352; Naftali, *George H. W. Bush*, 144–145; Perot, *United We Stand*, 98–109.

55. See James Baker note to Bush, December 9, 1991, GHWB Presidential Papers, Daily Files, GHWBL; Bush State of the Union Speech, January 28, 1992, APP; and David Broder, "Shame the GOP . . .," *Washington Post*, December 7, 1991.

56. See Bacevich, *The Age of Illusions*, 50–57.

57. Obama, *The Audacity of Hope*, 304.

58. Remnick, *The Bridge*, 345–347; Milne, *Worldmaking*, 429. Obama interview with Jim Lehrer on PBS's *Newshour*, December 23, 2009, APP.

59. Jeff Zeleny, "Obama Highlights His War Opposition," *New York Times*, October 2, 2007.

60. See Chollet, *The Long Game*, 41.

61. See Chait, *Audacity*, 229; Dionne, *Why the Right Went Wrong*, 299–300; and Boot, *The Corrosion of Conservatism*, 179.

62. This discussion draws on Chollet, *The Long Game*, 199–201; Rhodes, *The World as It Is*, 327–333; Obama speech at American University on the Iran Nuclear Deal, August 5, 2015, APP; and Julie Hirschfeld Davis, "It's Either Iran Nuclear Deal or Some Form of War, Obama Warns," *New York Times*, August 6, 2015.

63. Eisenhower quoted in 204th Meeting of the NSC, June 24, 1954, AWF, NSC Series, EL.

64. Quoted in Robin Wright, "Obama on War and Peace," *New Yorker*, August 6, 2015; Obama speech at American University, APP.

65. Quoted in Rhodes, *The World as It Is*, 312.

66. Quoted in Goldberg, "The Obama Doctrine"; Rhodes, *The World as It Is*, 312.

67. Obama speech to the nation, December 6, 2015, APP; Gardiner Harris and Michael D. Shear, "Obama Says of Terrorist Threat: 'We Shall Overcome It,'" *New York Times*, December 6, 2015; Greg Jaffe, "Obama's Oval Office Address Reflects Struggle to Be Heard," *Washington Post,* December 6, 2015.

68. See Meacham, *The Soul of America*, 15–16.

69. Goodwin interview with Obama; Eisenhower letter to Altschul.

70. See Remnick, *The Bridge*.

71. Ryan Lizza, "The Second Term," *New Yorker*, June 18, 2012; Chait, *Audacity*, xvii; Dionne, *Why the Right Went Wrong*, 3; Andersen, *Fantasyland*, 390–400; Mann and Ornstein, *It's Even Worse Than It Looks*; Destler, Gelb, and Lake, *Our Own Worst Enemy*, 11–30; and Boot, *The Corrosion of Conservatism*, 172.

72. Obama State of the Union Address, January 12, 2016, APP.

73. See Rhodes, *The World as It Is*, xvi–xvii.

74. David Remnick, "Obama Reckons with a Trump Presidency," *New Yorker*, November 18, 2016; Meacham, *Destiny and Power*, 114–115.

75. See Hoffer, *The True Believer*; Eisenhower letter to Robert J. Briggs, February 10, 1959, PDDE, vol. 19, pp, 1340–1343; Max Blumenthal, "Ike's Other Warning," *New York Times*, Sept. 2, 2009; Max Blumenthal, *Republican Gomorrah: Inside the Movement That Shattered the Party* (Nation Books, 2009); Hillary Clinton, *What Happened* (Simon and Schuster, 2017), 10.

76. Sestanovich, *Maximalist*, 333.

77. See Paul Lettow, "The Future of Conservative Foreign Policy: Political Realities and Electoral Viability," in The Future of Conservative Internationalism, Reagan Institute Strategy Group, July 2019.

CHAPTER 5

1. Peter Baker, "In Funeral of Pomp and Pageantry, Nation Bids Farewell to George Bush," *New* York Times, *December 5, 2018.*

2. See Susan Glasser, "George H. W. Bush's Funeral Was the Corny, Feel-Good Moment That Washington Craves," *New Yorker*, December 6, 2018; Peter Baker, "For Obama and Baker, a Lament for a Lost Consensus," *New York Times*, November 28, 2018; Obama interview at Baker Institute, November 27, 2018; Bower, *Team of Five*, 251–252

3. See Peggy McGlone, "With Groundbreaking, Elusive Eisenhower Memorial Moves from Dream to Reality," *Washington Post,* October 31, 2017; Michael Ruane, "Forever Ready for Battle," *Washington Post,* January 22, 2020.

4. Bush quoted in Updegrove, *The Last Republicans;* MacMillan, *Dangerous Games,* 15–31; Kammen, *Mystic Chords of Memory,* 9.

5. Remnick, "Going the Distance."

6. See Hitchcock, *The Age of Eisenhower,* xii–xvi; Greenstein, *The Hidden-Hand Presidency,* 5–11; Murray Kempton, "The Underestimation of Dwight D. Eisenhower," *Esquire,* September 1967; Wills, *Nixon Agonistes,* 114–145; Robert Wright, "Eisenhower's Fifties," *Antioch Review* (Summer 1980); Irwin F. Gellman, "Mr. President," *Prologue* (Fall 2015).

7. Eisenhower letter to Stanley High, August 15, 1960, with memo attached, WHCF, Confidential File, Eisenhower Administration, Subject Series, Box 24, EL; Timothy D. Rives, "Ambrose and Eisenhower: A View from the Stacks in Abilene," *History News Network* (2010); Richard Rovere, "Eisenhower Revisited," *New York Times,* February 7, 1971.

8. I owe the observation on war and memory to Viet Thanh Nguyen, *Nothing Ever Dies,* 4–19. For a description of Ike's experiences on the American Battle Monuments Commission, see Smith, *Eisenhower in War and Peace,* 76–79.

9. See Immerman, "Confessions of an Eisenhower Revisionist"; Hughes, *The Ordeal of Power;* Ewald, *Eisenhower the President,* 223–225; Hughes comment to Arthur Schlesinger Jr. in *Journals, 1952–2000* (Penguin Press, 2007), 514.

10. Neustadt, *Presidential Power and the Modern Presidents,* 295–305. Eisenhower's wisdom in staying out of Vietnam in the 1950s stands in contrast to his advice to President Johnson in the 1960s, when he declared the importance of "keeping Southeast Asia free" and worked to stiffen LBJ's spine to win the war quickly, at almost any cost. See H. W. Brands, "Johnson and Eisenhower: The President, the Former President, and the War in Vietnam," *Presidential Studies Quarterly* (Summer 1985).

11. Alan Brinkley, "A President for Certain Seasons," *Wilson Quarterly* (Spring 1990); Stephen G. Rabe, "Eisenhower Revisionism: A Decade of Scholarship," *Diplomatic History* (Winter 1993); Arthur Schlesinger Jr., "The Ike Age Revisited," *Reviews in American History* (March 1983); George H. Quester, "Was Eisenhower a Genius?" *International Security* (Fall 1979).

12. Haynes Johnson, "Eisenhower's Season of Ascendancy," *Washington Post,* October 14, 1990; Eliot Cohen, "The Party of Ike," *Atlantic,* April 22, 2018; Robert Kaplan, "Why We Need Someone Like Ike," *Wall Street Journal,* July 18, 2019.

13. See R. W. Apple, "On His Centennial, They Still Like Ike," *New York Times,* October 15, 1990; Susan Eisenhower, "A Man Ahead of His Time," *Washington Post,* October 14, 1990.

14. Brzezinski, *Second Chance,* 69; Bush letter to George and Jeb Bush, August 1, 1998, ATB, p. 615.

15. Meacham, *Destiny and Power,* 568–569; Weisberg, *The Bush Tragedy.*

16. John Solomon, "A Wimp He Wasn't," *Newsweek,* March 20, 2011; Updegrove, *The Last Republicans,* 400–401; Carlos Lozada, "The Memoir I Wish George H. W.

Bush Had Written," *Washington Post*, December 1, 2018. For a dissenting view on Bush's legacy, see David Greenberg, "Is History Being Too Kind to George H. W. Bush?" *Politico*, December 1, 2018.

17. Meacham, *Destiny and Power*, 595; Marjorie Williams, "Man of a Thousand Faces," in Timothy Noah, ed., *Reputation: Portraits in Power* (Public Affairs, 2008), 108–109; Paul Lettow and Kori Schake, "The Vision Thing," *National Review*, December 20, 2018; Jeff Greenfield, "George Bush, Comeback Kid," *Politico*, December 1, 2018.

18. See Jennifer Schuessler, "Historian's Assess Obama's Legacy Under Trump's Shadow," *New York Times*, November 13, 2016. The essays from this conference were published in Zelizer, *The Presidency of Barack Obama*.

19. Peter Baker, "Can Trump Destroy Obama's Legacy?" *New York Times*, June 23, 2017.

20. See Rockman and Rudalevige, *The Obama Legacy*.

21. See James Fallows, "Obama, Explained," *Atlantic* (March 2012); and Bacevich, *The Age of Illusions*, 120–121.

22. See Chollet, *The Long Game*, 219–220; Chait, *Audacity*, 158–160; Gideon Rose, "What Obama Gets Right," *Foreign Affairs* (September/October 2015).

23. Remnick, "Going the Distance"; Franklin Foer and Chris Hughes, "Barack Obama Is Not Pleased," *New Republic*, January 27, 2013; Ben Rhodes, "The 9/11 Era Is Over," *Atlantic*, April 6, 2020.

24. Robert Divine, *Eisenhower and the Cold War*, 154–155; Jon Meacham, "Our Better Angels," *Time*, December 17, 2018.

25. See Jonathan Rauch, "Father Superior," *New Republic*, May 22, 2000; and Elaine Kamarck, "The Fragile Legacy of Barack Obama," *Boston Review*, March 27, 2018.

26. See Lepore, *This America*, 45–46; Meacham, *The Soul of America*, 4–19

27. Eisenhower Diary, July 6, 1950, in Ferrell, ed., *The Eisenhower Diaries*, 176–177.

28. For an example of what a reinvented foreign policy along these lines might look like, see William J. Burns, "The United States Needs a New Foreign Policy," *Atlantic*, July 14, 2020.

29. See Dickerson, *The Hardest Job in the World*, 308.

30. Niebuhr, *The Irony of American History*, 5, 174.

31. George Kennan Diary, August 27, 1978, in *The Kennan Diaries*, Frank Costigliola, ed. (Norton, 2014), 511; Colin Dueck, "Reinhold Niebuhr and the Second World War," *Providence*, April 22, 2020.

32. Although Niebuhr did not support Eisenhower for president, he grudgingly credited him with being "politically and morally wiser" than his advisers. See Reinhold Niebuhr, *The Children of Light and the Children of Darkness* (1944), in Elizabeth Sifton, ed., *Reinhold Niebuhr: Major Works on Religion and Politics* (Library of America, 2015), 420; and Niebuhr, "Why Ike Is Popular," April 22, 1955, in *Reinhold Niebuhr*, 672.

33. Gawande, *Being Mortal*, 260; Nye, *Presidential Leadership and the Creation of the American Era*, 151.

34. Gawande, *Being Mortal*, 9; Groopman, *How Doctors Think*, 169; also see Gawande, *Better*, 162–163.

35. Eisenhower letter to Nelson Rockefeller, May 5, 1960, AWF, DDE Diary Series, Box 9, EL; Brianna Ehley, "Obama likens Obamacare to a starter home," *Politico*, October 20, 2016.
36. Bush Diary, December 31, 1989, ATB, p. 451; Obama interview with Marc Maron, WTF Podcast, Episode 613, June 22, 2015.
37. Adams quoted in Arthur M. Schlesinger Jr., "Editor's Note," in Naftali, *George H. W. Bush*, xvi.
38. Obama interview with Maron.
39. Eisenhower letter to Swede Hazlett, July 22, 1957, PDDE, vol. 18, , pp. 319–324.
40. Bush speech to Philadelphia World Affairs Council, June 6, 1979.
41. Charles Lindblom, "The Science of 'Muddling Through,'" *Public Administration Review* (Spring 1959); Atul Gawande, "The Heroism of Incremental Care," *New Yorker*, January 23, 2017.
42. Obama interview with Coates; John Dickerson, "The ultimate test of presidential character is restraint," *Washington Post*, June 15, 2020.
43. Dickerson, *The Hardest Job in the World*, 256–258; Suri, *The Impossible Presidency*; and Lowi, *The Personal President*.
44. See Venkataraman, *The Optimist's Telescope*; for a brilliant summation of strategic foresight, see J. Peter Scoblic, "Learning From the Future," *Harvard Business Review* (July–August 2020).
45. Eisenhower draft article entitled "Some Thoughts on the Presidency," July 1968, DDE Post-Presidential Papers, 1965 Principal File, Box 3, EL.
46. Eisenhower conversation with Merriman Smith, November 23, 1954, AWF, Ann Whitman Diary, Box 3, EL.
47. Sheehy, "Is George Bush Too Nice to Be President?"; Obama interview with Bill Simmons, *GQ*, November 17, 2015.
48. See Robert Kaplan, "The Tragic Sensibility," *New Criterion* (May 2017).
49. Eisenhower farewell address, January 17, 1961, APP.
50. See Bush speech at Texas A&M University, December 15, 1992, APP; and Michael Wines, "Bush, in Texas Valedictory, Defends His Foreign Policies," *New York Times*, December 16, 1992.
51. See Bush speech at West Point, January 5, 1993, APP; Ann Devroy, "4,000 Cadets Say Farewell to the Chief," *Washington Post*, January 6, 1993.
52. Obama speech to the nation, January 10, 2017, APP; David Nakamura, "Obama's Farewell Message on Democracy: 'Show Up. Dive In. Stay at It,'" *Washington Post*, January 11, 2017.
53. Brooks, *The Road to Character*, 71. See also Wehner, *The Death of Politics*, 152–155.
54. Jon Meacham, "Nostalgia for the Grace of George H. W. Bush," *New York Times*, October 15, 2016.
55. Remnick, "Going the Distance."
56. Obama interview at Baker Institute, November 27, 2018.
57. Eisenhower letter to Henry Luce, August 8, 1960, AWF Name Series, Box 21, EL.
58. See drafts in Ben Hibbs Papers 1961–69, Article Drafts, Middle Way Draft, Box 2, EL.

SELECTED BIBLIOGRAPHY

ON GEORGE H. W. BUSH:

Alfonsi, Christian. *Circle in the Sand: Why We Went Back to Iraq*. New York: Doubleday, 2006.

Baker, James A., III., with Thomas M. DeFrank. *The Politics of Diplomacy: Revolution, War, and Peace, 1989–1992*. New York: Putnam, 1995.

Baker, Peter. *Days of Fire: Bush and Cheney in the White House*. New York: Doubleday, 2013.

Beschloss, Michael, and Strobe Talbott. *At the Highest Levels: The Inside Story of the End of the Cold War*. New York: Little, Brown and Company, 1993.

Brands, Hal. *Making the Unipolar Moment: U.S. Foreign Policy and the Rise of the Post–Cold War Order*. Ithaca, NY: Cornell University Press, 2016.

Brzezinski, Zbigniew. *Second Chance: Three Presidents and the Crisis of American Superpower*. New York: Basic Books, 2008.

Bush, George W. *41: A Portrait of My Father*. New York: Crown, 2014.

Bush, George H. W. *All the Best: My Life in Letters and Other Writings*. Scribner, 1999.

Bush, George H. W., with Brent Scowcroft. *A World Transformed*. New York: Knopf, 1998.

Cramer, Richard Ben. *Being Poppy: A Portrait of George Herbert Walker Bush*. New York: Simon and Schuster, 2013.

Engel, Jeffrey A. *The China Diary of George H. W. Bush: The Making of a Global President*. Princeton, NJ: Princeton University Press, 2011.

Engel, Jeffrey A. *When the World Seemed New: George H. W. Bush and the End of the Cold War*. New York: Houghton Mifflin Harcourt, 2017.

Goldman, Peter, Thomas M. DeFrank, Mark Miller, Andrew Murr, and Tom Matthews. *The Quest for the Presidency 1992*. College Station: Texas A&M Press, 1994.

Haass, Richard. *War of Necessity, War of Choice: A Memoir of Two Iraq Wars*. New York: Simon & Schuster, 2009.

Halberstam, David. *War in a Time of Peace: Bush, Clinton, and the Generals*. New York: Scribner, 2001.

Leffler, Melvyn P., and Jeffrey W. Legro, eds. *In Uncertain Times: American Foreign Policy after the Berlin Wall and 9/11*. Ithaca, NY: Cornell University Press, 2011.

Mann, James. *The Great Rift: Dick Cheney, Colin Powell, and the Broken Friendship That Defined an Era*. New York: Henry Holt, 2020.

Mann, James. *Rise of the Vulcans: The History of Bush's War Cabinet*. New York: Viking, 2004.

Meacham, Jon. *Destiny and Power: The American Odyssey of George Herbert Walker Bush*. New York: Random House, 2016.

Naftali, Timothy. *George H. W. Bush*. New York: Times Books, 2007.

Nelson, Michael, and Barbara A. Perry, eds. *41: Inside the Presidency of George H. W. Bush*. Ithaca, NY: Cornell University Press, 2014.

Page, Susan. *The Matriarch: Barbara Bush and the Making of an American Dynasty*. New York: Twelve, 2019.

Sparrow, Bartholomew. *The Strategist: Brent Scowcroft and the Call of National Security*. New York: PublicAffairs, 2015.

Sununu, John H. *The Quiet Man: The Indispensable Presidency of George H. W. Bush*. New York: Broadside, 2015.

Updegrove, Mark K. *The Last Republicans: Inside the Extraordinary Relationship Between George H. W. Bush and George W. Bush*. New York: HarperCollins, 2017.

Weisberg, Jacob. *The Bush Tragedy*. New York: Random House, 2008.

Zelikow, Philip, and Condoleezza Rice. *To Build a Better World: Choices to End the Cold War and Create a Global Commonwealth*. New York: Twelve, 2019.

ON DWIGHT EISENHOWER:

Adams, Sherman. *Firsthand Report: The Story of the Eisenhower Administration*. New York: Harper & Brothers, 1961.

Blake, David. *Liking Ike: Eisenhower, Advertising, and the Rise of Celebrity Politics*. New York: Oxford University Press, 2016.

Bowie, Robert R., and Richard Immerman. *Waging Peace: How Eisenhower Shaped an Enduring Cold War Strategy*. New York: Oxford University Press, 2000.

Burke, John P., and Fred I. Greenstein, with Larry Berman and Richard Immerman. *How Presidents Test Reality: Decisions on Vietnam, 1954 and 1965*. New York: Russell Sage Foundation, 1989.

Divine, Robert A. *Eisenhower and the Cold War*. New York: Oxford University Press, 1981.

Eisenhower, David, with Julie Nixon Eisenhower. *Going Home to Glory: A Memoir of Life with Dwight D. Eisenhower, 1961–1969*. New York: Simon & Schuster, 2010.

Eisenhower, Dwight D. *At Ease: Stories I Tell to Friends*. New York: Doubleday, 1967.

Eisenhower, Susan E. *How Ike Led: The Principles Behind Eisenhower's Biggest Decisions*. New York: Thomas Dunne Books, 2020.

Ewald, William Bragg, Jr. *Eisenhower the President: Crucial Days, 1951–1960*. New York: Prentice-Hall, 1981.

Ewald, William Bragg, Jr. *Who Killed Joe McCarthy?* New York: Simon & Schuster, 1984.

Ferrell, Robert H., ed. *The Eisenhower Diaries*. New York: Norton, 1981.

Gaddis, John Lewis. *Strategies of Containment: A Critical Appraisal of American National Security Policy During the Cold War*, rev. ed. New York: Oxford University Press, 2005.

Galambos, Louis. *Eisenhower: Becoming the Leader of the Free World*. Baltimore: Johns Hopkins University Press, 2018.

Greene, John Robert. *I Like Ike: The Presidential Election of 1952*. Lawrence: University Press of Kansas, 2017.

Greenstein, Fred I. *The Hidden-Hand Presidency: Eisenhower as Leader*. New York: Basic Books, 1982.

Halberstam, David. *The Fifties*. New York: Villard Books, 1993.

Hitchcock, William I. *The Age of Eisenhower: America and the World in the 1950s*. New York: Simon and Schuster, 2018.

Hogan, Michael J. *A Cross of Iron: Harry S. Truman and the Origins of the National Security State*. Cambridge: Cambridge University Press, 1998.

Hughes, Emmet John. *The Ordeal of Power: A Political Memoir of the Eisenhower Years*. New York: Atheneum, 1963.

Johnson, Paul. *Eisenhower: A Life*. New York: Penguin, 2014.

Larson, Arthur. *A Republican Looks at His Party*. New York: Harper, 1956.

Larson, Arthur. *Eisenhower: The President Nobody Knew*. New York: Charles Scribner's Sons, 1968.

Ledbetter, James. *Unwarranted Influence: Dwight D. Eisenhower and the Military Industrial Complex*. New Haven, CT: Yale University Press, 2011.

Logevall, Fredrik. *Embers of War: The Fall of an Empire and the Making of America's Vietnam*. New York: Random House, 2012.

Melanson, Richard A., and David Mayers. *Reevaluating Eisenhower: American Foreign Policy in the 1950s*. Champaign: University of Illinois Press, 1987.

Neal, Steve. *Harry and Ike: The Partnership That Remade the World*. New York: Touchstone, 2001.

Newton, Jim. *Eisenhower: The White House Years*. New York: Random House, 2011.

Nichols, David A. *Eisenhower 1956: The President's Year of Crisis—Suez and the Brink of War*. New York: Simon & Schuster, 2012.

Nichols, David A. *Ike and McCarthy: Dwight Eisenhower's Secret Campaign Against Joseph McCarthy*. New York: Simon & Schuster, 2017.

Pickett, William B. *Eisenhower Decides to Run: Presidential Politics and Cold War Strategy*. Chicago: Ivan R. Dee, 2000.

Reichard, Gary W. *Politics as Usual: The Age of Truman and Eisenhower*, 2nd ed. Wheeling, IL: Harlan Davidson, 2004.

Rovere, Richard H. *The Eisenhower Years: Affairs of State, 1950–1956*. New York: Farrar, Straus and Cudahy, 1956.

Smith, Jean Edward. *Eisenhower: In War and Peace*. New York: Random House, 2012.

Thomas, Evan. *Ike's Bluff: President Eisenhower's Secret Battle to Save the World*. New York: Back Bay Books, 2013.

Wills, Garry. *Nixon Agonistes*. New York: Houghton Mifflin, 1969.

ON BARACK OBAMA:

Axelrod, David. *Believer: My Forty Years in Politics*. New York: Penguin Press, 2015.

Baker, Peter. *Obama: The Call of History*. New York: Callaway, 2019.

Chait, Jonathan. *Audacity: How Barack Obama Defied His Critics and Created a Legacy That Will Prevail*. New York: Custom House, 2017.

Chivvis, Christopher S. *Toppling Qaddafi: Libya and the Limits of Liberal Intervention*. New York: Cambridge University Press, 2014.

Chollet, Derek. *The Long Game: How Obama Defied Washington and Redefined America's Role in the World*. New York: PublicAffairs, 2016.

Clinton, Hillary Rodham. *Hard Choices*. New York: Simon and Schuster, 2014.

Dueck, Colin. *The Obama Doctrine: American Grand Strategy Today*. New York: Oxford University Press, 2015.

Garrow, David J. *Rising Star: The Making of Barack Obama*. New York: William Morrow, 2017.

Gates, Robert M. *Duty: Memoirs of a Secretary at War*. New York: Knopf, 2014.

Geithner, Timothy F. *Stress Test: Reflections on Financial Crises*. New York: Crown, 2014.

Gordon, Philip H. *Losing the Long Game: The False Promise of Regime Change in the Middle East*. New York: St. Martin's Press, 2020.

Kloppenberg, James T. *Reading Obama: Dreams, Hope, and the American Political Tradition*. Princeton, NJ: Princeton University Press, 2010.

Landler, Mark. *Alter Egos: Hillary Clinton, Barack Obama, and the Twilight Struggle over American Power*. New York: Random House, 2016.

Mann, James. *The Obamians: The Struggle Inside the White House to Redefine American Power*. New York: Viking, 2012.

Maraniss, David. *Barack Obama: The Story*. New York: Simon & Schuster, 2012.

McFaul, Michael. *From Cold War to Hot Peace: An American Ambassador in Putin's Russia*. New York: Houghton Mifflin Harcourt, 2018.

Obama, Barack. *The Audacity of Hope: Thoughts on Reclaiming the American Dream*. New York: Crown, 2006.

Obama, Barack. *Dreams from My Father: A Story of Race and Inheritance*. New York: Crown, 1995.

Power, Samantha. *The Education of an Idealist: A Memoir*. New York: Dey Street Books, 2019.

Remnick, David. *The Bridge: The Life and Rise of Barack Obama*. New York: Knopf, 2010.

Rhodes, Ben. *The World as It Is: A Memoir of the Obama White House*. New York: Random House, 2018.

Rice, Susan. *Tough Love: My Story of the Things Worth Fighting For*. New York: Simon & Schuster, 2019.

Rockman, Bert A., and Andrew Rudalevige, eds. *The Obama Legacy*. Lawrence: University Press of Kansas, 2019.

Sanger, David E. *Confront and Conceal: Obama's Secret Wars and Surprising Use of American Power*. New York: Crown, 2012.

Savage, Charles. *Power Wars: Inside Obama's Post-9/11 Presidency*. New York: Little, Brown and Company, 2015.

Todd, Chuck. *The Stranger: Barack Obama in the White House*. New York: Little, Brown and Company, 2014.

Warrick, Joby. *The Red Line: The Unraveling of Syria and America's Race to Destroy the Most Dangerous Arsenal in the World*. New York: Doubleday, 2020.

Zelizer, Julian E., ed. *The Presidency of Barack Obama: A First Historical Assessment.* Princeton, NJ: Princeton University Press, 2018.

ON US FOREIGN POLICY:

Bacevich, Andrew J. *The Age of Illusions: How America Squandered Its Cold War Victory.* New York: Metropolitan Books, 2020.

Bacevich, Andrew J. *The Limits of Power: The End of American Exceptionalism.* New York: Metropolitan Books, 2008.

Beinart, Peter. *The Icarus Syndrome: A History of American Hubris.* New York: HarperCollins, 2010.

Brands, Hal. *What Good Is Grand Strategy? Power and Purpose in American Statecraft from Harry S. Truman to George W. Bush.* Ithaca: Cornell University Press, 2014.

Burns, William J. *The Back Channel: A Memoir of American Diplomacy and the Case for Its Renewal.* New York: Random House, 2019.

Chollet, Derek, with James Goldgeier. *America Between the Wars: From 11/9 to 9/11.* New York: PublicAffairs, 2008.

Dallek, Robert. *The American Style of Foreign Policy: Cultural Politics and Foreign Affairs.* New York: Oxford University Press, 1983.

Destler, I. M., with Leslie Gelb and Anthony Lake. *Our Own Worst Enemy: The Unmaking of American Foreign Policy.* New York: Simon and Schuster, 1984.

Dueck, Colin. *Age of Iron: On Conservative Nationalism.* New York: Oxford University Press, 2019.

Dueck, Colin. *Hard Line: The Republican Party and U.S. Foreign Policy Since World War II.* Princeton, NJ: Princeton University Press, 2010.

Fitzgerald, Frances. *Way Out There in the Blue: Reagan, Star Wars and the End of the Cold War.* New York: Simon and Schuster, 2001.

Gaddis, John Lewis. *George F. Kennan: An American Life.* London: Penguin, 2012.

Gans, John. *White House Warriors: How the National Security Council Transformed the American Way of War.* New York: Liveright, 2019.

Gates, Robert M. *Exercise of Power: American Failures, Successes, and a New Path Forward in the Post–Cold War World.* New York: Knopf, 2020.

Gelb, Leslie H. *Power Rules: How Common Sense Can Rescue American Foreign Policy.* New York: HarperCollins, 2009.

Gelb, Leslie H., and Richard K. Betts. *The Irony of Vietnam: The System Worked.* Washington, DC: Brookings Institution Press, 2016.

Goldgeier, James M., and Michael McFaul. *Power and Purpose: U.S. Policy Toward Russia After the Cold War.* Washington, DC: Brookings Institution Press, 2003.

Hoffmann, Stanley. *Gulliver's Troubles; or, The Setting of American Foreign Policy.* New York: McGraw-Hill, 1968.

Jervis, Robert. *How Statesmen Think: The Psychology of International Politics.* Princeton, NJ: Princeton University Press, 2017.

Jervis, Robert. *Perception and Misperception in International Politics.* Princeton, NJ: Princeton University Press, 1976.

Kaplan, Fred. *The Bomb: Presidents, Generals, and the Secret History of Nuclear War.* New York: Simon & Schuster, 2020.

Kaplan, Robert D. *Earning the Rockies: How Geography Shapes America's Role in the World.* New York: Random House, 2017.

Kimmage, Michael. *The Abandonment of the West: The History of an Idea in American Foreign Policy.* New York: Basic Books, 2020.

Kissinger, Henry A. *White House Years.* Boston: Little, Brown and Company, 1979.

Kupchan, Charles A. *Isolationism: America's Efforts to Shield Itself from the World.* New York: Oxford University Press, 2020.

LaFeber, Walter. *America, Russia, and the Cold War 1945–1990,* 6th ed. New York: McGraw-Hill, 1991.

Leffler, Melvyn P. *For the Soul of Mankind: The United States, the Soviet Union, and the Cold War.* New York: Hill and Wang, 2007.

Leffler, Melvyn P. *Safeguarding Democratic Capitalism: U.S. Foreign Policy and National Security, 1920–2015.* Princeton, NJ: Princeton University Press, 2017.

Lippmann, Walter. *U.S. Foreign Policy: Shield of the Republic.* New York: Little Brown, 1943.

McDougall, Walter A. *The Tragedy of U.S. Foreign Policy: How America's Civil Religion Betrayed the National Interest.* New Haven, CT: Yale University Press, 2016.

Milne, David. *Worldmaking: The Art and Science of American Diplomacy.* New York: Farrar, Straus and Giroux, 2015.

Morgenthau, Hans. *Scientific Man Versus Power Politics.* Chicago: Chicago University Press, 1965.

Rapp-Hooper, Mira. *Shields of the Republic: The Triumph and Peril of America's Alliances.* Cambridge, MA: Harvard University Press, 2020.

Rothkopf, David. *National Insecurity: American Leadership in an Age of Fear.* New York: PublicAffairs, 2014.

Sestanovich, Stephen. *Maximalist: America in the World from Truman to Obama.* New York: Knopf, 2014.

Taft, Robert A. *A Foreign Policy for Americans.* New York: Doubleday, 1952.

Talbott, Strobe. *The Russia Hand: A Memoir of Presidential Diplomacy.* New York: Random House, 2002.

Wolfers, Arnold. *Discord and Collaboration: Essays in International Politics.* Baltimore: Johns Hopkins University Press, 1962.

Zoellick, Robert B. *America in the World: A History of U.S. Diplomacy and Foreign Policy.* New York: Hachette, 2020.

ON HISTORY, POLITICS, AND LEADERSHIP:

Andersen, Kurt. *Fantasyland: How America Went Haywire.* New York: Random House, 2017.

Avlon, John. *Washington's Farewell: The Founding Father's Warning to Future Generations.* New York: Simon & Schuster, 2017.

Boot, Max. *The Corrosion of Conservatism: Why I Left the Right.* New York: Liveright Publishing, 2019.

Bower, Kate Andersen. *Team of Five: The Presidents Club in the Age of Trump.* New York: HarperCollins, 2020.

Brands, Hal, and Charles Edel. *The Lessons of Tragedy: Statecraft and World Order.* New Haven, CT: Yale University Press, 2019.

Brooks, David. *The Road to Character.* New York: Random House, 2015.

Brower, Kate Andersen. *Team of Five: The Presidents Club in the Age of Trump.* New York: HarperCollins, 2020.

Crouter, Richard. *Reinhold Niebuhr: On Politics, Religion, and Christian Faith.* New York: Oxford University Press, 2010.

Dickerson, John. *The Hardest Job in the World: The American Presidency.* New York: Random House, 2020.

Dionne, E. J., Jr. *Why the Right Went Wrong: Conservatism—From Goldwater to Trump and Beyond.* New York: Simon & Schuster, 2016.

Frum, David. *Dead Right.* New York: Basic Books, 1994.

Gaddis, John Lewis. *On Grand Strategy.* London: Penguin, 2018.

Gaddis, John Lewis. *The Landscape of History: How Historians Map the Past.* New York: Oxford University Press, 2002.

Gawande, Atul. *Being Mortal: Medicine and What Matters in the End.* New York: Metropolitan Books, 2014.

Gawande, Atul. *Better: A Surgeon's Notes on Performance.* New York: Picador, 2007.

Gawande, Atul. *The Checklist Manifesto: How to Get Things Right.* New York: Metropolitan Books, 2009.

Goodwin, Doris Kearns. *Leadership in Turbulent Times.* New York, Simon and Schuster, 2018.

Grandin, Greg. *The End of the Myth: From the Frontier to the Border Wall in the Mind of America.* New York: Metropolitan Books, 2019.

Greenberg, David. *Republic of Spin: An Inside History of the American Presidency.* New York: W. W. Norton, 2016.

Greenstein, Fred I. *Leadership in the Modern Presidency.* Cambridge, MA: Harvard University Press, 1988.

Groopman, Jerome. *How Doctors Think.* New York: Houghton Mifflin, 2007.

Hoffer, Eric. *The True Believer: Thoughts on the Nature of Mass Movements.* New York: Harper & Row, 1951.

Hoganson, Kristin L. *The Heartland: An American History.* New York: Penguin, 2019.

Judis, John B. *William F. Buckley, Jr.: Patron Saint of the Conservatives.* New York: Simon & Schuster, 1988.

Kabaservice, Geoffrey. *Rule and Ruin: The Downfall of Moderation and the Destruction of the Republican Party, From Eisenhower to the Tea Party.* New York: Oxford University Press, 2012.

Kammen, Michael. *Mystic Chords of Memory: The Transformation of Tradition in American Culture.* New York: Knopf, 1991.

Kornacki, Steve. *The Red and the Blue: The 1990s and the Birth of Political Tribalism.* New York: Ecco, 2018.

Kruse, Kevin M., and Julian E. Zelizer. *Fault Lines: A History of the United States Since 1974.* New York: Norton, 2019.

Lepore, Jill. *These Truths: A History of the United States*. New York: Norton, 2018.

Lepore, Jill. *This America: The Case for the Nation*. New York: Liveright, 2019.

Lowi, Theodore J. *The Personal President: Power Invested, Promise Unfulfilled*. Ithaca, NY: Cornell University Press, 1985.

MacMillan, Margaret. *Dangerous Games: The Uses and Abuses of History*. New York: Modern Library, 2010.

Mann, Thomas E., and Norman J. Ornstein. *It's Even Worse Than It Looks: How the American Constitutional System Collided with the New Politics of Extremism*. New York: Basic Books, 2016.

Meacham, Jon. *The Soul of America: The Battle for Our Better Angels*. New York: Random House, 2018.

Mukunda, Gautam. *Indispensable: When Leaders Really Matter*. Boston: Harvard Business Review Press, 2012.

Nash, George H. *The Conservative Intellectual Movement in America Since 1945*, 30th anniversary ed. Wilmington, DE: Intercollegiate Studies Institute, 2006.

Neustadt, Richard E. *Presidential Power and the Modern Presidents*. New York: Free Press, 1990.

Nguyen, Viet Thanh. *Nothing Ever Dies: Vietnam and the Memory of War*. Cambridge, MA: Harvard University Press, 2016.

Niebuhr, Reinhold. *The Children of Light and the Children of Darkness*. New York: Scribner, 1944.

Niebuhr, Reinhold. *The Irony of American History*. New York: Scribner, 1952.

Nixon, Richard M. *Six Crises*. New York: Doubleday, 1962.

Nye, Joseph S., Jr. *Do Morals Matter? Presidents and Foreign Policy from FDR to Trump*. New York: Oxford University Press, 2020.

Nye, Joseph S., Jr. *Presidential Leadership and the Creation of the American Era*. Princeton, NJ: Princeton University Press, 2013.

Patterson, James T. *Grand Expectations: The United States, 1945–1974*. New York: Oxford University Press, 1996.

Patterson, James T. *Restless Giant: The United States from Watergate to Bush v. Gore*. New York: Oxford University Press, 2005.

Perot, Ross. *United We Stand: How We Can Take Back Our Country*. New York: Hyperion, 1992.

Suri, Jeremi. *The Impossible Presidency: The Rise and Fall of America's Highest Office*. New York: Basic Books, 2017.

Tooze, Adam. *Crashed: How a Decade of Financial Crises Changed the World*. New York: Penguin, 2018.

Venkataraman, Bina. *The Optimist's Telescope: Thinking Ahead in a Reckless Age*. New York: Penguin, 2019.

Wehner, Peter. *The Death of Politics: How to Heal Our Frayed Republic after Trump*. New York: HarperCollins, 2019.

White, Theodore H. *America in Search of Itself: The Making of the President, 1956–1980*. New York: Harper & Row, 1982.

Wilson, James Q. *On Character*. Washington, DC: AEI Press, 1995.

Zelizer, Julian E. *Arsenal of Democracy: The Politics of National Security—From World War II to the War on Terrorism*. New York: Basic Books, 2009.

For the benefit of digital users, indexed terms that span two pages (e.g., 52–53) may, on occasion, appear on only one of those pages.